STRATEGIC PLANNING
for Results

SANDRA NELSON

for the

PUBLIC LIBRARY ASSOCIATION

AMERICAN LIBRARY ASSOCIATION

Chicago   2008

Printed on 50-pound white offset, a pH-neutral stock, and bound in 10-point coated cover stock by Victor Graphics.

The paper used in this publication meets the minimum requirements of American National Standard for Information Sciences—Permanence of Paper for Printed Library Materials, ANSI Z39.48-1992. ∞

Library of Congress Cataloging-in-Publication Data

Nelson, Sandra S.
    Strategic planning for results / Sandra Nelson for the Public Library Association.
    p.   cm. — (PLA results series)
    Rev. ed. of: The new planning for results. 2001.
    Includes bibliographical references and index.
    ISBN 978-0-8389-3573-6 (alk. paper)
    1. Public libraries—Planning. 2. Public libraries—United States—Planning. 3. Public libraries—Administration. 4. Public libraries—United States—Administration. I. Nelson, Sandra S. New planning for results. II. Public Library Association. III. Title.
    Z678.N454 2008
    025.1'974—dc22   2007027926

ISBN-13: 978-0-8389-3573-6
ISBN-10: 0-8389-3573-7

Printed in the United States of America

12 11 10 09 08   5 4 3 2 1

Contents

Part Three
Tool Kits

Part Four
Workforms

Figures

Acknowledgments

June Garcia has been involved in the ongoing development of the Public Library Association's planning process since the early 1980s, and she has played a significant role in every planning book the PLA has published. June's in-depth knowledge of public library management issues has been a critical part of the success of the Results books.

June served as a member of the committee that worked with Chuck McClure and his team to write *Planning and Role-Setting for Public Libraries* (1987). She was a member of the committee that evaluated the effect of *Planning and Role-Setting for Public Libraries* in the mid-1990s and the committee that worked with Bill Wilson and Ethel Himmel to write the original *Planning for Results* (1998). She chaired the committee that worked with Diane Mayo, Ellen Altman, and myself to develop *Managing for Results* (2000). She served as a sounding board and unofficial editor for *The New Planning for Results* (2001), and we coauthored *Creating Policies for Results* (2003). Since 2003, June and I have worked together to edit the books in the Results series.

This book, like the others I have written in the Results series, is the product of a collaborative process. In particular, the new materials on organizational competencies and initiatives (Task 8) are based on concepts and practices that June developed over the past several years.

I would also like to thank the dozens of library managers and consultants who have participated in the PLA's *Planning for Results* Train the Trainer events over the past seven years. These trainers have introduced thousands of public librarians and trustees to the Results process and helped libraries across the country to develop strategic plans. The trainers have discussed and evaluated new ideas, field-tested workforms, and generously shared their successes and challenges with each other and with me. I would like particularly to thank Laura Sullivan, Bonnie Bruce, Wayne Piper, Deborah Duke, and Sara Dallas for reviewing the final manuscript and making excellent suggestions for revisions and additions.

Introduction

If anything is certain, it is that change is certain.
The world we are planning for today will not exist
in this form tomorrow. —Philip Crosby

This is the fifth planning guide produced by the Public Library Association (PLA) since 1980. The five planning guides have all been based on the same three assumptions:

1. Excellence must be defined locally. It results when library services match community needs, interests, and priorities.
2. Excellence is possible for both small and large libraries. It rests more on commitment than on unlimited resources.
3. Excellence is a moving target. Even when achieved, excellence must be continually maintained.[1]

Each of the five planning guides reflects the concerns and priorities of public library managers and boards at the time it was written. The first guide, *A Planning Process for Public Libraries,* was published in 1980.[2] At that time, few libraries had completed a planning process of any kind, and excellence was defined by national or state standards. *A Planning Process for Public Libraries* introduced the concept of community-based planning.

The second guide, *Planning and Role-Setting for Public Libraries* (1987), introduced the concept of library roles.[3] Library roles were based on work done by Lowell Martin, who believed that libraries needed to focus on providing a few services well rather than providing many services poorly. Libraries in the late 1980s and early 1990s were dealing with reduced budgets and a proliferation of formats. The library roles provided a way for planners to identify service priorities.

The third guide, *Planning for Results: A Public Library Transformation Process*[4] (1998), built on the concept of roles and introduced thirteen service responses, which were defined as *what a library does for, or offers to, the public in an effort to meet a set of well-defined community needs.*[5] The earlier planning guides had focused almost exclusively on planning. This was the first process to put an emphasis on implementing the strategic plan, and it included a number of tools to help library managers reallocate resources to support the service priorities identified during the planning process.

By the time the fourth guide, *The New Planning for Results: A Streamlined Process* (2001), was written, it was obvious that libraries were being profoundly affected by the Internet and other changes in information technology.[6] Planning was more important than ever, but the process needed to be streamlined. A planning process that took fifteen months to complete would be out-of-date before it was published. Therefore, the planning process was simplified and the time line was reduced to four or five months. The focus on implementation, introduced in the first *Planning for Results,* was intensified in *The New Planning for Results.*

There were several clear trends in the progression from one planning guide to the next. The time it takes to complete a library strategic plan was reduced from years to months, accurately reflecting the rapidly changing environment in which libraries operate today. The number of tasks required to complete a plan was reduced from twenty-three to twelve, resulting in a more streamlined process appropriate for the shorter planning time frame. The number of possible library priorities (roles in 1987 and service responses in 1998 and 2001) was increased from eight to thirteen to provide a more accurate picture of the array of services provided by public libraries. Finally, each new version of the PLA planning guide placed a greater emphasis on implementing the plan. All of these trends continue in this book, the fifth PLA planning guide. The recommended planning time line has been reduced to four months, there are ten planning tasks instead of twelve, and the number of library priorities (service responses) has been increased from thirteen to eighteen.

How Is This Book Different?

There have been two significant changes in this book. The first is a reflection of the current planning environment for public libraries. Each of the earlier planning guides used the term *long-range planning* to describe the planning process. In this book, the process is referred to as *strategic planning.* This is more than a semantic change. It is an acknowledgment that the future is too fluid to make firm "long-range" plans. The Alliance for Nonprofit Management describes the difference between long-range planning and strategic planning clearly:

> Long-range planning is generally considered to mean the development of a plan for accomplishing a goal or set of goals over a period of several years, with the assumption that current knowledge about future conditions is sufficiently reliable to ensure the plan's reliability over the duration of its implementation. . . . On the other hand, strategic planning assumes that an organization must be responsive to a dynamic, changing environment (not the more stable environment assumed for long-range planning). . . . Strategic planning, then, stresses the importance of making decisions that will ensure the organization's ability to successfully respond to changes in the environment.[7]

The second change in this book is also a reflection of current conditions, but in this case it is the current conditions within libraries that need to be addressed. In far too many libraries planning has become an end in itself. At the end of the planning process everyone breathes a sigh of relief and thinks, "Thank goodness that's over. Now we can go back to our *real* work." Needless to say, the *real* work these staff want to return to is exactly the same work they were doing before the planning process started. That raises the interesting question of why these staff think the library went through the planning process at all.

There really isn't much point in planning if library staff don't make the changes needed to implement the library's new service priorities. Implementation will require changes in the way staff spend their time, the types and number of materials they purchase, the way library space is allocated, and the use of the library's technology. Earlier planning guides tried to integrate the planning and implementation processes into a single volume and ended up shortchanging both. The planning processes included little or no guidance for library managers and boards struggling to actually create a change-ready environment. The implementation guidelines were far too general—and brief—to do more than encourage managers to reallocate resources to support their new priorities.

This book deals with these two problems in two ways. It includes a great deal of information about understanding and managing the change process—and it includes almost nothing about implementation. This is in recognition of the fact that implementation issues are more complex than planning issues and require a separate and clearly defined process. That process is described in *Implementing for Results: From Ideas to Action,* the companion volume to this book.[8]

A Preview of the Process

This book has been divided into six chapters. The first five chapters correspond to the five phases of the planning process, and the sixth sets the stage for implementation.

> *Plan to Plan.* In this chapter you will learn to create a successful planning foundation.
>
> *Identify Service Priorities.* In this chapter you will learn to establish a collaborative planning environment that includes community leaders, library staff, and the members of the library board, and you will select the library's service priorities.
>
> *Set the Stage.* In this chapter you will learn to assess the change readiness of your library and to prepare managers, frontline staff, and library board members to implement the changes that will come from the strategic plan. You will also learn how to identify library values and craft a mission statement or tagline.
>
> *Describe the Future.* In this chapter you will learn how to write goals and objectives, and to identify desired organizational competencies and related initiatives.
>
> *Communicate the Plan.* In this chapter you will learn how to put all of the decisions you made during the planning process into a written strategic plan that is clear, concise, credible, logical, and persuasive. You will also learn to communicate effectively about the plan with different target audiences.
>
> *The Rest of the Story.* In this very brief chapter you will be introduced to the book *Implementing for Results: From Ideas to Action.*

Figure 1 lists all of the tasks and steps in the *Planning for Results* process.

There are forty-four figures scattered throughout the six chapters of this book. The figures provide illustrations of key parts of the planning process. Many of the figures include examples of work done by the staff in two fictional libraries, the Tree County Public Library and the Anytown Public Library. The Tree County Public Library is a mythical county library somewhere in the United States that serves a population of 300,000 people

FIGURE 1

Planning for Results Tasks and Steps

Task 1: Design the Planning Process
    Step 1.1: Identify the reasons for planning
    Step 1.2: Define planning responsibilities
    Step 1.3: Prepare a planning schedule and budget
    Step 1.4: Develop a communication plan
    Step 1.5: Design and present a staff orientation

Task 2: Start the Planning Process
    Step 2.1: Obtain board approval
    Step 2.2: Select community planning committee members
    Step 2.3: Invite committee members
    Step 2.4: Prepare and distribute community and library information packets

Task 3: Identify Community Needs
    Step 3.1: Present an orientation for the members of the planning committee
    Step 3.2: Develop community vision statements
    Step 3.3: Define current conditions in the community
    Step 3.4: Decide what needs to be done to reach community vision

Task 4: Select Service Responses
    Step 4.1: Present an overview of the library to committee members
    Step 4.2: Select preliminary service responses
    Step 4.3: Describe the effect of preliminary service responses on current library services
    Step 4.4: Select final service responses

Task 5: Prepare for Change
    Step 5.1: Assess the library's readiness for change
    Step 5.2: Plan to create a positive environment for change
    Step 5.3: Review and revise communication plans
    Step 5.4: Train supervisors and managers

Task 6: Consider Library Values and Mission
    Step 6.1: Define values
    Step 6.2: Consider the library mission

Task 7: Write Goals and Objectives
    Step 7.1: Write system goals
    Step 7.2: Write system objectives
    Step 7.3: Determine the priority of goals and measures of progress for each unit

Task 8: Identify Organizational Competencies
    Step 8.1: Understand organizational competencies and initiatives
    Step 8.2: Identify organizational issues
    Step 8.3: Write organizational competencies and initiatives

Task 9: Write the Strategic Plan and Obtain Approval
    Step 9.1: Write and review the strategic plan
    Step 9.2: Submit the strategic plan for approval

Task 10: Communicate the Results of the Planning Process
    Step 10.1: Define the target audiences
    Step 10.2: Develop a communication plan
    Step 10.3: Develop communications to target audiences

from seven branches. The Anytown Public Library is an equally mythical city library serving a population of 75,000 from a single building.

Some Basic Definitions

Before you start to use this book, it will be helpful if you understand how some basic terms have been used. These words mean different things in different libraries, but this is how the words are defined in this book.

> *Branch.* A separate library facility.
>
> *Central library.* The largest library facility, usually in a downtown area; referred to as the main library in some places.
>
> *Department.* A unit within a single facility that is normally a central library.
>
> *Library.* The entire organizational entity and its units.
>
> *Library board.* The authority board that governs the library, and to which the library director reports; in some cases this may be a city or county government. An authority board hires the director, sets library policy, and has fiduciary responsibility. The library may have an advisory board if the director reports to a city or county government.
>
> *Library management team.* The senior managers in a library; typically this team includes the director, assistant director, head of branches (if any), head of the central library, and any senior staff positions (personnel, marketing, finance, etc.). In very small libraries, the library administrative "team" is the director.
>
> *Manager.* A generic term that refers to the staff member or staff members who are responsible for resource allocation in a particular area; in some libraries the "manager" is actually a team of staff members.
>
> *Team.* A group of staff members brought together to work on a specific project or program; it may include members from different departments and with different job classifications.
>
> *Unit.* A term used to refer to individual library departments and branches (if any).

Other Resources

The six chapters described above make up part 1 of the book. There are three additional parts of the book that provide planning resources. Part 2 presents the eighteen library service responses. Part 3 contains four tool kits that present information that you will use again and again throughout the planning process. Part 4 provides copies of all of the workforms that support the process.

Part Two: Public Library Service Responses

This book contains eighteen service responses, which are defined as what a library does for, or offers to, the public in an effort to meet a set of well-defined community needs. Service responses serve multiple purposes in a library strategic planning process. Service responses can

- describe the primary service roles or priorities of public libraries
- provide a common vocabulary that can be used by librarians, trustees, and community leaders to identify service priorities for specific libraries
- suggest target audiences for some services
- include a list of organizations that might partner with the library to offer the service
- identify possible policy implications that library managers will need to address if the service response is selected as a priority
- define the resources (staff, collections, facilities, technology) required to support specific service priorities
- provide suggested measures that can be used to evaluate services in priority areas

The eighteen service responses in this book were developed through an open process that included three open meetings at the 2006 American Library Association (ALA) Annual Conference, postings on the PLA blog, and a final open hearing at the 2007 ALA Midwinter Conference.

Part Three: Tool Kits

There are four tool kits included in this part. The first tool kit provides guidelines for presenting data. You will be presenting data about the library and the community to members of the community planning committee, and you will be working with data as you develop your objectives. The guidelines in this tool kit will help you present data in easily understandable ways.

The next two tool kits provide information on dealing with groups: Groups: Identifying Options and Groups: Reaching Agreement. As you can see, both of these tool kits focus on helping people in groups to reach decisions. You will be working with groups of community leaders, staff, and board members throughout the planning process, and the tips and aids in these tool kits will be valuable.

The final tool kit provides a brief overview of internal communication practices. As you work through the tasks and steps in the planning process, you will be repeatedly reminded to "communicate, communicate, communicate," and the information in this tool kit will help you to ensure that the messages you send are effective.

Part Four: Workforms

There are fourteen workforms associated with this planning process. They serve a variety of functions. They provide a place to record decisions that are made during the process. They provide a framework for discussion and help you to understand the issues you need to resolve. They can be used as worksheets during the community planning committee meetings and the staff review meetings. Finally, they can be used as training tools with staff. There is an example of a partially completed copy of each of the fourteen workforms among the figures in the first section of this book. You may download electronic copies of all fourteen workforms from http://www.elearnlibraries.com. The electronic versions of the workforms were created using Microsoft Word and can be modified to meet the needs of your library.

How to Use This Book

This book was written to be used by staff in public libraries of all sizes and in all parts of the country. Any book that is written for everyone will have to be modified by each user to reflect the unique local environment. This means that you will need to read the entire book before you start using any part of it. As you read through the book, think carefully about conditions in your library. Are there any special circumstances that would require you to alter the process? What kinds of changes might be needed? There are multiple options described for a number of the steps in the planning process, and you will need to decide which of those options will be most effective in your library.

There is one particular issue that you should consider before you start planning, and that is the current organizational culture in your library. In Task 5 in chapter 3 you will learn to assess the change readiness in your library. If you follow the structure recommended in this book, that assessment will occur after the two meetings of the community planning committee. However, in some libraries that might be too late. After you and your colleagues read Task 5 in chapter 3, you may decide to start the process with Task 5 and wait to begin the rest of the planning process until you have made the changes needed to create an organizational culture in the library that is more conducive to change.

Putting It All Together

All of the tools you will need to develop a strategic plan for your library have been included in this book. All that is left is to "just do it!"

Notes

1. Charles R. McClure and others, *Planning and Role-Setting for Public Libraries: A Manual of Options and Procedures* (Chicago: American Library Association, 1987), 1.
2. Vernon Palmour, Marcia C. Bellassai, and Nancy V. DeWash, *A Planning Process for Public Libraries* (Chicago: American Library Association, 1980).
3. Charles R. McClure and others, *Planning and Role-Setting for Public Libraries: A Manual of Options and Procedures* (Chicago: American Library Association, 1987).
4. Ethel Himmel and William James Wilson, *Planning for Results: A Public Library Transformation Process* (Chicago: American Library Association, 1998).
5. Ibid., 54.
6. Sandra Nelson, *The New Planning for Results: A Streamlined Approach* (Chicago: American Library Association, 2001).
7. Alliance for Nonprofit Management, http://www.allianceonline.org/FAQ/strategic_planning/what_is_strategic_planning.faq.
8. Sandra Nelson, *Implementing for Results: From Ideas to Action* (Chicago: American Library Association, forthcoming 2008).

Part One

The Planning Process

Chapter 1

Plan to Plan

Organizing is what you do before you do something,
so that when you do it, it is not all mixed up.

—A. A. Milne

MILESTONES

By the time you finish this chapter you will be able to

- describe the reasons you are developing or updating a strategic plan
- define the responsibilities of planning committee members, library staff, library board members, and local government officials
- decide if you need to hire an outside facilitator for your planning process
- prepare a plan to communicate with library staff, library board members, the members of the planning committee, and other stakeholders throughout the planning process
- provide an effective orientation on the planning process for the staff
- identify and invite community leaders to participate on the planning committee

Most public library staff have participated in at least one planning process or work in a library that has a long-range plan. In some libraries, staff have had good planning experiences. The planning process was a collaborative effort among the staff, board, and community leaders; staff input was sought and valued; the process was completed in a relatively short period of time; and the final strategic plan was used as a blueprint for meaningful change. Unfortunately, in other libraries staff have had very different experiences. In those libraries, managers or the board members developed the plan, staff felt excluded from the process, the planning process dragged on for months or even years, and the final strategic plan was printed, filed, and forgotten. People's past experiences inevitably color their perceptions of the value of library planning, and it is hard to step away from personal feelings and look dispassionately at the bigger picture.

Even positive past experiences do not guarantee that future planning efforts will be well-received by staff. Planning is a lot of work, and it inevitably creates tension. Planning is intrinsically about change, and some staff have seen more than enough changes in the past decade. They are not interested in looking for yet more new and different ways to change. Other staff believe that the information environment is changing so rapidly that planning is futile. Still others believe that planning restricts their choices rather than defining them.

In view of these staff issues, is it worth it to initiate a planning process? It is if you consider the alternative. In libraries that do not have current strategic plans, decisions are based on personal opinions and values, or on past experience, the squeaky wheel, or the management theory of the day. There are no clear priorities and no agreed-upon measures of success. In the absence of agreed-upon priorities, staff compete for available resources, rather than collaborating to provide services. Both frontline staff and managers may find it difficult to initiate new services or programs, even if the demand for current services and programs is declining, because they are vested in the status quo. There is no way to measure success because there are no clearly defined targets.

The *Planning for Results* process has been designed to address these issues and others. This process has multiple benefits:

> It engages community leaders in a discussion of how the library could meet the needs of community residents.
>
> It helps community leaders understand the full range of services that might be provided by the library.
>
> It involves community leaders, staff, and board members in a collaborative process to identify library service priorities.
>
> It leads to realignment of library services in response to community needs.
>
> It includes all staff in the identification of the core values of the library.
>
> It assesses organizational capacity and identifies areas that need improvement.
>
> It defines clear targets and establishes procedures to track the progress made toward reaching those targets.
>
> It provides a framework for creating an organization that can respond quickly and effectively to change.

Note that these results all focus on the *services* the library provides and not on the *resources* the library needs. One of the underlying assumptions in this process is that you can't make effective resource allocation decisions until you know what you are trying to accomplish with your resources. During the planning process, you will work with the board and your colleagues to identify the values that shape the library's services and programs. At the end of the process, everyone will have a shared sense of purpose and a clear understanding of *why* the library is providing the services it provides. This provides the framework needed to effectively adopt new programs and services and to adapt to changing customer expectations.

Getting Started

Although it may seem oxymoronic (and to some just plain moronic), there is no way to develop an effective strategic plan for your library without planning to plan. Any library planning process is a complex endeavor that involves multiple stakeholders working together to make important decisions about service priorities, values, and organizational capacity.

These are critical issues, and the processes used to address them will have an effect on the decisions that are made. If you fail to involve all of the community stakeholders, your plan may be too limited in scope or vision. If you schedule your planning process to start in November and end in February, you will find that the holiday season makes it very difficult to bring people together. If you forget to communicate with one or more of the stakeholder groups during the process, you may find that some people actively resist the final plan because they feel disenfranchised. Each of these potential problems, and many others as well, can be eliminated through careful planning before you start the strategic planning process.

This planning process has been divided into ten tasks, and each task has been subdivided into a series of sequential steps. The first task in the process is to design the planning process. The decisions you make in this first task will affect the implementation of the other nine tasks.

TASK 1: DESIGN THE PLANNING PROCESS

Task 1:   Design the Planning Process
    Step 1.1:   Identify the reasons for planning
    Step 1.2:   Define planning responsibilities
    Step 1.3:   Prepare a planning schedule and budget
    Step 1.4:   Develop a communication plan
    Step 1.5:   Design and present a staff orientation
Task 2:   Start the Planning Process
Task 3:   Identify Community Needs
Task 4:   Select Service Responses
Task 5:   Prepare for Change
Task 6:   Consider Library Values and Mission
Task 7:   Write Goals and Objectives
Task 8:   Identify Organizational Competencies
Task 9:   Write the Strategic Plan and Obtain Approval
Task 10:   Communicate the Results of the Planning Process

The steps in Task 1 will be completed by the library director, the members of the library management team, and the members of the library board. It will take two to three weeks to accomplish the steps in this task. The first step includes a meeting of the library board.

Step 1.1
Identify the Reasons for Planning

Library boards and managers enter into strategic planning processes for a variety of reasons, and those reasons are not always compatible. For example, the board of the Tree County Public Library might want the library to complete a strategic plan to establish the need for a new library facility. Library managers in Tree County might want to go through the planning process to identify library service priorities and allocate scarce resources more effectively. The frontline staff might hope that the planning process will "prove" that the library needs to hire more staff to manage the library's public access computers. The board of the Friends of the Library may expect the library planning process to focus on marketing library services and programs. Advocates for the growing Hispanic population in Tree County may expect the plan to focus on identifying and meeting the needs of this new service group. Perhaps Tree County has a new county manager who wants the library to participate in a countywide planning process designed to streamline services. The state library agency may require the Tree County Public Library to have a plan to be eligible for state aid. It is unlikely that a single planning process will produce all of these desired results, and any process that tries to do so will probably disappoint everyone.

Obviously then, an effective planning process starts by clearly identifying the reason or reasons for developing a plan. Any process used to determine the reasons for planning has to start with the expectations of the person or group that first initiated the planning discussion. This does not mean, however, that the discussion has to be restricted to those initial expectations.

The suggestion that the library initiate a strategic planning process might come from a variety of sources, but in most cases it comes from the library management team or from one or more board members. The decision to actually begin such a process must be made by the board and should be based on clearly defined expectations. Before the meeting during which the board is scheduled to discuss the possibility of initiating a planning process, the library director should develop a brief summary of the status of the current library plan (if there is one), a brief list of the reasons why the library should begin a planning process at this time, and an overview of the proposed *Planning for Results* process (see figure 2 for a sample).

During the meeting, the director will review the status of the current plan (if there is one) with the board. The director will then briefly list the reasons why she thinks the library should initiate a *Planning for Results* process at this time. Members of the board may believe there are additional reasons for planning. All of the possible reasons for planning should be listed and discussed.

It will be important for the board chair and the director to look for unrealistic or mutually exclusive planning expectations. As noted above, the countywide planning process initiated by the county manager is unlikely to produce a planning document that will meet the requirements of the state library agency. It is equally unlikely that a strategic plan intended to identify service priorities for the library will include a list of facility enhancements needed. Some board members may expect a strategic plan to focus on acquiring additional resources, and will be disappointed unless they know from the beginning that this is not the case.

If the director and the board decide to develop a strategic plan that focuses on identifying library service priorities, the director will introduce the *Planning for Results* process and explain why staff are recommending that it be used during the upcoming planning cycle. This discussion should focus on the rationale for using a community-based planning committee (there is information on this in the next step) and should include the fact that the members of the board will be selecting the people to serve on the planning committee during their next meeting. Board members should be asked to think about those people who represent important constituencies in the community in preparation for that meeting.

There is no need for formal board action at this point, but the director and the members of the board should reach consensus about the planning process and its expected benefits. Two of the tool kits in part 3 may be useful for the person managing this discussion: Groups: Identifying Options; and Groups: Reaching Agreement. When the board

FIGURE 2
Planning for Results Assumptions and Key Points

ASSUMPTIONS

EXCELLENCE MUST BE DEFINED LOCALLY. It results when library services match community needs, interests, and priorities.

EXCELLENCE IS POSSIBLE FOR BOTH SMALL AND LARGE LIBRARIES. It rests more on commitment than on unlimited resources

EXCELLENCE IS A MOVING TARGET. Even when achieved, excellence must be continually maintained.

KEY POINTS

COMMUNITY-BASED PLANNING. The *Planning for Results* process begins by asking key community stakeholders to define a vision for the community served by the library and to identify what needs to happen in the community to reach that vision. These community needs provide the framework to determine how the library can make a contribution toward achieving the community vision. This in turn helps to answer the question, "What difference does the library make?"

LIBRARY SERVICE PRIORITIES. *Planning for Results* includes eighteen public library priorities (service responses) and encourages library planners to select

the priorities that match the community needs identified through the visioning process. This will ensure that the library board members, managers, and staff are using their energies and resources to provide the services that matter most to the people of the community.

MEASURES OF PROGRESS. There is a strong emphasis on measurement and evaluation in *Planning for Results,* which includes four categories of measures:

> Number of people who use a service or program
>
> Those users' perceptions of the service or program
>
> The difference the service or program makes in the individual user's knowledge, skill, attitude, behavior, or condition
>
> The number of units of library service delivered (circulation, number of programs presented, etc.)

MANAGING CHANGE. Planning is ultimately about change, and *Planning for Results* includes guidelines and suggestions to help library board members, managers, and staff use the results of the planning process to reshape the services and programs offered by the library. Public libraries are being transformed, and this planning process provides the framework that library leaders need to manage that transformation effectively.

---

members have agreed on the reasons for developing a plan, those reasons should be included in the board minutes. The agreed-upon reasons for planning provide the rationale for the entire planning process and will be referenced throughout the process.

The director will conclude by telling the members of the board that they will receive more information about the proposed planning process during their next scheduled meeting. That information will include a proposed time line and budget, a list of the planning participants and their responsibilities, and a recommendation about using an outside consultant or facilitator. The board members will be asked to formally approve the plan to plan after reviewing that information.

Step 1.2
Define Planning Responsibilities

Once you have agreed on the outcomes you expect from the planning process, you are ready to decide how you will reach those outcomes. You will start by defining the planning responsibilities of each of the groups that will participate in the planning process, and then you will decide who will facilitate the process.

Who Will Participate in the Process and What Will They Do?

There are four groups that must be involved in the *Planning for Results* process: the library management team, the library board or governing agency, the other library staff, and people representing the various constituencies in your community. Deciding who should represent each of these groups is a fairly straightforward process in libraries with an authority board operating out of a single building and serving a single community or county. However, it is more complex for staff working in libraries operating from multiple buildings that serve a single community or county, libraries that serve multiple communities within a county, or libraries that report to a city or county government and have an advisory board. These staff will have several additional issues to consider as they work through the decisions in this step.

LIBRARY BOARD OR GOVERNING AUTHORITY

Although library governance structures vary widely throughout the country, virtually every library director reports either to an authority board or to a city or county manager or her designee. As noted in the introduction, when the term *library board* is used in this book, it means an "authority board that governs the library, and to which the library director reports; in some cases this may be a city or county government." Library boards that serve in an advisory capacity are always referred to as "advisory boards."

There is no point in beginning a planning process—this one or any other—without the explicit approval and support of your library board. The members of your library board are responsible for setting library policy and determining library priorities. The *Planning for Results* process is designed to provide board members with the information they need to make these decisions.

The members of the board will be asked to officially approve the products of the planning process at several steps during the process (see figure 3 for a list of the board approval points), and it will be imperative that the members of board be kept informed about the process through every task and step. One member of the library board should be appointed to serve as the board liaison for the planning process. This person will serve as the board's representative to the community planning committee and will be responsible for keeping lines of communication open between the board and the committee. If the library reports to a city or county manager or her designee, that person should serve on the committee or should appoint a person to serve for them.

Libraries that are a part of city or county government and have advisory boards, and libraries serving people who live in more than one community or county may want to include additional representatives in the process.

Library advisory boards. If your library is part of a city or county government and you have a library advisory board, you will need to decide how to include the members of that board in the process. In some libraries, the advisory board is largely ceremonial and the members have little or no interest in actively participating in events such as the planning process. The members of these boards will want a brief report summarizing the process as you work through its tasks and steps, and little more.

There are also library advisory boards that take a more active role in the library's policy decisions. Some members of these boards may want to be more involved in the

This is a list of points during the planning process when the members of the library board review and take formal action to accept, revise, or reject the recommendations from the community planning committee or the library management team.

1. The board agrees in principle to initiate a planning process using the *Planning for Results* process and reaches consensus on planning outcomes (Step 1.1).

2. The board reviews and accepts, revises, or rejects the responsibilities of the participants, the planning time line, the planning budget, and the use of outside consultants or facilitators (Step 2.1).

3. The board makes the final selection of the members of the community planning committee (Step 2.2).

4. The board reviews the preliminary service responses and makes recommendations to the planning committee. The board recommendations are presented to the community planning committee before they make their final recommendations (Step 4.3).

5. The board reviews and accepts, revises, or rejects the service responses recommended by the community planning committee (Step 4.4).

6. The board reviews and accepts, revises, or rejects the library's values and mission statements (Steps 6.1 and 6.2).

7. The board reviews and accepts, revises, or rejects the goals, objectives, organizational competencies, and initiatives (Steps 7.2 and 8.3).

8. The board reviews and accepts, revises, or rejects the final strategic plan (Step 9.2).

planning process. In these instances, it makes sense to appoint a member of the advisory board as a liaison to the community planning committee. This liaison will have the same responsibilities as the liaisons from authority boards, as described earlier.

Multiple governing authorities. Some libraries are supported by both city and county governments. Others receive support for several communities. This is the most complex environment in which to develop a strategic plan. You will have to decide whether or not to include a representative from each governing authority. If there are only two such authorities, the answer is probably yes. But what if there are three or four governing authorities—or even more? As you will see in Step 2.2, the situation becomes even more complicated when you begin to consider who should serve on the community planning committee.

LIBRARY MANAGEMENT TEAM

Every library has a management team. In very small libraries, the "team" is a single person. In very large systems, the team can include more than a dozen people in both staff and line positions. This team is responsible for administering all aspects of library services, and all members of the team should be informed about and involved in every task of the planning process. These are the people who will have to implement the final plan, and it is critical that each and every one of them understands and supports that plan.

One way to ensure that everyone on the management team is involved in the planning process is to appoint a member of the team as the planning coordinator. The planning coordinator will be responsible for managing all of the tasks and steps throughout the process. She will work with the board liaison to answer questions and address concerns from board members. She will report regularly to the other members of the management team to keep them informed about the progress of the planning process, and she will work with the members of the team to identify and resolve current or potential problems. She will also serve as the liaison with an outside consultant or facilitator, if the decision is made to use one.

The coordinator will need to be familiar with the *Planning for Results* process and be able to answer questions from other members of the management team and from the other library staff. She can become familiar with the process by reading this book, by talking to staff in other libraries of similar size and structure that have completed the *Planning for Results* process, or by taking the online *Planning for Results* course offered by the Public Library Association—or by doing all three. What is important is that the coordinator has a clear understanding of all the tasks and steps of the process before the process begins. This is not a process that can be managed by reading about the next task and steps after you finish the steps in the preceding task. The tasks are too integrated for that approach to work. Decisions you make during each task will affect the options available in later tasks. The coordinator is the person who has to keep the big picture in mind while working through each task in the process.

LIBRARY STAFF

This planning process is driven by community needs that are defined by community members and not staff, and that makes it easy for staff to feel disenfranchised. Therefore, it is critical to keep all members of the library staff informed and involved every step of the way. Throughout the process, the staff will be responsible for reviewing and reacting to work done by others. Initially, some staff may see this as a passive or peripheral role. As the process moves forward, most staff come to understand that the contributions they make to the process are just as important as the contributions made by the other stakeholders.

The staff's knowledge about library programs, services, and users provides a vital reality check at key points. They will first review and respond to the community planning committee's initial recommendations about service priorities. Later, they will have a chance to recommend changes in the draft goals, objectives, and organizational competencies that will be included in the final plan. See figure 4 for a complete list of the staff's responsibilities during the planning process.

Although staff play a supporting role in the planning process, they will be the lead actors in the implementation process that follows the approval of the plan (described in detail in *Implementing for Results: From Ideas to Action*).[1] That is when staff will identify and evaluate both current and proposed activities for the new planning cycle—and that is when the value of the work they do during the planning process will become apparent. The library goals will reflect the service priorities recommended by the community planning committee, and the library objectives will describe how progress toward the goals will be measured. Activities, in turn, will be expected to support the goals and objectives. Staff will have a chance to influence the selection of the service priorities, the target audiences in the goals, and the measures in the objectives before they are made final. After the board has approved the priorities, goals, and objectives, staff will be expected to support them.

One excellent way to keep staff involved with and informed about the planning process is to appoint a staff member who has credibility with the rest of the staff to serve on the community planning committee. The staff representative will be a full and participat-

FIGURE 4
Staff Participation

This is a list of points during the planning process when the members of the library staff will have an opportunity to review and react to recommendations from the community planning committee or the library management team. This list also includes the points in the process when staff will be making recommendations to the library management team.

1. The staff are encouraged to submit the names of people to be included on the community planning committee (Step 2.2).

2. The staff review the preliminary service responses that are recommended by the community planning committee and complete a SWOT (Strengths, Weaknesses, Opportunities, and Threats) analysis of each one. The results of the staff SWOT analysis are presented to the board during the board discussion of the preliminary service responses and are presented to the community planning committee before they make their final recommendations (Step 4.3).

3. The staff review the draft value and mission statements and suggest revisions or additions (Steps 6.1 and 6.2).

4. The staff review the draft goals and objectives and the organization competencies and initiatives that are developed by the library management team and suggest revisions or additions (Steps 7.1 and 7.2).

5. The staff in each branch or unit may be involved in determining the priority of the system goals for their branch or unit (Step 7.3). [This is optional and not all libraries will do this.]

---

ing member of the committee. In addition to that responsibility, the staff member will work with the planning coordinator and the members of the library management team to keep the other staff informed about the process. The staff member you appoint should not be the planning coordinator and probably should not be a library administrator at all. The most effective staff representatives are usually frontline staff members or supervisors. If you work in a union environment, you will want to make plans to keep the union members involved and informed, as well. The processes used will differ depending on union agreements and other local conditions.

COMMUNITY PLANNING COMMITTEE

The fourth stakeholder group in the process is composed of people who represent the various constituencies in your community and who agree to serve on the community planning committee. The community planning committee will meet twice early in the planning process. During their first meeting, the members of the committee will articulate a community vision, describe current conditions in the community, identify what needs to be done to reach the community vision, and select preliminary library service priorities. During their second meeting, the members of the committee will hear feedback from the library management team, the library board, and the library staff about their preliminary recommendations and will make final recommendations about the community needs that could and should be addressed by the library during this planning cycle.

Sometimes library board members may wonder why they should appoint another community-based committee to participate in the planning process. After all, these members say, the library board was specifically appointed or elected to represent the interests of local residents. This is a good question, and there are two good answers. The first answer reflects the perceptions that people have about publicly funded institutions; the second answer focuses on demographics.

Take a moment and think about the use of your tax dollars by the federal government, your state government, your county government, and your city government. If you are like most people, you are not enthusiastic about how your tax dollars are being spent at any level. Many people feel that they have little or no say in how government agencies determine priorities and allocate resources, even though many of the agencies have citizen boards. The public tends to link the members of the boards with the staff of the agency and to think of both collectively as "them" and not "us." The community-based planning committee brings together representatives from all segments of the community. It sends a clear message that the library decision makers want to involve everyone, not just those who have an official connection with the library, in the planning process.

The second reason for the board to appoint a community planning committee has to do with the size and demographic profile of the members of the board. Most library boards have five to seven members. They are often appointed or elected to represent geographic areas within the community. Although many boards make serious efforts to attract members who represent the ethnic diversity in their communities, library board members are still predominantly older, white, well-educated, and relatively affluent. The final composition of the community planning committee should reflect the community's demographics: age, ethnicity, race, gender, education, and so on. It should also include people who live in different parts of the library's service area and represent the various groups within the service area: parents, business owners, literacy students, educators, service organizations, religious institutions, and so on. It is almost impossible to be as inclusive as this on a board with five to seven members. You will learn more about selecting committee members in Step 2.2.

Figure 5 is a visual representation of the responsibilities and relationships of the community planning committee, the library staff, and the library board.

FIGURE 5
Planning Responsibilities

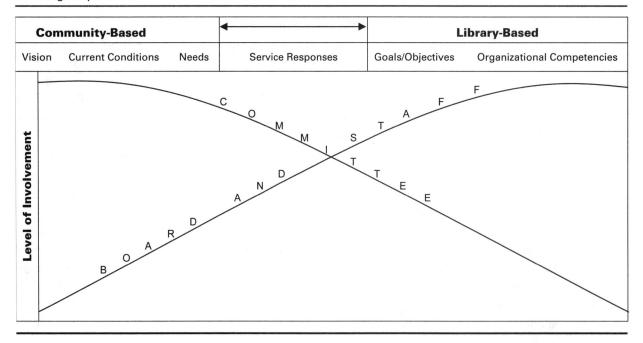

Who Will Facilitate the Planning Process?

There are several decisions to be made as you consider who will facilitate the planning process. The big question to resolve first is whether you want to ask an outside consultant to work with the planning coordinator and other library staff to manage the planning process. This book is designed to provide library staff with the information and skills they need to manage the planning process without the services of an outside consultant. However, in some circumstances, an outside consultant will make the process run more smoothly.

To make your decision, start by considering the library's planning environment. Does the library have a current strategic plan? When was it developed? Was the plan developed using the *Planning for Results* process? Did the planning process include a community planning committee? Was the plan well-received by the staff? By the board? Were most of the activities in the plan implemented? Did the library collect the data needed to track progress toward reaching the goals? If your answers to these questions indicate that there have been problems with previous strategic planning efforts, consider asking an outside consultant to assist with the planning process.

Next consider the amount of staff time available to manage the planning process. Is the planning coordinator fully committed to other duties that cannot be reassigned? Will library administrators be engaged in other initiatives at the same time the planning process is taking place? Are there—or do you anticipate there will be—vacancies on the management team? If finding time to manage the planning process is an issue in your library, consider asking an outside consultant to help the planning coordinator to manage the process.

Now think about the organizational climate. Do the members of the management team work well together or are there conflicts? Are there disagreements between the library director and the board? Between the library director and the staff? Is staff morale low? Has the library been through a lot of changes recently? Have one or more change projects stalled or failed? Is library funding stagnant or dropping? Are there labor relations issues? If there are significant interpersonal or organizational issues in your library, consider asking an outside consultant to help the planning coordinator to manage the process.

Finally, consider the complexity of your organization. Does the library report to more than one governmental unit? Does the library have facilities in more than one community or county? If so, does the library have multiple advisory boards? Does the library have intergovernmental agreements to operate joint-use facilities with other organizations? If the library environment is complex, consider asking an outside consultant to help the planning coordinator to manage the process.

As you see, cost is not the only factor, or even the primary factor, to consider when deciding if you want to ask an outside consultant to help manage the planning process. If you are concerned about cost, there are a number of options open to you, based on your budget and the complexity of your environment. There are professional library consultants who specialize in assisting public libraries to use the *Planning for Results* process to develop strategic plans, and their fees vary.[2] However, there are also a number of consultants who work for systems or state library agencies and who have been trained by the PLA to assist library staff to use *Planning for Results* to develop strategic plans.[3] These consultants typically facilitate planning processes as part of their jobs, and they charge the library little or nothing. The key factor is not cost but skill. The person you ask to manage your planning process needs to know about libraries, be familiar with the *Planning for Results* process, and be a skilled facilitator. If you plan to use an outside consultant, you might find the information in the article "Getting Your Money's Worth: How to Hire the Right Consultant" helpful.[4]

If you decide to ask an outside consultant to work with the planning coordinator throughout the planning process, that consultant will facilitate the two main meetings of the community planning committee as part of her responsibilities. If you decide that you will manage the planning process in-house, you will still have to decide who will facilitate the meetings of the committee. This is best done by someone other than a library staff member. If a member of the management team facilitates the community planning meetings, some staff may believe the results of process were predetermined. Even the members of the community planning committee may find it difficult to see the library manager as a neutral facilitator.

As noted earlier, if you decide to hire a consultant to manage your entire planning process, you will want someone who is knowledgeable about both libraries and *Planning for Results* and who is a skilled facilitator. The requirements for the person who is hired solely to facilitate the community planning meetings are simpler. The person needs to be a skilled facilitator who is willing to read this book (or at least chapters 1 and 2 of this book) and follow the steps in Tasks 3 and 4.

Of course, if you want to hire someone with both subject expertise and facilitation skills, you could hire a professional library consultant to facilitate the meetings, or you could ask one of the consultants who has been trained by the PLA to assist library staff to facilitate the meetings. However, there are a number of people in your community who could facilitate the two main meetings of the community planning committee and would probably charge only a nominal fee. They include someone from the city or county planning office, school guidance counselors, someone from the county extension service, clergymen, psychologists, and communication instructors from the local community college or university, among others.

When you have identified the participants in the planning process, defined their responsibilities, and decided who you will recommend to manage or facilitate the process, you are ready to begin Step 1.3.

Step 1.3
Prepare a Planning Schedule and Budget

The key to developing an effective planning time line is to remember that planning is a means to an end and not the end itself. The whole point of the process is to identify priorities for change—and then to actually change. If you spend too much time identifying priorities, you are in danger of running out of energy before the real work of implementing the plan begins.

How Long Should the Process Take?

Most library managers feel overworked and stressed out. There is too much to do and no way to get everything done. Adding a planning process to an already hectic schedule is difficult, and there is a tendency to want to spread the process out over a period of months in order to reduce the amount of time that will be required in any given day or week. The thinking seems to be that it will be easier to work on the planning process occasionally during a six- or eight-month period than to work on the process regularly during a two- or three-month period. The truth, of course, is that the process will take more time if it is spread out over a longer planning period. It is a matter of momentum. It takes a lot of energy to get a process started, but once you are moving forward it is easier to keep on going than to stop. A process that starts and then is put on hold for a month or two and then starts again only to be put on hold again after a couple of weeks will take at least twice as many hours to complete as a process that moves forward steadily from start to finish.

Staff perceptions also play a part in determining the appropriate planning time frame. If your planning process starts in January and you don't develop goals and objectives until September, staff are likely to feel that you have been planning forever before you ever start considering implementation issues. On the other hand, a planning process that starts in January and results in goals and objectives in mid-March should keep staff involved and engaged. Figure 6 is a suggested planning time line for you to consider.

When Should the Process Start?

The library year has a rhythm of its own. Spring brings an increased number of school visits and lots of students doing research papers. Summer is dominated by the summer reading program and staff vacations. In the fall students are back in school, and in the winter the holiday season starts in mid-November and doesn't end until early January. There is also the annual management cycle to consider. Managers move from preparing budgets to monitoring expenditures, and from performance planning to performance appraisal.

FIGURE 6
Suggested Planning Time Line

Task	Planning Activity	Month
Task 1	Design the Planning Process	Month One
Task 2	Start the Planning Process	
Task 3	Identify Community Needs	Month Two
Task 4	Select Service Responses	
Task 5	Prepare for Change	Month Three
Task 6	Consider Library Values and Mission	
Task 7	Write Goals and Objectives	
Task 8	Identify Organizational Competencies	
Task 9	Write the Strategic Plan and Obtain Approval	Month Four
Task 10	Communicate the Results of the Planning Process	Ongoing

There are regular monthly reports to write and complex annual reports to compile. You can't ignore weather cycles either. Many libraries in northern states avoid scheduling any major activities during heavy snow months.

The cycle of events in your library (and the climate in which you work) will affect your choice of starting and ending dates for the planning cycle. You probably won't want to start a planning process in June or December because scheduling will be too complicated. In fact, for all of the reasons listed in the preceding paragraph, most libraries start their planning processes in February or March or in August or September.

What Will the Process Cost?

There will be costs associated with every planning process. All libraries will have to pay to provide coffee, tea, and pastry at the beginning of each meeting of the community planning committee and lunch during each meeting of the committee. The food cost will vary dramatically depending on who provides the food. If you buy a can of coffee, a box of tea bags, and two dozen doughnuts at the grocery store, the total cost may be less than ten dollars. If you pay a caterer to provide the morning coffee and food, the total cost may be as much as ten dollars per person. You will face the same choices for lunch. You can buy sandwiches from a sub shop and chips, sodas, and cookies from the grocery store, or you can have a caterer provide the complete lunch. The sub sandwiches will be relatively inexpensive. The caterer won't be. On the other hand, if you don't hire a caterer, you or another staff member will have to manage the morning and lunch food preparation and service. You will have to go to the grocery store and the sub shop. You will have to make the coffee. You will have to set up the lunch buffet. It comes down to a choice between time and money.

The biggest variable in the cost of managing a planning process is the consultant or facilitator. As noted above, you can hire a full-time library consultant who specializes in library planning. If you do, you will pay a daily fee and travel expenses. The costs for consultants vary, and so will the travel expenses. If you use a local facilitator to manage the two meetings of the community planning committee, you may have to pay a modest honorarium and you probably won't have any travel expenses. If you are fortunate enough to be able to use a consultant from your system or state library agency, you won't have any consultant-related expenses.

You will have to decide if you want to reimburse the members of the community planning committee for their mileage and parking. Very few libraries provide reimbursement, but if your committee members are traveling a long way, or if parking near your library is expensive, you may want to consider it. You may also want to purchase a small gift for each member of the committee to thank them for their time and effort. Typical gifts include library-themed coffee cups, pens, or tote bags.

At one time, many libraries budgeted a considerable amount of money to have the final strategic plan typeset and printed, often in full color. The advent of desktop publishing and laser printers reduced these publication costs considerably. In fact, the whole concept of printing one beautifully produced and bound copy of the plan is outdated. As you will see in chapter 5, the "final" plan that you publish will be short and may be changed depending on the target audience for the publication. In essence, you may have multiple "final" plans, in both print and electronic formats.

Step 1.4
Develop a Communication Plan

Effective communication is a critical component of any successful planning effort. There are a number of groups participating in the planning process, and their responsibilities change as the process moves forward. It is easy to get so involved with the group or groups that have responsibility for the current part of the process that you forget to keep other stakeholders informed. This can have very negative consequences.

Think of your planning process as a square table supported by four legs (see figure 7). The first leg is the library board, the second leg is the library management team, the third leg is the library staff, and the fourth leg is the community planning committee. Remove any one of these four legs and you will have a very shaky table. Remove two or more and your table won't stand at all.

Communication is the key to keeping all four groups involved with and supporting your planning process. Most of the communications you develop throughout the process will be for one of two purposes: to inform or to persuade. As you begin to develop your communication plan, you will realize that the old saying "one size fits all" is not true.

The members of each of the groups know different things about the library, have different roles in the planning process, and will be affected differently by the results of the process. For instance, early in the process you will want to keep staff informed while persuading the members of the board to approve your planning design, budget, and time line. Later in the process, you will want to keep the board informed, while you are persuading staff to fully participate in the selection of activities. Because the roles and responsibilities of the stakeholder groups evolve throughout the planning process, it makes sense to develop a communication plan for each task within the process.

This becomes clearer as you consider the six questions to answer when developing your communication plan.

> *Why do the members of the group need to know about this task?* The first thing to decide is why you are communicating with the members of the group at all. Is there a reason for them to be informed about the task? Will they have to take some action? Will they be affected by actions that others take? Every communication should have a clearly defined purpose. You need to know what you expect from the recipient before you develop the message.

FIGURE 7
Stakeholders Support the Process

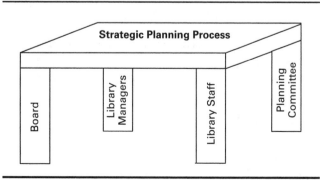

What do they know now? Once you define the purpose of the message, think about what the members of the group know about the task now. In this instance, you will want to consider both what the members of the group have learned through official communications and what they may have heard through the grapevine or other unofficial channels.

What will they need to know? You have defined the purpose of your communication and the information that the recipients of the communication currently have that might affect that purpose. Now you need to decide what additional information they will need to fulfill your intended purpose.

When will they need to know it? Almost all communications pertaining to the planning process will be time-sensitive. Once you begin to plan, the process moves forward quickly. Effective communications must reach the intended recipients in time to influence their actions or reactions.

How will you inform them? There are a variety of media and methods that can be used to communicate with the stakeholders in the planning process. They are described in detail in the Library Communication tool kit in part 3.

Who will be responsible for informing them? Nothing gets done unless someone or some group is assigned to do it.

Workform A, Communication Plan, provides a framework for you to use when developing your communication plans for each of the ten tasks in the planning process. Figure 8 illustrates how the Tree County Public Library completed the workform for Task 1.

What Is the Most Effective Way to Communicate with Staff?

The easiest and most effective way to keep all library staff and board members informed about the status of the planning process and to solicit staff input is to develop and maintain a web-based planning site on the library intranet. The site should have a home page that provides a brief introduction to the *Planning for Results* process and has links to five subordinate pages, each of which provides information for a separate phase of the planning process:

Phase 1: Plan to Plan

Phase 2: Identify Service Priorities

Phase 3: Define Library Values

Phase 4: Write Goals and Objectives

Phase 5: Identify Organizational Competencies and Initiatives

You will note that the five phases on the staff website do not correspond exactly with the ten tasks in this process. This is because the staff will not be involved in all ten tasks. Tasks 2 (Start the Planning Process), 5 (Prepare for Change), 9 (Write the Strategic Plan and Obtain Approval), and 10 (Communicate the Results of the Planning Process) will be managed by the members of the library management team. Task 3 (Identify Community Needs) is completed by the community planning committee, and their work will be reported to staff on the Phase 2 web page.

The staff planning website has two purposes: it can be used to provide instructions for staff to provide their input into the planning process, and it provides a means to keep

FIGURE 8

Workform A: Communication Plan—Example

TASK 1: Design the Planning Process

A. Start Date: September 25, 2XXX

B. End Date: October 23, 2XXX

	C. Why do they need to know about this task?	**D.** What do they know now?	**E.** What will they need to know?	**F.** When do they need to know it?	**G.** How will they be informed?	**H.** Who will be responsible for informing them?
1. Board/ Governing Authority	They need to formally approve the facilitator, responsibilities, time line, and budget They need to appoint committee members	They approved the use of *PFR* to develop a new library strategic plan during their September board meeting and knew that they would be appointing the planning committee at the October meeting	The planning process and responsibilities; the planning time line and budget The issues to consider when appointing the planning committee	Before the October 23 board meeting	One-page summary of process and responsibilities One-page summary of time line and budget List of possible committee members	Planning coordinator Director Director
2. Library Managers	They will be responsible for working with staff throughout the process	The board approved the use of *PFR* during the September board meeting They can recommend people to serve on the committee	The *PFR* process is more inclusive than our previous planning process	Before the October 23 board meeting	Attend a one-day management retreat on *PFR*	Director; head of staff development
3. Library Staff	They will be involved throughout the process and will be affected by the results	The board approved the use of *PFR* during the September board meeting They can recommend people to serve on the committee	Staff orientation meetings are scheduled for [date]	As soon as the board approved using the *PFR* process	Through a planning web page on library intranet Unit meetings	Planning coordinator; online services manager Unit managers
4. Planning Committee Members	They don't					
5. Other: Friends of the Library	The members need to be kept informed	A planning process is going to be initiated by the library	The planning process, responsibilities, time line	As soon as the board approved using the *PFR* process	A short presentation at the Friends' board meeting	Director

Note: Be sure the planning website is completed by October 1.

the staff informed about decisions made during the planning process. The subordinate pages can link to draft documents that staff can review and react to, and to instructions and workforms that staff are expected to complete. The pages can also include the planning products produced during each phase of the process.

At the end of Phase 1, you could post the planning time line and the names of the members of the community planning committee. During Phase 2, you could post the minutes of the meetings of the planning committee, the committee's preliminary recommendations, the staff and board reactions to those recommendations, and final service responses as approved by the board. During Phase 3, you could post the draft value statements, forms for staff comments, and the final versions when approved. During Phases 4 and 5 you could do the same thing for the goals, objectives, and organizational competencies and initiatives.

There is more information on communicating effectively in the Library Communication tool kit in part 3 of this book.

Step 1.5
Design and Present a Staff Orientation

This planning process is based on the belief that each community is unique, that library priorities need to reflect community needs, and that representatives from various constituencies in the community are the most appropriate people to take the lead role in defining that community's needs.

While many staff members may agree with and support this belief, it is not universally endorsed. There are those who feel strongly that only library professionals have the knowledge and expertise to identify library priorities. They fear that the community planning committee will select the "wrong" priorities or that it will "dumb down" the library because it lacks a clear understanding of the underlying principles of public librarianship. It is probably impossible to change the perceptions of staff who believe these things (beliefs are notoriously difficult to change). You will need to acknowledge that some people feel this way and address their concerns.

The most effective way to address staff concerns is to make the responsibilities of each of the stakeholder groups very clear before the process begins. After the board has endorsed the idea of planning and reached consensus that the plan will focus on identifying service priorities (Step 1.1) and before the board meets to approve the plan to plan (Step 2.1), all staff should be asked to attend a two-hour program designed to provide them with an orientation to the *Planning for Results* process. You will probably need to repeat the orientation at least twice to be sure that all staff can attend, and you may need to repeat it three or even four times if your library has a large staff.

The orientation programs will be presented by the outside library consultant, if you choose to use one. If you decide not to use an outside consultant, the orientation programs can be presented by the library director or the member of the management team who was selected to be the planning coordinator. The information that the staff receive about the planning process will be the same no matter who is presenting the program.

Why is the library starting a new planning process? The planning outcomes endorsed by the board (Step 1.1) provide this information.

What planning process will be used? Figure 2 provides a succinct summary of the process.

Who will be involved in the planning process? Figure 7 lists all four stakeholder groups and illustrates the need for all to be involved throughout the process.

How will staff be kept informed about the planning process? The presenter can use a data projector to give staff a short tour of the planning website on the library intranet.

What will the community planning committee do? Figure 5 illustrates the responsibilities of all of the planning stakeholders.

Who will select the community planning committee? The presenter should tell staff that while the board will make the final selections, staff members are encouraged to recommend the names of potential members. The presenter might want to use figure 9 to help staff understand the issues to consider when selecting people to recommend. Workform B, Select Planning Committee Members, can be posted on the Phase 1 page of the staff planning website for staff to use to submit their recommendations.

What role will staff have in the selection of the library's priorities? Staff need to know that the members of the planning committee will not be making their recommendations in a void. Staff will have a chance to review the committee's preliminary recommendations and to comment and make suggestions. The members of the committee will receive a report about the staff reactions before they make their recommendations.

What other responsibilities will staff members have in the process? Figure 4 lists all of the points during the process that staff will be given an opportunity to participate.

What is the time line for the process? The presenter can share the tentative time line developed during Step 1.3 but should make it clear that the board has not yet approved the time line.

It is worth reminding staff both during the orientation program and throughout the process that if they choose not to participate when given an opportunity to do so, they will still have to live with the results of the decisions made. Too many staff ignore the initial parts of the process because they aren't interested in the library's priorities or goals, both of which can seem pretty vague and theoretical to frontline staff. When it comes time to develop measurable objectives for those goals, staff may find they have strong opinions about the implications of the library's new priorities and goals. However, by that time, the priorities have been selected and the goals have been established and it is too late.

TASK 2: START THE PLANNING PROCESS

The steps in Task 2 will be completed by the library director, the members of the library management team, and the members of the library board. It will take two to three weeks to accomplish the steps in this task. Actually, the selection of community planning committee members will have begun during Task 1. This second task, like the first, begins with a meeting of the library board.

Step 2.1
Obtain Board Approval

The library director will develop an information packet about the planning process for board review and approval. The packet will include the proposed time line and budget (Step 1.3). If the management team has decided to recommend that the board hire an outside consultant or facilitator, that recommendation will be included as well. When the director has completed the information packet, she will review it with the board chair, and then it will be sent to the members of the board for their review before the meeting.

The information packet will also include a reminder that the members of the board will be suggesting names of people to be invited to participate in the community planning committee during the board meeting. It might be helpful to include a copy of Workform B in the packet for the members of the board.

The business part of the board meeting will open with a review and discussion of the proposed planning budget, time line, and consultant or facilitator (if applicable). When the members have concluded their discussion, the chair will ask for a motion to approve the recommendations and a vote will be taken.

After the board has formally approved the planning time line, budget, and consultant or facilitator (if any), the members will be ready to begin to select the people they want to invite to serve on the community planning committee. Before the selection process begins, the director may want to make a short presentation that includes information on the approximate size of the committee, the characteristics of effective committee members, and the process that has been used to generate recommendations from staff and others. If there are special issues to consider when selecting community planning committee members, such as selecting representatives from multiple governmental jurisdictions, they should be identified now.

Step 2.2
Select Community Planning Committee Members

The members of the community planning committee play a critical role in the library's strategic planning process. They will be responsible for identifying the community needs that the library could and should address. In other words, they provide the foundation for the remainder of the process. If the foundation is shaky, the rest of the structure is in danger. That is why it is so important that everyone involved take the time to select and appoint the "right" people to the committee. In this instance, "right" simply means a combination of people who can speak for all of the constituencies in your community and who reflect the demographics of your community.

The community planning committee usually has twelve to eighteen members, most of whom are not involved with the library in any official capacity. A fifteen-member committee typically has thirteen community members, the staff representative, and the board liaison. In addition, some libraries include a representative from the library foundation or Friends group. As a rule, no more than 15 percent of the committee members should be library staff, board members, or affiliated with a library support group. Remember, this is a *community* planning committee. Use figure 9 as a starting point for identifying the groups that should be represented on the planning committee.

FIGURE 9
Community Organizations and Groups

Businesses/ Chambers of Commerce/ Economic Development Organizations

Major employers, minority business owners, small business owners, visitors' centers, chambers of commerce (city, county, and ethnic, if any), economic development councils, industry councils, unions

Community Services Organizations/Associations/ Clubs

Rotary, Lions, Kiwanis, United Way, AARP, AAUW, American Red Cross, literacy organizations, Soroptimists, National Organization for Women, YWCA, YMCA

Cultural Groups

Theater groups, art leagues, dance supporters, arts commission

Educational Organizations

Public schools, private schools, colleges/universities, PTA or PTO, school boards, homeschool organizations

Ethnic Organizations

Ethnic chambers of commerce, NAACP, tribal councils, Latino/Hispanic groups, Asian groups, Urban League, refugee rights associations

Family Services Organizations

County department of social services, family service agency

Financial Representatives

Bankers, credit unions, financial planners, stockbrokers

Government/Political Representatives

Mayor, city/county manager, city council, county supervisors, city/county fiscal office, city/county planning office, law enforcement officers, job training programs

Health Organizations

American Cancer Society, American Heart Association, hospitals, public health nurses, public health clinics

Legal Organizations

Legal aid, ACLU

Library Representatives

School media center staff, college or university librarians, special librarians

Media Representatives

Newspaper, radio, TV, ethnic media, local magazines and newsletters

Organizations Serving the Disabled

Center on Deafness, Council of the Blind, state/county/ city health and human services, Easter Seal, Goodwill, independent living centers, United Cerebral Palsy

Professional Groups

Medical associations, board of realtors, bar association, business and professional women's groups

Religious Groups

Ministerial alliance, youth groups, faith-based community centers

Senior Centers/Service Organizations

Area Agency on Aging, senior centers

Youth Services Organizations

Big Brother/Sister, Boy Scouts, Girl Scouts, FFA, FHA, child abuse agencies, city/county recreation programs, Junior Achievement, Head Start, Even Start, child care associations, local Association for the Education of Young Children, school-age care and enrichment programs

Who Should Be Invited to Participate on the Committee?

The most effective planning committee members hold leadership positions in the groups they represent. After all, the members of the various community groups have selected their leaders to speak for them. If you ask Nancy Smith, the president of the Parent-Teacher Organization, to represent parents on the committee, you will probably find that she is aware of the issues that concern parents and has been involved in planning to address those issues. Ms. Smith will find it easy to speak for that group during the planning committee meeting.

On the other hand, if you decide to ask Mary Jones, mother of three children and a regular library user, to represent parents, Ms. Jones will only be speaking for herself, her family, and perhaps her friends and neighbors. When the time comes to inform the groups in the community about the library planning process, Ms. Smith will have an official venue and a built-in audience, while Ms. Jones can only talk to her friends and family.

Not all groups have formal elected leaders, but most groups without elected leaders have unofficial leaders. In one community, child care providers are required to attend classes at the local community college to be certified. The woman who coordinates and teaches the community college classes is perceived by most child care providers as their spokesperson. In another community, a young woman operating a small not-for-profit newspaper for new immigrants from Central America is the unofficial leader of that immigrant community. She helps people fill out forms, get jobs, locate places to learn English, and do all of the other things people moving into a new society need to do. In a third community, a nun who operates a shelter for homeless women also serves on the boards of virtually every private, public, and not-for-profit social service agency in the county. She is the logical representative for that segment of the population.

The members of the community planning committee should be selected from within the library's service area. After all, the people who pay the bills (taxes) should have a say in what they are paying for (library services). If the community you serve is fairly large, you will want to be sure to include people from the different neighborhoods throughout the city. Managers and boards in urban systems with many branches throughout the city may wonder if they should appoint planning committees for each branch and then find a way to compile the recommendations from each group into citywide recommendations. This is a very labor- and time-intensive process and it is not recommended. An urban library system should appoint a citywide committee to identify systemwide goals that reflect the needs of the entire community. Later in the process, during Task 7, staff in branch libraries will be given an opportunity to recommend the priority of the system goals for their branch clientele.

The question of how to include representatives from throughout the library service area is more complex for county library systems serving multiple communities within their service area. There are three choices listed below, along with the pros and cons of each. However, most libraries are encouraged to use the single county planning committee unless there is a compelling local reason to use one of the other two alternatives.

A single county planning committee. The process can be managed in exactly the same way that was recommended for urban systems. First appoint a committee with representatives from throughout the county to identify service priorities, and then during Task 7 encourage staff in branch libraries to determine the priority of the system goals for their communities. The benefit to this approach is obvious—it is the fastest and most efficient way to identify priorities. The prime drawback is equally obvious—the leadership in the separate communities may feel disenfranchised on the front end of the process, which may make it more difficult to get their buy-in as the process moves forward.

A single county planning committee with subcommittees from each community. In this model, three or four representatives from each community served by the system are invited to participate in the planning process. The representatives from each community will work together during Task 3 to identify the vision for their communities and the current conditions in their communities. Then the community groups are merged and redivided into mixed small groups to identify service priorities for the system. If you use this process, you will again encourage staff in branch libraries to determine the priority of the system goals for their communities in Task 7. They will be able to use the vision and current conditions from the community-based subcommittees to identify those priorities.

The benefit is that community leaders feel their voices have been heard. The drawback to this approach is that, depending on the number of communities served by the library, the committee can get quite large. In one case, the committee had twenty-eight members, which made it difficult to ensure that all of the members had a chance to participate. It definitely takes a trained facilitator to manage a committee this size. If the group has more than twenty participants, you and the facilitator may want to consider having three meetings of the committee to complete Tasks 3 and 4, rather than the two meetings that are recommended in chapter 2.

Separate planning committees in each community that send representatives to a county planning committee. In this model, the library appoints separate planning committees in each community served by the library, plus a planning committee for county residents who do not live in any of the communities. Each of these individual planning committees completes the steps in Tasks 3 and 4 and identifies service priorities for the local branch libraries. Representatives are selected from each community committee to meet in a countywide committee that is responsible for identifying systemwide service priorities. This is the most complex process and one that definitely requires a professional facilitator, preferably a library facilitator. It will add at least three months to your planning time line.

What Is the Most Effective Way to Identify Possible Committee Members?

The community planning committee will serve in an advisory capacity to the library board, and the library board will be responsible for making the final selection of the committee members. This does not mean, however, that the responsibility for identifying possible members of the community planning committee should be limited to board members. Staff should be encouraged to suggest people to be included on the community planning committee during the staff orientation programs (Step 1.5). Members of the management team should also recommend names. You might even want to ask the board of the library's Friends group or foundation to make suggestions.

Ask everyone who plans to recommend committee members to submit their recommendations to the planning coordinator in writing, and tell them to include a phone number or address for each person and a brief statement about why each is being recommended. Remind everyone that they are simply recommending names and that the board will make the final decisions. No one should tell a potential committee member that he or she is being recommended. There will be dozens of people recommended, and there is no way to know who will be selected. It is not a good idea to raise expectations that may not be met. Be sure that everyone knows the deadline by which recommendations must be received. The deadline should be several days before the scheduled board meeting in order to allow time to consolidate the recommendations into a single list.

The board chair will start the process by distributing Workform B to the members. The format of the workform will provide the framework for the board members to make their recommendations. They can suggest an organization, an individual, or both, but they have to include the reason for their suggestions. As the members make their recommendations, someone will record them on a flip-chart. When all of the recommendations from the board have been recorded, the chair will distribute the composite list of recommendations from the staff and others. The group will compare the names recommended by the board and the names recommended by the staff and create a final list of names from which to select. You can see a part of the list developed by the staff and board of the Tree County Public Library in figure 10.

The final selection process will probably be too time-consuming to be managed during this meeting. If that is the case, the chair will appoint a subcommittee to complete the work. The subcommittee will be authorized to make the final selections and to work with the members of the management team to invite the selected individuals to participate. The subcommittee will want to select two or three names for each slot on the committee in case one of the invitees declines.

FIGURE 10

Workform B: Select Planning Committee Members—Example

A. Organization/Group/Skill	B. Name(s) to Consider	C. Reason for Selection
Chamber of Commerce		Includes most small business owners
City Manager's Office		He controls our budget
Redwood School District	Superintendent	The library works with a lot of students
	Naomi Gregg	She is an African-American small business owner and she is VP of Rotary this year
	Bill James	President of the high school student council
Ministerial Alliance		They know about the social services in town
	Henry Kramer	Retired chief of police; has lived in town all his life and knows everyone
Someone who knows about the future of technology		Things keep changing and we need to keep up

FIGURE 11
Committee Checklist

Demographics

1. Does the committee include members in the following age groups?
   a. Teens
   b. Adults 18–30
   c. Adults 31–50
   d. Adults over 51
2. Are the ethnic and racial groups in your community represented equitably?
3. Does the committee include people with various levels of education?
4. Are men and women equitably represented?
5. Does the committee include newcomers to the community as well as long-time residents?

Location

1. Are all of the geographic areas served by the library represented?
2. Are any of the areas served by the library overrepresented compared to others?

Local government

1. Is local government represented?
2. Should representatives from more than one local government be represented? If so, how?

Employers and occupations

1. Are various employers and occupations represented?
2. Are any employers or occupations overrepresented compared to others?

Agencies and organizations

1. Does the committee include representatives from the following groups?
   a. Local school districts
   b. Key social service agencies

Other

1. Is there a representative from the library staff?
2. Is there a representative from the library board?

Balancing all of the things that need to be considered when selecting people to serve on the community planning committee can be challenging. Before the list of people to be invited to serve on the planning committee is completed, the members of the board (or the subcommittee of the board) will want to answer the questions in figure 11. This will ensure the final list of people to be invited is exactly "right" for your community. You will also want to keep those questions in mind if someone declines to serve on the committee and you have to ask an alternate.

Step 2.3
Invite Committee Members

It takes a lot of time, energy, and thought to identify exactly the right mix of people to serve on the community planning committee, but it is all wasted if the people you invite to participate decline your invitation. It is just as important to think carefully about how you issue your invitations as it was to think carefully about who to invite.

Think for a minute about the invitations you have received to participate in some activity in your school, in a club or organization, in your place of worship, or in your community. What influenced your decision? If you are like most people, you were more likely to agree to serve if you were asked by a friend or colleague than if you were asked by a complete stranger. You were more likely to agree if you cared about the endeavor. You were more likely to agree if you thought you had something to contribute than you were if you didn't know anything about the endeavor. You were more likely to agree if you thought that you or someone or something that you cared about would receive some benefit from your participation. You were more likely to agree if you knew exactly what you were being asked to do and how much time it would take.

These same feelings will motivate the people that you invite to serve on the planning committee. In view of this, you will probably want to have several people issue the invitations to serve. If you are lucky, everyone on your list of potential committee members will be known by at least one of the members of your board, and that board member will be willing to issue the invitation. If you are not that lucky, don't despair. It is likely that your potential committee members are at least "friends of friends" of one or more board members, and those board members can arrange for a personal introduction before issuing the invitation to serve.

Before any invitations are issued, the people who are doing the inviting need to be prepared to explain a number of things to the invitees:

What is the purpose of the committee? The members of the planning committee will be responsible for identifying a vision for the future of the community (and particularly the segments of the community they represent), for describing current conditions, and for defining what needs to happen to move the community from where it is now to the future described in the vision. Committee members will then work with library staff and board members to identify the services that the library should provide to help meet the needs and move the community toward the identified vision.

What is the relationship of the planning committee and the library board? The planning committee is advisory to the board.

What benefits will the invitee or the group(s) he or she represents receive as a result of serving on the committee? The needs of the group(s) he or she represents will be addressed as part of the library planning process, and the services for the group may be enhanced. The invitee will have an opportunity to meet with other community leaders to discuss the future of the community and may make connections with other participants that will enhance services to the group he or she represents. The invitee will participate in creating a vision for the future of the community. The invitee can use that vision in planning for the groups he or she represents.

Why is the invitee being asked to serve on the committee? Be prepared to explain why the invitee was selected, the segment or segments of the community that he or she represents, and the knowledge, skills, or experiences he or she has that will contribute to identifying a community vision, describing current conditions, and defining what needs to happen to move toward the vision.

Who else will be serving on the committee? If the invitee is interested, you could list some of the organizations or groups that will be represented on the committee. You may also provide the names of people who have agreed to serve. However, be careful not to provide information about pending invitations.

What is the timetable for the planning process? The total planning time line is four months, but the committee's work will be completed during two meetings held three to four weeks apart.

When and where will the first meeting be held? When will the second meeting be held? There is no point in asking people to serve on the committee and then going back to those people to schedule the meetings. Inevitably, some of the people who agreed to serve will be unable to participate on any meeting date you select. Therefore, you should select the date and time for both meetings before issuing any invitations and try to ensure that everyone who agrees to serve will be able to participate. Invitees who are unable to attend meetings on the selected dates will not be included on the committee.

What is the process for reimbursement of any expenses incurred (mileage, parking, etc.), if applicable? If the library is planning to reimburse any expenses, tell the invitee and explain how the reimbursement process will work.

There are also several practical details to decide before you start to issue invitations to potential committee members. If you are planning to have several people issue invitations, you will want to have one person coordinate the process, probably the planning coordinator appointed in Step 1.2. Agree on a time frame for issuing invitations and decide how long you will wait for someone to say "yes" or "no," typically no more than two or three days. Remind the people doing the inviting that there are several possible names for each slot on the committee, and the person being invited cannot send an alternate to serve in his or her place—unless the person being invited is an elected official. Finally, ask the people issuing invitations to inform the coordinator immediately after they receive an answer to the invitation, so that the coordinator can maintain a master list of those who accept and decline.

Step 2.4
Prepare and Distribute Community and Library Information Packets

The members of the planning committee were selected because they represent various constituencies and demographic groups in your community. It is very likely that each will have a different set of assumptions about the community and the library. It is helpful to provide the members with a packet of information about the community and the library prior to the first committee meeting, to help everyone develop a common frame of reference for the process.

The packet typically includes information about the library such as:

Welcome letter from the director or the library board chair

Roster listing names and contact information for planning committee members

Library organization chart

Library locations—size, hours, and communities served

Library budget—broken down by major expenditures (personnel, materials budget, etc.)

Library use—circulation, number of programs, program attendance, number of reference questions, number of registered borrows, website hits, etc., for the past five years. This is best presented in charts so the planning committee members can see the trends.

Number of staff—by location or function

Collection information—by location and type of materials

Copies of library publications that describe services the library offers

In addition, the packet should include some basic demographic information about the community from the past five years or ten years (from the city, county, or state planning office). This is also best presented in charts so the planning committee members can see the trends. Earlier versions of the Public Library Association's planning process included a data collection form to record information about the community. Experience has shown that committee members rarely needed all of the information included on that form. In fact, dense information packets tend to impede the committee's work, rather than enhance it. The members of the committee were selected because of their firsthand knowledge of the community, and that is what should drive their decision making.

What's Next?

In this chapter you planned your planning process, developed a communication plan, prepared the staff to participate in the process, and selected the members of the planning committee. The next chapter will focus on the two meetings of the planning committee and the staff and board meetings that take place between the two committee meetings. You will learn more about the community visioning process, identifying community needs, and selecting service priorities. You will also get a better understanding of the interactions among the members of the committee, the staff, and the board.

Key Points to Remember

You must plan to plan. Otherwise you may end up like the Stephen Leacock character who "flung himself upon his horse and rode madly off in all directions."

It is important to clearly define your reasons for planning.

There are key roles for everyone to play during the planning process, and each role is important.

The key to successful planning is communication. You developed a communication plan in this chapter. As you implement that plan, continuously monitor your results. Make changes that are needed to be sure that everyone is kept informed throughout the process.

Use an outside facilitator to manage the two meetings of the planning committee. If a library manager facilitates the process, the members of the committee may not see the facilitator as impartial.

The staff orientation is a critical part of the planning process. Make sure that as many staff as possible attend one of the orientation programs.

You are appointing a *community* planning committee. It is important to keep the number of library representatives on the committee to a minimum.

Select the people to serve on the planning committee based on their knowledge of the community and not on their knowledge of the library.

Notes

1. Sandra Nelson, *Implementing for Results: From Ideas to Action* (Chicago: American Library Association, forthcoming 2008).
2. A list of library consultants is available at http://www.libraryconsultants.org.
3. A current list of trained *Planning for Results* facilitators is available from the Public Library Association, 800-545-2433, extension 5027.
4. Sandra Nelson and Paula Singer, "Getting Your Money's Worth: How to Hire the Right Consultant," *Public Libraries* (July/August 2004): 223–26, available at http://www.ala.org/ala/pla/plapubs/publiclibraries/43n4.pdf.

Chapter 2

Identify Service Priorities

Priority is a function of context.

—Stephen R. Covey

MILESTONES

By the time you finish this chapter you will be able to

- ensure that the members of the planning committee understand their responsibilities
- work with the planning committee to describe the ideal future for your community and to identify what needs to be done to achieve that ideal future
- provide planning committee members with a concise overview of current library services and programs
- use the library service responses to identify how the library can help to achieve the ideal future for the community
- provide board members and staff with an opportunity to respond to the preliminary recommendations from the planning committee
- share the board and staff reactions to the preliminary recommendations with the members of the planning committee
- select the library's service priorities for the current planning cycle

It is relatively easy to reach consensus on abstract ideals. Everyone wants world peace. Disagreements arise when people start talking about the means that should be used to reach world peace. In the same way, library managers, staff members, and board members have no problem agreeing that they want to provide the best possible public library service to people in the community. The problem, as anyone who has ever been involved in a library strategic planning process knows, is defining "the best possible public library service." There are as many definitions of that phrase as there are people working in and with libraries.

The process of identifying the service priorities that result in "the best possible public library service" can rapidly degenerate into a battle of wills among the planning participants. When that happens, the person who is loudest, or most stubborn, or who has the most authority (or all three), normally imposes her will on the rest of the group, and that is clearly not the strongest foundation for a collaborative planning effort.

In *Getting to Yes,* Robert Fisher and William Ury write:

> No negotiation is likely to be efficient or amicable if you pit your will against theirs, and you have to back down or they do. And whether you are choosing a place to eat, organizing a business, or negotiating custody of a child, you are unlikely to reach a wise agreement as judged by any objective standard if you take no such standard into account. If trying to settle differences of interest on the basis of will has such high costs, the solution is to negotiate on some basis independent of the will of either side—that is, on the basis of objective criteria.[1]

For this reason, effective strategic planning processes start by identifying the objective criteria that will be used to evaluate potential service priorities in order to determine "the best possible public library services." In the *Planning for Results* process, these criteria are community needs. In fact, the whole planning process is based on a belief that "the best possible public library services" cannot be defined in the abstract. The only valid definition is one that takes into consideration the needs of the people being served in each community.

Consider two communities: one in an isolated, economically disadvantaged area with limited public services, and the other in an affluent suburban community for seniors. It seems obvious that "the best possible public library services" would be quite different in these two communities. In the poor, isolated community, the library might be the only provider of literacy services or Internet access. In the senior community, the library might be a central meeting place, a source of leisure materials, and a place to explore topics of personal interest. The needs of community residents and the other services and organizations available in the community provide the external criteria by which to establish priorities.

This, of course, raises the next question. How can you identify community needs? If you follow the recommendations in chapter 1, your planning committee will be composed of representatives from a variety of constituencies in your community, each with a different set of needs. This seems to put us right back where we started. The person who is loudest, or most stubborn, or who has the most authority will impose her group's needs on the committee. This, in turn, suggests that you will need to identify a set of objective criteria to establish community needs before you can use the community needs as the criteria to determine the services that are "the best possible public library services" in your community. This may seem to be spinning into a convoluted process like one described in the following rhyme, but it really isn't.

> For want of a nail the shoe was lost.
> For want of a shoe the horse was lost.
> For want of a horse the rider was lost.

For want of a rider the battle was lost.

For want of a battle the kingdom was lost.

And all for the want of a horseshoe nail.

The "horseshoe nail" in the planning process is a series of vision statements describing the ideal future for the community. Once that nail is in place, the rest of the process flows naturally. The vision statements provide the objective criteria by which to determine community needs. The community needs, in turn, provide the criteria for determining library service priorities. The library service priorities are then translated into goals and objectives and ultimately into services and programs, which are evaluated by measuring how much progress is being made toward reaching the library goals, which were based on the original vision statements. These relationships are illustrated in figure 12.

FIGURE 12
Community Vision: The Beginning and the End

Getting Started

During the first task in this chapter, Task 3, members of the community planning committee will describe the ideal future for your community and identify what needs to happen to reach that ideal. During Task 4, you and your colleagues will work with the members of the community planning committee to select the service priorities that will be recommended to the library board for the current planning cycle, and the board will act upon the recommendations.

Most of the steps in both tasks in this chapter take place during and between the first two meetings of the community planning committee, which are typically scheduled three to four weeks apart. The two meetings of the planning committee will be facilitated by the outside consultant or facilitator you selected during Step 1.2. The library director and a small group of library managers will attend the meetings as observers. They will not participate in the small group discussions, will not contribute to the discussions about community vision, current conditions, and needs, will not express a preference among the library service responses, and will not take part in any process used to establish the library's service priorities. Those responsibilities are assigned to the members of the planning committee.

The director and the members of the library management team do have three important responsibilities during these two tasks, however. The director or his or her designee will make a presentation about the library (Step 4.1), which will set the stage for the identification of preliminary service priorities for the library. Following the first meeting of the planning committee, the members of the library management team will facilitate meetings of staff and board to hear their reactions to the preliminary service responses (Step 4.3). During the second meeting of the planning committee, the library director will discuss the staff and board reactions with the members of the committee (Step 4.4).

TASK 3: IDENTIFY COMMUNITY NEEDS

Task 1:   Design the Planning Process
Task 2:   Start the Planning Process
Task 3:   Identify Community Needs
      Step 3.1:   Present an orientation for the members of the planning committee
      Step 3.2:   Develop community vision statements
      Step 3.3:   Define current conditions in the community
      Step 3.4:   Decide what needs to be done to reach community vision
Task 4:   Select Service Responses
Task 5:   Prepare for Change
Task 6:   Consider Library Values and Mission
Task 7:   Write Goals and Objectives
Task 8:   Identify Organizational Competencies
Task 9:   Write the Strategic Plan and Obtain Approval
Task 10: Communicate the Results of the Planning Process

All of the steps in Task 3 occur during the first three hours of the first meeting of the planning committee. The full meeting is five hours long and typically includes either lunch or dinner, depending on the starting and ending time. The last two hours of the meeting are allocated for the activities described in Steps 4.1 and 4.2.

Figure 13 is a sample of the meeting agenda to be distributed to the meeting participants. The agenda starts with a list of the meeting objectives and then provides a general outline of the work to be accomplished during the meeting. The only times listed on the agenda are the beginning time, lunch time, and the ending time. This allows the meeting facilitator the flexibility to take more time on one part of the process and less on another, depending on the group interactions. When an agenda has specific times for each activity, meeting participants usually expect those times to be followed. If the first activity is scheduled to start at 10:30 and end at 11:15 and actually takes until 11:45 to complete, meeting participants get anxious and wonder if the meeting is going to run thirty minutes over schedule. They may also lose confidence in the facilitator's ability to manage the meeting.

Figure 14 is the facilitator's version of the same meeting agenda. This agenda has tentative times listed for each of the activities in the meeting and lists the handouts to be used during each activity. The handouts in the participants' packet will be based on the figures noted in the agenda. The agenda and handouts serve as the outline of the script the facilitator will follow throughout the meeting. If one part of the process takes longer than expected, the facilitator will need to adjust another part of the process to compensate.

TREE COUNTY PUBLIC LIBRARY

Meeting One of the Planning Committee

[Date]

MEETING OBJECTIVES

Participants will understand the roles and responsibilities of all participants in the *Planning for Results* process

Participants will describe the ideal future for Tree County

Participants will identify the current strengths and weaknesses of Tree County and potential opportunities or threats that might affect achieving the ideal future

Participants will identify the needs that must be addressed to reach the ideal future of the county

Participants will develop an understanding of the current conditions in the library

Participants will make a preliminary selection of future library service priorities

MEETING AGENDA

10:00   *Planning for Results*

        Defining the Ideal Future: Vision Statement

        Reviewing Where the Community Is Now: SWOT Analysis

12:00   Lunch

        Determining Community Needs

        Reviewing Where the Library Is Now: Director's Presentation

        The Library Can Make a Difference: Service Responses

3:00   Adjourn

TREE COUNTY PUBLIC LIBRARY

Meeting One of the Planning Committee

[Date]

MEETING OBJECTIVES

Participants will understand the roles and responsibilities of all participants in the *Planning for Results* process

Participants will describe the ideal future for Tree County

Participants will identify the current strengths and weaknesses of Tree County and potential opportunities or threats that might affect achieving the ideal future

Participants will identify the needs that must be addressed to reach the ideal future of the county

Participants will develop an understanding of the current conditions in the library

Participants will make a preliminary selection of future library service priorities

MEETING AGENDA

10:00	Introductions—All
10:15	*Planning for Results*—Presentation by Facilitator
	Handout: *Planning for Results* (based on figure 2)
	Handout: Planning Responsibilities (based on figure 5)
	Handout: Planning Time Line
10:30	Defining the Ideal Future: Vision Statement—Small Groups and Round-Robin Reporting
	Handout: Demographic Data in Committee Orientation Packet
	Handout: Workform C, Community Vision
11:45	Reviewing Where the Community Is Now: SWOT Analysis—Small Groups
	Handout: Workform D, Community SWOT Analysis
12:15	Working Lunch—Round-Robin Reporting from SWOT Analysis
1:00	Determining Community Needs
	Handout: Needs Decision Tree (based on figure 17)
1:15	Reviewing Where the Library Is Now: Director's Presentation
	Handout: Library Data in Committee Orientation Packet
	PowerPoint Presentation
1:45	The Library Can Make a Difference: Service Responses—Presentation by Facilitator
	Handout: Service Responses (based on figure 18)
2:15	Identify Preliminary Service Responses—Group
3:00	Adjourn

Step 3.1
Present an Orientation for the Members of the Planning Committee

The meeting begins with introductions. Each member should be asked to give his or her name and the organization or group he or she represents. When the introductions are complete, the facilitator will briefly introduce the *Planning for Results* process. The facilitator can use the same overview of the process (figure 2) and the picture illustrating the responsibilities of the planning participants (figure 5) that were presented to the board and staff in chapter 1.

The orientation ends with a review of the information about the community that was in the orientation packet you prepared and distributed prior to the meeting during Step 2.4. While most of the members of the committee will have looked at the materials, you cannot assume that they have all read the information with equal care. (The information about the library included in the packet will be discussed in Step 4.1.)

Step 3.2
Develop Community Vision Statements

The real work of the committee begins with a discussion of what the community would look like in ten years if all the aspirations of all of the residents had been achieved. Derek Okubo of the National Civic League defines *community vision* as a shared sense of the future. He goes on to say:

> A community's vision should reflect the common values of that community; at the same time, however, it needs to be inclusive of the diverse populations which make up that community. Moreover, a community vision is not a "cookie cutter" type of document. A vision should reflect those qualities that make a community unique.[2]

The facilitator may want to start this part of the process by reading Okubo's statement and discussing it with the members of the committee to be sure that everyone understands three things. First, and most important, this visioning process is about the community and *not* the library. Second, the vision statements should focus on specific target audiences whenever possible. The members of the small groups should try to avoid statements that target "all residents." Third, vision statements always refer to the future, and there may be differing perceptions about the future. The visioning process may not result in a consensus on every vision statement, but it should result in a set of vision statements that taken together reflect the unique qualities of the community.

What Is the Best Way to Manage Group Work and Reporting?

Typically, the facilitator divides the members of the committee into groups of three members each. After a brief introduction to the process by the facilitator, the members of each of the small groups begin their discussions. They use Workform C, Community Vision, to structure their discussions and record their work. The facilitator goes from group to group to answer any questions about the process, to be sure that all of the groups are talking about the community and not the library, and to encourage group members to focus on specific target audiences. In figure 15, you can see examples of the kinds of vision statements that were identified by the Tree County Library committee members.

As the facilitator moves from group to group, she can judge how much time the groups will need for this step. Normally, this group work takes about twenty minutes, but that varies. When the groups have completed their discussions, the facilitator will begin to record their work on a flip-chart. The fastest and most effective way to record group work is to start by asking one group to read a vision for a target audience. Record that vision statement and then ask if other groups had vision statements for that target audience too. Record all of the vision statements for the first target audience and then ask another group to read a vision statement that focuses on a different target audience. Again record all of the vision statements from all of the groups for that target audience, and then move on to a third target audience. Continue until all of the vision statements from all groups have been recorded. When the facilitator is finished, someone should tape the sheets containing all of the vision statements on a wall that can be seen by the meeting participants.

FIGURE 15

Workform C: Community Vision—Example

A. Who Will Benefit	B. Benefit and Result
Children	will receive the education they need to secure employment that provides a living wage
Seniors	will have affordable and accessible health care to maintain a high and active quality of life
Seniors	will have volunteer opportunities to use their skills and keep them involved in the community
Immigrants	will get the education they need to assimilate and become citizens
Families	will have programs and services that support strong family values across cultures
Local businesses	will continue to grow and the local economy will be strong
Local businesses	will have a stable tax environment to encourage growth
County agencies	will all collaborate and provide services in a manner in which the roles of each are clearly identified and understood
Working people	will have easily accessible and affordable public transportation to their places of employment
Children and teens	will have the transportation they need to participate in after-school and weekend activities
Teens	will have access to group and individual activities after school and on weekends that are exciting, informative, and interactive
Young adults	will return to the community after they graduate from college

What If Your Community Already Has a Vision Statement?

Some communities already have vision statements created through a community-wide process initiated by local officials. If you are lucky enough to live in such a community, you will use the official community vision statement as a starting point for the process. The facilitator will start by reviewing the community vision statement with the members of the committee. It is likely that one or more members of the committee participated in the process that resulted in the community vision, and if so they should be encouraged to tell the others about the process that was used to identify the vision.

Sometimes the final product of a community-wide visioning process is condensed into two or three sentences that describe a vision for all residents. In these instances, the members of the committee should be divided into groups of three and asked to deconstruct the broad vision statement by identifying specific target audiences and the desired future for each. The group reports should be recorded using the process described in the preceding section.

Step 3.3
Define Current Conditions in the Community

In some ways, this process is like planning a trip. First you decide on your destination, and then you make plans to get there from where you are now. Let's say you want to plan a trip to Chicago. Your plans will be quite different if you are starting from Elmhurst, a Chicago suburb, than they will be if you are starting from San Francisco, and they will be different yet again if you are starting from Moscow. In the same way, the vision statements developed by the committee only provide half of the information required to determine community needs. Before the committee members can make recommendations about how to reach their visions, they will have to describe where they are now—the current conditions in the community.

Community A might have an excellent school system and a 95 percent graduation rate. Community B, on the other hand, might have a school system that has been plagued with problems and graduates only 60 percent of its students. The committee members in both communities could easily have identified the same vision: "Students will receive a first-class education that will enable them to attend the colleges or trade programs of their choice." In Community A, there is little that needs to be done to achieve the vision except to maintain the already first-rate school system. In Community B, making progress toward the vision will require significant effort.

How Will the Committee Analyze Current Conditions in the Community?

The committee members will use a standard strategic planning tool called a SWOT analysis to describe the current conditions in the community. The SWOT mnemonic stands for Strengths, Weaknesses, Opportunities, and Threats. The members of the committee will use Workform D, Community SWOT Analysis, to structure their discussion and record their comments. Strengths and weaknesses refer to current conditions within the community. Opportunities and threats relate to current or potential issues outside of the community. Strengths and opportunities support achieving the vision, while weaknesses and threats can obstruct progress.

This step of the process is not intended to identify every possible community strength, weakness, opportunity, or threat. That would take hours and would not be very helpful. In this step, the members of the committee are looking at the vision statements they developed in Step 3.2, which are posted on the wall, and defining current conditions *that relate to those vision statements.*

The committee members will work in groups of three to complete this step. In most cases, the facilitator will want to leave people in the same groups that identified vision statements during Step 3.2. However, if one or more members of the committee are domineering or difficult, it might be fairer to everyone to change the composition of the small groups after each step.

The groups will use Workform D to structure their discussions and record their work. The facilitator will go over the instructions for Workform D with the entire group to be sure that everyone understands what they are to do, and then the group work will begin. The facilitator will again move from group to group to answer questions and judge the time required to complete the work. Normally, this takes between fifteen and twenty minutes. About halfway through the time allocated for the group work, the instructor should remind people of the time and encourage them to address all four types of current conditions.

The groups will report their work using the same round-robin process they used to report their vision statements. As you saw in figure 14, the round-robin reporting for this step normally takes place while the participants are eating their lunches.

The facilitator will start by asking each group to identify a community strength that will support achieving one or more of the vision statements and recording their answers on a flip-chart. When all of the groups have reported all of the strengths they identified, the flip-chart sheets will be posted in the meeting room, and the facilitator will move on to the opportunities. When these have all been recorded and posted, the facilitator will move on to weaknesses and, finally, to threats. In figure 16, you can see examples of the current conditions that members of the Tree County Library planning committee identified in relation to their vision statements.

Step 3.4
Decide What Needs to Be Done to Reach Community Vision

By the time the members of the committee reach this step in the process, they have all of the information required to identify what needs to be done to make progress toward reaching the community vision statements. In fact, in some cases the identification of needs occurs as the groups are reporting about current conditions. In the example in the preceding section, the members of the planning committee in Community B would have identified conditions in the local school system as a weakness and might have said that the rumor that the state legislature was going to reduce funding for schools was a threat. During the discussion of these two items, it would not be surprising to hear someone say, "We really need to get together and do something about the schools." When this spontaneous needs identification occurs, the facilitator should write the need on a second flip-chart before continuing to record the group's comments about current conditions.

FIGURE 16
Workform D: Community SWOT Analysis—Example

A. **Support Achieving the Vision**	B. **Obstruct Achieving the Vision**
A1. County Strengths Good K–12 schools Programs for children 6–12 offered by the Parks and Recreation Dept. in the summer New senior centers in two communities in the county and two more being planned Growing number of neighborhood associations English Language Learning classes offered by the school district for immigrants	**B1.** County Weaknesses Strip malls erode support for downtown businesses No strategic plan for the county No senior centers in some areas of the county No formal activities for teens after school or on weekends Limited health care services outside of the county seat
A2. External Opportunities for the County Governor's initiative to establish universal preschool programs for children ages 3 and 4 The possibility of a new community college in the county Regional transportation planning State and regional economy is strong State is growing and there are a number of small companies thinking about locating in our region	**B2.** External Threats to the County Economic recession State legislators who favor developers over environmentalists State laws that override local values Globalization and its effect on jobs State is ranked in bottom quarter for per pupil K–12 funding Increasing pollution from nearby metropolitan area There is no state or national safety net for health care

The facilitator cannot count on serendipity to identify all of the community needs that will have to be addressed to make progress toward reaching the vision, but there is rarely any reason to go through yet another small-group discussion process either. In most cases, the needs are clear when the group compares the vision statements and the current conditions for each target audience. This can be done during a brief general discussion.

The facilitator can use the identification and recording of community needs onto the flip-chart as a way to summarize the meeting to this point. If the process has truly focused on the community and not the library, many of the needs will address issues like health care, housing, transportation, and safety, which may seem peripheral to the library. This is absolutely as it should be. The final list should be as usable in a discussion of priorities for the Parks and Recreation Department or the Health Department as it is in this process.

TASK 4: SELECT SERVICE RESPONSES

The first two steps in Task 4 take place during the last two hours of the first meeting of the community planning committee. The third step takes place between the first and second meetings of the planning committee. The fourth and final step begins during the second meeting of the planning committee and ends when the members of the library board act on the committee's recommendations.

The steps in the preceding task all focused on the community. The members of the committee spent the first three hours of the first planning committee meeting defining a vision for the community, describing current conditions in the community, and identifying community needs to be addressed to make progress toward the vision. Some committee members get so involved in this process that they forget that the real purpose of the committee is to recommend service priorities for the library. During this task, the spotlight shifts from the community to the library.

Step 4.1
Present an Overview of the Library to Committee Members

The members of the planning committee were selected for their community expertise, not for their library expertise. It is a sad but true fact that some of the community leaders on the committee may not be regular library users, and others may not even have a library card. Even those committee members who use the library regularly are probably only familiar with the services they personally use. A young mother might know about the library's children's programs and the library's new book section but not know—or care—about the library's services for businesspeople or the local history resources that are available. On the other hand, a businessperson might know about the library's business resources and be completely unaware of library services for students.

Before the members of the committee begin to consider how the library might meet some of the community needs identified during Task 3, they should all have a common understanding of the library's current services and programs and how those services and programs are used by community residents. The orientation packet sent to the committee members in Step 2.4 included information about the library, but as noted earlier, you can't be sure that everyone read and understood that information.

Who Should Present the Library Overview?

The library director is the most appropriate person to provide this overview of the library. Up to this point in the meeting, the facilitator has been the face of the process and the director has been an observer. Now it is time for the library director to step forward as the official representative of the library.

The director probably knows some, but not all, of the members of the planning committee. They may have served together on committees or boards, or go to the same church, or belong to the same organizations. They may even be neighbors. However, even the people who know the director may not have seen her act in her official capacity. During this presentation, the director can provide evidence that the library is being managed by a skilled library professional and that the public is being well-served by a caring and effective staff.

What Should Be Included in the Library Overview?

The director's presentation should be relatively brief—fifteen to thirty minutes—and should present information in a value-neutral manner. Think of the presentation as a documentary and not as an infomercial. The purpose of the presentation is to provide committee members with a context for making decisions about the future service priorities for the library, not to persuade the members that the library is perfect as it is. During the presentation, the director may want to refer to some or all of the materials about the library that were included in the orientation packet. However, the director will want to avoid overwhelming the members of the committee with statistics.

Strings of numbers that may mean something to librarians (number of items purchased, number of items processed, number of reference questions asked, turnover rate, etc.) are less likely to have meaning to people who are not closely associated with the library. The director will want to select data elements that reflect community use and support, and provide trend data rather than data from a single year whenever possible. It is always more effective to present data in chart or graph form than in tabular form, particularly trend data. There is more information on this topic in the Presenting Data tool kit in part 3.

The director's presentations typically include some or all of the following data elements:

Percentage of people in the service area with library cards (five-year trend data)

Annual door count (five-year trend data)

Circulation of materials by format (five-year trend data)

Circulation of materials by age (five-year trend data)

Program attendance (five-year trend data)

Regular programs (summer reading program, one city-one book)

Number of reference questions answered (five-year trend data)

New or exciting programs or services

Awards or honors

Budget (five-year trend data)

Budget by expenditure (five-year trend data)

Number of facilities

Number of staff

Many directors develop PowerPoint presentations as part of their library overview. PowerPoint presentations are particularly effective when used to present data in graph or chart form. People learn in different ways, and PowerPoint presentations make it possible for people to both see and hear the information being presented. As a result, the messages are more likely to be received and remembered by the committee members. PowerPoint presentations also provide an easily manageable outline of the director's presentation and help the director to stay focused and on track. The director may want to distribute copies of the PowerPoint presentation to committee members, who can use them as a place to take notes.

Step 4.2
Select Preliminary Service Responses

The director's overview of the library sets the stage for the final step of the first planning committee meeting—and by now you are no doubt thinking that the first meeting of the planning committee lasts for days or weeks instead of a mere five hours. It is true that during the first meeting, the members complete all four steps in Task 3 and two of the four steps in Task 4. However, look back at the facilitator's agenda for the first committee meeting (figure 14) and you will see that the time frame for each of the steps is reasonable. It is the descriptions of how to manage the steps that are time-consuming, not the steps themselves. During the meeting, the steps flow naturally from one to the next, and committee members almost never feel that they didn't have enough time to complete each of the steps.

How Can the Committee Identify the Needs the Library Might Address?

During this last step of the first meeting, the members use everything they have discussed and learned throughout the meeting to identify a list of library services that would help to meet the needs of the community. The process begins immediately after the identification of community needs in Step 3.4 and starts with a review and discussion of the Needs Decision Tree (see figure 17).

The Needs Decision Tree is not intended to be used with each of the needs individually. It would take too long for the facilitator to go through the list of needs one-by-one and it is not necessary. The members of the committee are smart people, and they have spent most of the meeting identifying the issues used to create the needs list. The Needs Decision Tree provides a visual picture of the questions that the members of the committee should consider as they work together to link community needs and library service priorities.

First they will want to consider if the library is suited to address certain needs. A community might have a serious need to provide more low-income housing units, but the library is not the appropriate agency to take the lead in meeting this need. The library might provide information about available low-income housing, but that does little to meet the need for additional housing units. Meeting this need would not be a priority for the library.

Even if the library could meet a community need, it might not be the only—or best—agency that could do so. Before making that decision, committee members will want to consider what other agencies and organizations are working to meet the need already. There are plenty of needs that will have to be met to make progress toward the

FIGURE 17

Needs Decision Tree

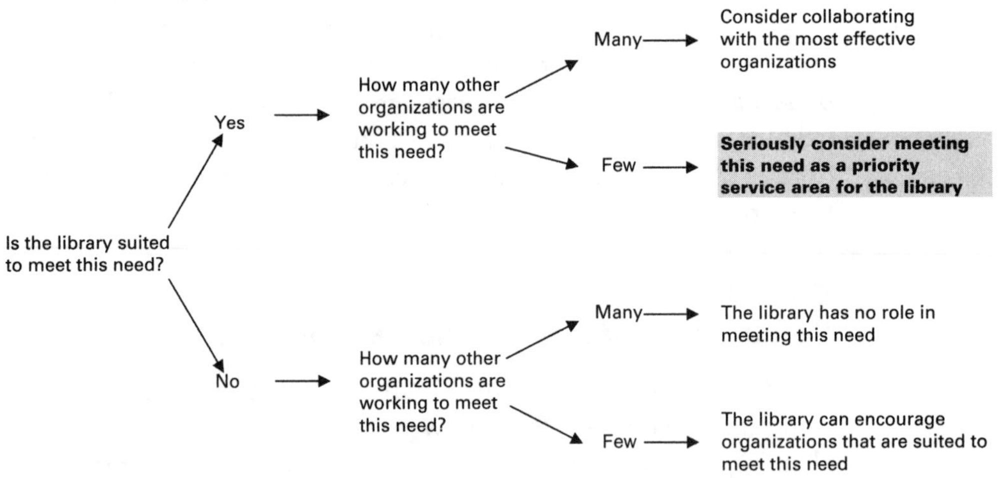

community vision. There is no reason for agencies and organizations to get into turf wars about who should provide what services. If there is an active Literacy Council in the community that recruits, trains, and schedules volunteers, there is no reason for the library to make providing literacy services a priority. This doesn't mean that the library won't continue to purchase high-interest, low-vocabulary materials for new readers or provide space for tutors to meet with students. It simply means that the library will acknowledge that the Literacy Council is the lead agency in providing literacy services and that the library's role is to collaborate with the council and support its efforts.

There will be some needs that the library is suited to meet and that are not being addressed effectively by other organizations. These are the needs that should be considered when identifying possible library service priorities. In these instances, the library would be the agency that takes the lead in meeting the need, and other agencies might collaborate with the library and support the library's efforts.

When the members of the planning committee have reviewed the Needs Decision Tree, they are ready to consider what the library might do to meet the needs it is suited to address. However, before the members can do that, they need to have a clearer understanding of the services that their public library could provide. Remember, most members of the committee only know about the library services that they use or the services that their friends and family use. It is highly unlikely that any of them are aware of the broad array of services available in public libraries today. That is why library service responses are a core element of the *Planning for Results* process.

What Are Library Service Responses?

Library service responses are the links between the community's needs, interests, and priorities and the programs and services that the library offers. Specifically, *a service response is what a library does for, or offers to, the public in an effort to meet a set of well-defined community needs.* There are eighteen service responses, and they are listed in figure 18. A complete description of each service response can be found in part 2 of this book. Each description

FIGURE 18

Library Service Responses

Be an Informed Citizen: Local, National, and World Affairs Residents will have the information they need to support and promote democracy, to fulfill their civic responsibilities at the local, state, and national levels, and to fully participate in community decision making.

Build Successful Enterprises: Business and Nonprofit Support Business owners and nonprofit organization directors and their managers will have the resources they need to develop and maintain strong, viable organizations.

Celebrate Diversity: Cultural Awareness Residents will have programs and services that promote appreciation and understanding of their personal heritage and the heritage of others in the community.

Connect to the Online World: Public Internet Access Residents will have high-speed access to the digital world with no unnecessary restrictions or fees to ensure that everyone can take advantage of the ever-growing resources and services available through the Internet.

Create Young Readers: Early Literacy Children from birth to five will have programs and services designed to ensure that they will enter school ready to learn to read, write, and listen.

Discover Your Roots: Genealogy and Local History Residents and visitors will have the resources they need to connect the past with the present through their family histories and to understand the history and traditions of the community.

Express Creativity: Create and Share Content Residents will have the services and support they need to express themselves by creating original print, video, audio, or visual content in a real-world or online environment.

Get Facts Fast: Ready Reference Residents will have someone to answer their questions on a wide array of topics of personal interest.

Know Your Community: Community Resources and Services Residents will have a central source for information about the wide variety of programs, services, and activities provided by community agencies and organizations.

Learn to Read and Write: Adult, Teen, and Family Literacy Adults and teens will have the support they need to improve their literacy skills in order to meet their personal goals and fulfill their responsibilities as parents, citizens, and workers.

Make Career Choices: Job and Career Development Adults and teens will have the skills and resources they need to identify career opportunities that suit their individual strengths and interests.

Make Informed Decisions: Health, Wealth, and Other Life Choices Residents will have the resources they need to identify and analyze risks, benefits, and alternatives before making decisions that affect their lives.

Satisfy Curiosity: Lifelong Learning Residents will have the resources they need to explore topics of personal interest and continue to learn throughout their lives.

Stimulate Imagination: Reading, Viewing, and Listening for Pleasure Residents who want materials to enhance their leisure time will find what they want when and where they want them and will have the help they need to make choices from among the options.

Succeed in School: Homework Help Students will have the resources they need to succeed in school.

Understand How to Find, Evaluate, and Use Information: Information Fluency Residents will know when they need information to resolve an issue or answer a question and will have the skills to search for, locate, evaluate, and effectively use information to meet their needs.

Visit a Comfortable Place: Physical and Virtual Spaces Residents will have safe and welcoming physical places to meet and interact with others or to sit quietly and read and will have open and accessible virtual spaces that support networking.

Welcome to the United States: Services for New Immigrants New immigrants and refugees will have information on citizenship, English Language Learning, employment, public schooling, health and safety, available social services, and any other topics that they need to participate successfully in American life.

includes the following information: the title, the description, suggested target audiences, typical services and programs in libraries that select this as a priority, potential partners, policy implications, critical resources, and possible measures. These sections are described in detail in the introduction to the service responses in part 2.

One of the most important functions of the library service responses is to provide a common vocabulary that can be used by library staff, library board members, and the members of the planning committee when they are discussing service priorities. Consider the term *reference.* If a staff member is talking about reference, she may be talking about answering ready-reference questions, or about helping a user do research, or about helping a student decide how to find the information he needs for his report, or about spending three or four hours tracking   down the answer to an obscure request from a user, or she may even be talking about the reference books and databases that are used to answer questions. When a community member thinks about the word *reference,* the most common association is someone who recommends a person for a job. If you ask him to think about the term *reference* in a library context, he is going to be thinking about his high school or college term papers.

Obviously, if the librarian and the community member are having a conversation about the relative priority of reference services, they will be speaking at cross-purposes. The librarian will be thinking about a complex and multilayered service, and the community member will be thinking about job interviews or completing school assignments.

There are other examples of this problem as well. What is "information and referral" or the even more confusing "I & R"? What are "government documents"? Does that mean income tax forms? Who are "young adults"? Are they teenagers or adults in their early twenties? Are seniors "old adults"? Does "remote access" mean providing services to people who live in rural areas? What is "public access computing"? Who is accessing what, and how are they doing it?

If the members of the planning committee and the members of the library staff and the library board all use the service responses to describe potential library priorities, they can be relatively sure that the choices they make mean the same things to all of them. This will be critical as the process moves forward and the library management team begins to reallocate resources to support the library's new priorities.

HOW DO THE MEMBERS OF THE COMMITTEE LEARN ABOUT THE SERVICE RESPONSES?

Before the members of the committee can use the service responses, they need to know more about them. Just asking the members to read through the handout in their packet based on figure 18 won't be sufficient. There is not enough information in the handout to ensure that the committee members really understand the scope of each service response. On the other hand, there is way too much information in the full descriptions of the service responses in part 2 for the committee members to be able to read and absorb in the time available.

The best way to introduce the service responses is to have someone discuss each service response with the committee, giving a one- or two-minute summary of the typical services offered by libraries that make the service a priority. If the meeting facilitator is a library consultant, this can and should be done by the facilitator. If the meeting is being facilitated by a nonlibrarian, there are two choices. The full descriptions of the service responses in part 2 include lists of typical services, and if the facilitator is willing, he or she can develop a presentation based on those lists. However, if the facilitator is uncomfortable talking about library services, this information can be presented by the library director or her designee, again based on the lists in part 2. No matter who introduces the service responses, the information about each service response should be presented in a neutral manner. This is not the time to talk about what the library does in each of the areas covered by the service responses. There will be plenty of time for that during the second meeting of the community planning committee.

No matter who presents the introduction to the service responses, it will be critical to manage the time effectively. If the presenter takes two minutes to talk about each service response, it will take thirty-six minutes to cover all eighteen service responses, and that is six minutes over the maximum time allocated (see the facilitator's agenda in figure 14). It would be better if the presenter could discuss all of the service responses in twenty to twenty-five minutes.

HOW DO THE MEMBERS OF THE COMMITTEE LINK NEEDS AND SERVICE RESPONSES?

The first meeting of the planning committee is almost over. The final thing the committee members have to do is to identify the service responses that they think might meet the community needs that were identified earlier in the meeting. Keep in mind that this is simply a preliminary selection. In fact, it may be easier to think of it as a de-selection. The members of the committee are actually eliminating from consideration those service responses that do not meet any of the identified community needs, or that address needs that are being met by other agencies or organizations.

The service responses that remain after the de-selection process will not all be included in the final recommendations made by the committee during its second meeting, but the members will need more information to make those decisions. Before the second meeting, the members of the committee will have had a chance to read the full descriptions of their preliminary choices, and the library management team will have discussed the preliminary service responses with the staff and board. The second meeting of the committee will include a complete report on what the staff and board had to say about the implications of the preliminary service responses with regard to current library services.

There are at least two ways to identify the preliminary service responses. One way is to use the dot exercise described in the Groups: Reaching Agreement tool kit in part 3. In brief, the names of the eighteen service responses are written on flip-chart paper and posted on the walls of the meeting room. Each member of the committee is given nine colored dots and asked to place those dots by the service responses that seem most reflective of community needs and that are not being addressed by other agencies. Members can "bullet" vote, or place more than one dot by a service response, if they feel strongly about a specific service response. At the end of the process, the service responses with few or no dots are eliminated and those that remain become the preliminary service responses. The only real question here is what constitutes a "few" votes, and that depends on the number of members on the committee and the spread of the votes across the service responses. It is a judgment call.

Another approach is to ask the members of the committee to make a check mark by the service responses that they don't think meet any of the community needs or that they think are being addressed by other groups; this is done during the time the presenter is describing each service response in more detail. The members are then asked to vote for the service responses they think should be excluded from the preliminary list. The members vote by raising their hands as each service response is named if they think that service response should be eliminated from further consideration. If you use this process, the service responses with many votes are eliminated from further consideration and those with few votes remain. What constitutes "many" and "few" remains a judgment call.

No matter what process is used to identify preliminary service responses, there are two important things to remember. First, the committee members are basing their votes on their limited understanding of the service responses. If one committee member feels very strongly that a service should remain under consideration, it should be included in the preliminary service responses, even if no one else agrees. The issues of inclusion and priority can be dealt with during the next meeting of the committee, when everyone is better informed.

Second, there is no magic number of preliminary service responses that the committee should select. The only reason the list of eighteen is being reduced is to allow everyone involved in the process to focus their attention on the service responses that are likely to be selected as library priorities during the second meeting. There is no point in everyone wasting their time and energy learning a lot about library service responses that are not appropriate for the community and will never be selected as priorities. Typically, the planning committee includes eight to ten service responses on the preliminary list, but some committees have included as few as six and others have included as many as twelve.

The selection of the preliminary service responses concludes the first meeting of the planning committee. The facilitator should remind the members of the date of the next committee meeting and encourage them to read the detailed information about the service responses they have selected, which they will receive from the library before that meeting.

What Happens after the First Meeting?

After the meeting, someone (probably the facilitator or the planning coordinator) should prepare a brief report that summarizes the work of the committee. The report should include the list of vision statements, the results of the SWOT analysis, the list of community needs (if there is a formal list), and the preliminary service responses. This report, along with photocopies of the full descriptions of the preliminary service responses from part 2, should be sent to each member of the planning committee and to each member of the board within a day or two of the meeting. The same information, along with a copy of the director's presentation about the library, should be posted on the staff *Planning for Results* website, or one complete print copy should be sent to each unit in the library.

Step 4.3
Describe the Effect of Preliminary Service Responses on Current Library Services

There is one thing that all libraries have in common: they are all currently providing collections, services, and programs that fully utilize the library's available resources. When the staff and board start discussing the possibility of new priorities, the first question that comes to mind for many is "How are we going to pay for this?" The only realistic answer to that question is "By reallocating our current resources." There is little likelihood that the library will receive a substantial increase in public funding to support newly defined priorities, so that the staff won't have to change the way they provide services that have been determined to have a lower priority. In other words, the planning process is about "putting your money where your mouth is."

If "Build Successful Enterprises" is selected as a new service priority, library staff will have to do more than purchase a few additional business titles. They will be expected to build partnerships with local business organizations, develop a strong web presence to support business and nonprofit organizations, participate in local business blogs, and build and maintain a current collection of print and online resources. In other words, they will have to approach the service in a completely new way. This is going to take time that is currently allocated to other things, technology resources that are currently allocated to other things, and collection dollars that are currently allocated to other things, and it may take additional facility resources as well.

All of this boils down to a single word: change. Two of the fundamental principles of change management are to keep everyone involved in the change process from the beginning and to provide a mechanism for all staff to contribute to the change process. That is the purpose of this step.

What Is the Best Way to Get the Staff Involved?

Most staff members will attend one of the orientation programs presented before the planning process begins (Step 1.5), and even those who do not will know that the library is involved in a planning process. However, the fact that a community-based planning committee is talking about abstract ideas such as community vision and community needs may make some staff feel that the process has little or nothing to do with the actual work they do every day. That will change once the results of the first meeting of the planning committee have been posted on the staff *Planning for Results* website or sent to all of the units in print form. When staff start reading about the proposed service responses, the process will seem much more real to them and they are going to be interested in discussing the possible ramifications of new priorities.

The whole point of this step is to allow as many staff as possible to participate in the process of identifying the final service responses. To do this, you will want to establish multiple ways for staff to provide their input. You might want to set up a blog with separate entries for each proposed service response and an entry for general comments. This will allow everyone to track comments about each service response easily. The blog entries should encourage staff to focus on the library's strengths and weaknesses and on the potential opportunities and threats of each service response.

Even in this age of ubiquitous electronic communication, the best way to be sure that all staff are included in the process is to hold a series of meetings to discuss the service responses. The meetings can be scheduled in several ways, depending on how many staff work in your library and how much time you have between the first and second meetings of the planning committee.

Open meetings. You could schedule a series of meetings that are open to any staff members who wish to attend. The benefit of this approach is that staff with different experiences and points of view will come together to talk about the preliminary service responses, which should result in a lively and informative meeting. The only real drawback to this approach is time, both the amount of time each meeting might take and the amount of time that will be required to hold enough meetings to accommodate all of the staff who wish to attend.

Unit meetings. You could ask each unit manager to schedule time to let unit staff talk about the service responses. In this instance, the units would probably have to hold more than one meeting to ensure that all staff have a chance to participate. The benefit of this approach is that every staff member will participate in the discussion. There are two drawbacks, however. The first is that every staff member will *have* to participate in the discussion, whether they want to or not. People tend to be more positive and engaged in discussions they choose to join. The second disadvantage of this approach is that each of the unit managers who will be facilitating the unit meetings will have a different understanding of the process, a different relationship with the unit staff, and a different level of facilitation skill. This disadvantage can be addressed by having members of the library management team facilitate all of the unit meetings, but that obviously depends on the number of units in the library system and the number of members on the library management team.

Invitational meetings. Some libraries appoint cross-functional teams to discuss the preliminary service responses. Staff members from different job classifications and library units and with different areas of expertise are invited to attend meetings to review and discuss the preliminary service responses. The benefit of this approach is that the feedback that comes from the meeting may be more representative of the feelings of all of the staff than the feedback that comes from unit meetings or from open meetings that may have a disproportionate number of staff from one unit, classification, or area of expertise. The drawback is that only selected people get to participate, and those not selected may feel that their opinions don't matter. You might hold several invitation meetings to involve more staff, but this process inevitably excludes some staff members who would have liked to participate.

Specialist meetings. In many library systems, groups of staff with similar job assignments meet regularly. Children's librarians, young adult librarians, reference librarians, branch managers, and others come together monthly or quarterly to discuss their common interests, design new programs or services, and look for solutions to issues that affect them all. These groups might be asked to review and respond to the preliminary service responses. The benefit of this approach is that you might get a deeper understanding of how the preliminary service responses will affect the various specialists in your organization than you would through any of the preceding processes. However, the drawbacks may outweigh this benefit. First, you may have the same problem with facilitation of the meetings that you would have with unit meetings. A potentially more significant problem is that the specialists tend to be proprietary about their services. This may lead them to put too much emphasis on service responses that seem to support their specialties and too little on others that don't.

Regardless of who is in attendance, the staff review meetings will last between one and a half and two hours, depending on the number of preliminary service responses. The staff review meetings are usually facilitated by a member of the library management team and the staff representative on the planning committee, although, as you saw above, there are exceptions to this.

The staff review meetings should include time for staff to talk in small groups about the service responses of most interest to them, and time for them to hear what others in the larger group have to say about other service responses. If you have more than thirty participants, the easiest way to do this is to write the title of each of the preliminary service responses on a separate piece of flip-chart paper and post the titles around the meeting room. Place a few chairs near each title. At the beginning of the meeting, tell the members of the group that they will be able to select two service responses to discuss in small groups and that they will be able to add their comments about other service responses during the reporting period. Ask the participants to self-select a service response and join others who wish to discuss that service response in the chairs near the title. Give them ten or fifteen minutes to discuss the service response and then ask the participants to select a second service response and repeat the process. During the final hour of the meeting, the facilitator will record the comments from the small groups about each service response and will then give the other participants a chance to add their comments.

The process described in the preceding paragraph works best with larger groups. For groups with ten to thirty participants, start by posting half of the preliminary service responses in the room. Let participants self-select and go through the process described above. When the first groups have completed their discussions, post the second half of the service responses and let participants select from them for the second discussion period. The group reports and general discussion occur during the last hour of the meeting. In meetings with fewer than ten participants, there is no need to break into small groups. The group as a whole can discuss each of the preliminary service responses.

During their small group meetings, the staff will use the SWOT analysis process to describe the potential consequences of making the preliminary service responses the library's priorities. This SWOT analysis is similar to the one used by the committee in Step 3.3, although the questions are slightly different. The staff will be looking at the library's current strengths and weaknesses in relation to each of the preliminary service responses. Then they will consider the external opportunities and threats that might affect the library's ability to implement each of the preliminary service responses.

Finally, the staff should be encouraged to consider the service responses that were not included on the list of preliminary recommendations. Are any of the excluded service responses current library priorities? If so, what are the potential consequences of reducing or eliminating a current library priority? Is the current priority used by many people occasionally or is it heavily used by a few people? Has the use of the services in the priority area been growing, declining, or remaining steady over the past five years? Is the library the only source for the services in the priority area, or are other organizations providing similar services? Will the reduction or elimination of services in the priority area lead to negative publicity? Workform E, Library SWOT Analysis, is a tool that can be used to structure the staff discussions and record staff comments. Figure 19 shows how one group of Tree County library staff members evaluated the preliminary service response "Express Creativity."

What Is the Best Way to Get Board Input?

The community planning committee serves in an advisory capacity to the board. The members of the board will want to review and respond to both the preliminary service

FIGURE 19
Workform E: Library SWOT Analysis—Example

A. Library Service Response: EXPRESS CREATIVITY: CREATE AND SHARE CONTENT (FOR TEENS)

B. For Selecting the Service Response	C. Against Selecting the Service Response
B1. Library Strengths The library currently offers poetry writing classes and sponsors poetry readings The library has gallery space currently used by local artists The library has a teen advisory board	**C1.** Library Weaknesses The library has no production equipment, nor are there staff who know how to use such equipment The teen advisory board is small and not very active The library has never been very successful at attracting teens The library has no way to monitor copyright and fair use of teens using library equipment The library has too few staff to start trying to publish things There is no space for production facilities
B2. External Opportunities for the Library The library might be able to work in partnership with the community college to offer services that support this service response	**C2.** External Threats to the Library Services that support this service response may be seen as a frivolous waste of taxpayers' money The technology is changing so fast that the library will have to keep updating equipment and software It is difficult to monitor content in online sites and the library might be liable for things teens did Library-sponsored wikis and other collaborative information resources may make people lose trust in the library

responses recommended by the committee and the staff reactions to those recommendations. The members may also want to discuss the implications of the service responses that were not selected by the community planning committee.

When all of the staff meetings are complete, the library management team will meet to review the staff comments, add their own comments, and prepare a report of the staff and management reactions to be presented to the library board. The members of the board should receive a summary of staff reactions rather than verbatim reports from all of the staff meetings. The board doesn't need that much information, and the members may find it difficult to synthesize the data from several different meetings. The summaries for the board should be no longer than one page per service response.

Some of the members of the board are probably unfamiliar with the SWOT process, and there won't be time for them to do a complete SWOT analysis during their meeting. In view of this, consider organizing the information in the board summary into two sections: comments for selecting each service response as a priority, and comments against selecting each service response as a priority. This will allow you to merge the strengths

FIGURE 20
Director's Report to the Board on the Staff SWOT Analysis

EXPRESS CREATIVITY: CREATE AND SHARE CONTENT

**Teens* will have the services and support they need
to express themselves by creating original print, video, audio,
or visual content in a real-world or online environment.**

STAFF COMMENTS

The comments came at four open staff meetings and a meeting of the library management team that were held to discuss the proposed service responses.

A. For selecting "Express Creativity" as a service response:

- The library has gallery space
- The current programming for teens includes poetry writing classes and performances
- The library has a relatively new teen advisory board
- The library has a full-time teen librarian
- The library has a good relationship with the high schools in the county
- Tree County Community College is teaching several courses on creating animated and live-action videos
- This program will be very popular with teens
- Staff members will learn new skills that will help to make other services more interactive

B. Against selecting "Express Creativity" as a service response:

- The library currently has no video or audio production equipment
- The library will have to find a way to monitor copyright and fair use by teens using library equipment
- The technology is changing so fast that the library will have to keep updating equipment and software
- It is difficult to monitor content on collaborative online site, and the library might be held liable for things teens created or said
- If the library officially creates and supports wikis and other collaborative information resources, people may lose trust in the accuracy of library information
- Few libraries have done this and there are no accepted models to follow

*The members of the community planning committee thought this service should be targeted at teens.

and opportunities into a single list and the weaknesses and threats into a single list. This will be a delicate process. You want to be sure that the contents of the report reflect the staff's reactions, but you don't want to overemphasize either the positives or the negatives. Figure 20 illustrates how the Tree County Library management team summarized the staff comments and their own perceptions for the service response "Express Creativity."

The summary does not need to be sent to the members of the board prior to the meeting. The information in the summary will be easier to understand if it is presented by the director and if the board members have an opportunity to ask questions. After the board meeting, the summary should also be posted on the *Planning for Results* website on the staff intranet or sent to the units in print form.

The board should probably hold a special meeting to discuss the committee's recommendations, rather than trying to include the discussion in a regularly scheduled meeting of the board. The board meeting needs to be held after all of the staff meetings have been completed and before the second meeting of the community planning committee. For many libraries, that is going to be a relatively short time period.

The part of the board meeting devoted to the discussion of the preliminary service responses is normally facilitated by the library director with assistance from the board representative on the community planning committee. This meeting will be structured somewhat differently than the staff meetings. Rather than going through a full SWOT analysis for each service response, the person facilitating the meeting will review the staff reactions to that service response with the board (see figure 20). Board members will then be asked to comment on both the inclusion of the service response on the list of preliminary recommendations and the staff's reactions to the service response.

The board members are likely to have a somewhat different reaction to the preliminary service responses than the staff. Sometimes board members see a political threat or opportunity that is not as apparent to the staff. They may also be more aware of the resource implications of certain choices, particularly if those choices will help raise money from external sources.

When the Tree County Library Board reviewed the staff's reaction to the preliminary service response "Express Creativity" (figure 20), they saw more opportunities and fewer threats than staff. The board members were particularly aware of the potential for positive publicity and the opportunities for partnerships and acquiring outside funding to support the "Express Creativity" service response. The members of the board acknowledged staff concerns about resources, but noted that any changes in service priorities would require a shift in resource allocation. The board members spent the most time talking about the issues of fair use, copyright, and liability for online postings. They agreed with staff that these were potential threats, but finally decided that the threats could be addressed through the development of clear library policies.

What Is the Best Way to Report the Staff and Board Reactions to the Committee?

After the board meeting, the library director or the planning coordinator will prepare a report about the staff and board's reactions to the preliminary service responses, which will be presented to the planning committee during their second meeting. This report will be briefer than the report created for the board and will summarize the combined reactions of the staff and board. Whoever writes the report will have to be careful to reflect the intent of the staff and board when combining and merging comments. The summary presented to the community planning committee will be a public document and it will be shared with staff. They should be able to see their opinions reflected in the final document.

The members of the planning committee will have used the SWOT process to identify current conditions in the community during their first meeting, so they will be familiar with the terms and process. In view of that, it makes sense to use the SWOT terms when presenting the reactions of the staff and board, although you can continue to merge the strengths and opportunities in one list and the weaknesses and threats in another list. The summary of the comments about "Express Creativity" that was prepared by the Tree County Library director is shown in figure 21.

Step 4.4
Select Final Service Responses

The activities in this step occur during the second meeting of the community planning committee and during a formal meeting of the board held after the second planning committee meeting.

EXPRESS CREATIVITY: CREATE AND SHARE CONTENT

Teens will have the services and support they need to express themselves by creating original print, video, audio, or visual content in a real-world or online environment.

STRENGTHS AND OPPORTUNITIES

- The main library has a teen program with a staff of three and a teen advisory board
- The library has a good relationship with the high schools, arts groups, and community colleges in the county and could collaborate with them on this service
- This program would be very popular with teens and would generate excellent publicity for the library
- This program offers an opportunity to obtain funding through grants, gifts, or partnerships

CHALLENGES AND RISKS

- The library does not currently have the resources required to support this program; the library would need to purchase equipment, reallocate space, and train staff
- The library board would have to develop policies relating to copyright, fair use, and sharing online information
- Staff are concerned that if the library officially creates and supports wikis and other collaborative information resources, people may lose trust in the accuracy of library information

Figure 22 is a sample of the agenda for the second meeting of the community planning committee to be distributed to the meeting participants. Like the agenda for the first meeting, this agenda starts with a list of the meeting objectives, provides a general outline of the work to be accomplished during the meeting, and lists starting, lunch, and ending times. Figure 23 is the facilitator's version of the same meeting agenda, which again includes tentative times for each of the activities in the meeting and lists the handouts to be used during each activity.

This meeting will be facilitated by the same person who facilitated the first meeting of the planning committee. The facilitator will start with a brief review of the first meeting. The members of the committee will have received the notes from the first meeting, along with the full descriptions of the service responses still under consideration. The facilitator should ask if the members have questions about the notes or if they have any additions they would like to make. Sometimes committee members have discussed the process with friends or colleagues and have identified additional needs to be considered.

Then the facilitator will give the members a chance to discuss what they learned about the preliminary service responses when they read the full descriptions of those service responses. Almost all of the committee members will have read all of the descriptions, and this will be their first opportunity to discuss them. This is not the time for members to lobby for the service responses they think are most important. Rather, it is the time for members to share their reactions to the new things they discovered. The facilitator could start the discussion by asking members to share what surprised them when they read the descriptions. What did they find that was unexpected? What questions, if any, did the members have after reading the full descriptions?

The library director or his or her designee will take the lead in the next part of the meeting. The director will distribute a written report summarizing the staff and board's reactions to the preliminary service responses (see figure 21 for an example). The

TREE COUNTY PUBLIC LIBRARY

Meeting Two of the Planning Committee

[Date]

MEETING OBJECTIVES

Participants will discuss the preliminary service responses selected during the
first meeting

Participants will learn how the adoption of the preliminary service responses would affect
current library services and resource allocation

Participants will make the final selection of service responses to recommend to the
library board

Participants will identify potential target audiences for each service response

MEETING AGENDA

10:00	Where We Are Now: Review of the First Meeting
	Thoughts since Meeting One
	The Effect of the Preliminary Service Responses on the Library
12:00	Lunch
	Further Discussion of Service Responses
	Selection of Final Service Responses in Priority Order
	What's Next?
3:00	Adjourn

director will have between an hour and an hour and a half to discuss the highlights of
the report and to respond to questions from the committee members. Just as with the
earlier presentation the director made, this is a documentary and not an infomercial. The
director should be presenting facts and not trying to sell a point of view. Many directors
use a PowerPoint presentation to reinforce the information that they are presenting. The
PowerPoint slides help both the director and the committee members stay focused on the
service response under discussion.

After the director's report, the facilitator will give the members of the committee an
opportunity to discuss what they have learned and to lobby for the inclusion of specific
service responses in the final recommendations. Occasionally, a member may want to
revisit the decision to exclude a specific service response from further consideration that
was made during the first meeting. It is quite possible that committee members thought
of additional needs after the first meeting or during the presentation of the library director. Perhaps staff made a strong case for meeting the needs of a current client group
whose needs were not addressed by the service responses on the preliminary list. If the
group agrees, the service response can be added to the list of service responses that will
be considered during this meeting.

TREE COUNTY PUBLIC LIBRARY

Meeting Two of the Planning Committee

[Date]

MEETING OBJECTIVES

Participants will discuss the preliminary service responses selected during the first meeting

Participants will learn how the adoption of the preliminary service responses would affect current library services and resource allocation

Participants will make the final selection of service responses to recommend to the library board

Participants will identify potential target audiences for each service response

MEETING AGENDA

10:00	Where We Are Now: Review of the First Meeting
10:15	Thoughts since Meeting One
10:30	The Effect of the Preliminary Service Responses on the Library
12:00	Lunch
12:45	Further Discussion of Service Responses
1:30	Selection of Final Service Responses in Priority Order
2:30	What's Next?
3:00	Adjourn

How Will the Committee Members Determine Priority?

When everyone has had an opportunity to talk, it will be time to determine the service responses to be included in the committee's final recommendations. These recommendations will present the service responses in priority order, with the understanding that the library will work toward achieving progress in the areas of high priority before addressing service responses with lower priority.

The facilitator will introduce this final part of the meeting by reminding the members of the committee that their recommendations should be based on community needs and not on personal values or preferences. The facilitator will then briefly remind the committee members of the consequences of their choices. The selected service responses will be used as the framework for allocating library resources, and the service responses with the highest priority will receive a larger portion of the available resources than service responses with a lower priority. *Planning for Results* is based on the premise that most changes in libraries have to be supported by reallocating resources rather than by obtaining new resources. This means that every increase in resources for services that have a high priority will come from a reduction in resources from services that have lower priorities. The facilitator will want to keep the discussion of reallocating resources general. It is not appropriate—or useful—for the members of the community planning committee to hypothesize about the effect that selecting certain service responses will have on existing library collections and programs. That responsibility rests with the library board and staff.

There are a variety of ways to determine the priority of the final service responses to be recommended to the board (see the Groups: Reaching Agreement tool kit in part 3), but almost all involve some sort of voting. One of the most common methods of determining the priority of the service responses is to use the dot exercise described in the Groups: Reaching Agreement tool kit and in Step 4.2. In the description in Step 4.2, each committee member was given nine dots to use to identify his or her priorities and was allowed to "bullet vote" those dots by placing more than one dot on a service response. In this step, members should receive three dots of one color and one dot of another color. The single dot is a "super-dot," and members should be encouraged to place it by the service response they believe has the highest priority. The other three dots can be used to identify service responses that should be included in the final recommendations. Again, members can "bullet vote" their dots if they choose to.

After everyone has used their dots to vote, the facilitator should count the number of "super-dots" and regular dots placed by each service response. In most instances, the service responses with highest priorities are easy to identify. They are the service responses with the most "super-dots" and, often, the most regular dots as well. If two or three service responses receive about the same number of total dots, the number of "super-dots" that each received can be used to determine priority.

The second way to organize the voting process is to ask the committee members to imagine they live in a world with library police who have mandated that the library can only select one service response. The facilitator reads through the list of preliminary service responses, asking the members to vote for the one service response they would choose in that world. There is almost always agreement on the most important service response, although occasionally two service responses receive about the same number of votes. If that happens, the easiest thing to do is to consider both top priorities and move on to determining the priority of the remaining service responses on the preliminary list.

When the service response with highest priority has been determined, it is removed from the voting list and the facilitator asks the group the same question: "If you could only offer one of these remaining service responses, which would it be?" As the process continues, it often becomes apparent that some of the preliminary service responses are getting few or no votes. The facilitator then asks the committee members if they wish to remove those from the list of final recommendations. The answer is almost always "yes." When all of the service responses that the committee wishes to include in the final recommendations have been placed in priority order, the process is complete.

Should the Recommendations Be Limited to a Specific Number of Service Responses?

There is no magic number of service responses that every committee should select. There are too many factors that affect the library's ability to support the selected service responses. The first, of course, is the level of support the library has. Libraries with per capita support well below the national average will probably be able to support fewer service responses than libraries with per capita support considerably above the national average. Another factor to consider is size. A library with three staff members, no matter what kind of per capita support it has, will not be able to manage as many service priorities as a library with 300 staff members. A third factor is the degree to which the selected service responses differ from the library's current service priorities. If the changes are significant, the library staff will probably be able to address fewer priorities. If the changes are minor, it will be easier for the staff to add new priorities. Then there is the question of the library's current infrastructure and past history. A well-managed library with a sound infrastructure and a history of providing excellent library services will be able to manage more service responses than a library that has serious infrastructure issues and a troubled past.

In some ways, this whole discussion of the number of service responses to be included in the final recommendations misses the most important point. The recommendations will be presented in priority order. The library board and management team allocate the resources needed to provide excellent library services in support of the highest priority. They will then allocate resources to provide excellent library services in support of the second-highest priority. When they are out of resources, they will not be able to support any further service responses. In some libraries, making real progress toward the two service responses with the highest priority takes all available resources. In others, there are sufficient resources to address the top four or five priorities.

The facilitator will end the meeting by telling the members about the next tasks and steps in the process. The committee's recommendations will be taken to the library board for action, and then staff will develop goals and objectives based on the approved service responses. Staff will also assess the current library infrastructure and identify the organizational competencies that will be required to implement any or all of the goals and objectives. The planning committee will receive a draft copy of the goals, objectives, and strategic initiatives and will meet one final time for two hours to discuss the final draft of the strategic plan (Step 9.1).

The library director will want to thank all of the meeting participants for the work they have done and then the meeting will adjourn. This second meeting of the planning committee is often over early, particularly if the members of the group have little difficulty reaching consensus on the final service responses to recommend to the board.

Is Final Board Action Required?

The library director will send the committee's final recommendations to the members of the board prior to the board's next scheduled meeting. During that meeting, board members will discuss and act on the committee's recommendations. In almost every instance, that action will be to approve the recommendations as submitted, but in rare cases, the board might make adjustments to the relative priority of the service responses.

What's Next?

At the conclusion of Step 4.4, the community planning committee's responsibilities are ended and the service priorities for the current planning cycle have been determined. In the next chapter, the focus of the process shifts from defining priorities to creating an organizational environment that will support the newly defined priorities. Creating that environment can start by informing all staff of the committee's final recommendations immediately after the second meeting of the planning committee and by transmitting the board's action on those recommendations immediately after the board meeting. As you will see in the next chapter, communication will be critical to the success of your planning process.

Key Points to Remember

The most effective way to reach agreement on issues is to first identify objective criteria.

It is called a *community* planning committee for a reason. The director's presentations should be informative and not persuasive. The director already knows what she and the staff think. The purpose of the planning meetings is to find out what community members think.

There is no need to work to reach consensus on the community vision, current conditions, or needs. There is room for several points of view in this process.

The identification of library service priorities is a collaborative process that includes community leaders, library staff, and the members of the library board.

The library service responses will be selected to meet identified community needs. The personal beliefs and values of the people selecting the service responses should not be a factor.

There is no magic number of service responses that can be selected. The appropriate number of service responses is different for every library.

Communicate, communicate, communicate.

Notes

1. Robert Fisher, William Ury, and Bruce Patton, *Getting to Yes: Negotiating Agreement without Giving In,* 2nd ed. (New York: Penguin Books, 1991), 81–82.
2. Derek Okubo, "Community Vision: A Shared Sense of a Desired Future," National Civic League, http://www.ncl.org/cs/articles/okubo10.html.

Chapter 3

Set the Stage

Ask librarians about future prospects and you get a tale of woe. Old ways are clutched firmly. Clearly, there is uncertainty of purpose. —Lowell A. Martin

MILESTONES

By the time you finish this chapter you will be able to

- help staff understand the changes that are affecting all public libraries
- assess the library's readiness for change
- prepare managers, frontline staff, and library board members to implement the changes that will come from the strategic plan
- keep the staff and board involved and informed throughout the remainder of the planning process
- develop and implement an inclusive process to define the library's core values
- determine if the library needs a mission statement or a tagline

If people really did learn from experience, librarians should have become experts on change in the past twenty-five years. However, there is considerable evidence that they have not. The quotation above is from Lowell Martin's 1982 Bowker Memorial Lecture, "The Public Library: Middle-Age Crisis or Old Age?" but it could have come from a library blog in 2007. In his Bowker lecture, Martin went on to say: "Morale is down, at the service desk as well as in the administrator's office." That, too, will sound familiar to anyone who has talked to the staff or managers of many of the public libraries in this country today.

It is in this environment that you will be developing and ultimately implementing your strategic plan. There is little point in going through all of the effort in Tasks 1–4 if you are not prepared to address the challenges that will face you as primary responsibility for the planning process moves from the community planning committee to the library staff and board.

The library management team, and particularly the library director and the planning coordinator, will be very involved in every step of Tasks 1, 2, 3, and 4. It may be hard for them to remember that the rest of the staff will be somewhat more isolated from the process. Yes, staff will be encouraged to react to the preliminary service responses recommended by the planning committee, but most of them will react during a one- or two-hour meeting that focuses on vision and service priorities. That is very different from the hours and hours that senior managers will spend on the planning process. Furthermore, some frontline staff may have difficulty relating a broad discussion of library priorities to the very specific work they do every day. Even staff who can easily see the relationship will be uneasy because they understand that it is too early in the process to know exactly what changes will be required.

Library staff have many reasons to be uneasy. There has been a lot written about the "new" public library. The public library, it is said, will be transformed into Library 2.0, a place that is interactive and user-driven. In their widely read white paper on Library 2.0, Ken Chad and Paul Miller defined the four principles of Library 2.0:

> The library is everywhere.
>
> The library has no barriers.
>
> The library invites participation.
>
> The library uses flexible, best-of-breed systems.[1]

These principles may seem like a radical departure from traditional library services to many staff, particularly staff members who have worked at the library for a long time. These staff think of libraries as buildings and not as some ethereal "everywhere." Their customer interactions are governed by policies, regulations, and procedures, many of which create barriers to use. They do not see their services as participative—quite the opposite, in fact. These librarians were trained to be "experts" and to see users as the recipients of their expertise. Many of these staff are even leery of "flexible, best-of-breed systems." They have been involved in too many beta tests and seen too many technology solutions that became technology problems.

Yet, when you look at the five laws of library science articulated by S. R. Ranganathan in 1931, you will see that the principles of Library 2.0 are not that contrary to the historic principles of librarianship. Figure 24 lists Ranganathan's five laws and a reinterpretation of those laws that was done by a group of library students in 2007. The most interesting thing about the two lists is how much alike they are. Libraries are still about connecting users and resources in ways that are meaningful to the users. Libraries are still about looking for ways to make it easy for users to take advantage of the resources that are available. Libraries are certainly still growing organisms.

Now compare the two sets of library laws with the principles of Library 2.0 above. If Library 2.0 is everywhere, then the chances that resources will be used are enhanced, it is likely that every resource will find a user, and that every user will find the needed resource. If Library 2.0 has no barriers, then it will clearly save time and energy for the user. "The library uses best-of-breed systems" is certainly one aspect of the fifth law, "The library is a growing organism."

It is the fourth principle of Library 2.0, "The library invites participation," that is most foreign to many library professionals. Yet even this principle is more evolutionary than revolutionary. Public libraries all over the country sponsor and support book clubs, where

FIGURE 24

Five Laws of Library Science

S. R. Ranganathan's Five Laws of Library Science, 1931	Reinterpretation of the Five Laws of Library Science, 2007
1. Books are for use	1. Resources are for use
2. Every person his or her book	2. Every resource its user
3. Every book its reader	3. Every user his resource
4. Save the time of the reader	4. Save time and energy of user
5. A library is a growing organism	5. The library is a growing organism
Source: Shiyali Ramamrita Ranganathan. *The Five Laws of Library Science* (London: Edward Goldston, 1931).	*Source:* http://tametheweb.com/2007/01/would_you _rewrite_ranganathans.html. The original list posted on the blog substituted the word "collection" for "book." Diana Rodríguez's post said that when her library school class reinterpreted the five laws, they substituted "resources" for "book" and that is the version used here.

people come together to discuss a book they have all read. Many public libraries have teen advisory boards, whose members are encouraged to develop and deliver programs for other teens. Many libraries encourage library users to recommend titles for purchase. Libraries hold writing workshops, sponsor poetry readings, and display works by local artists. This participation is face-to-face and not electronic, but it is undeniably participation. Perhaps Library 2.0 is more in keeping with traditional librarianship than it appears on first reading.

What does all this have to do with planning? It provides a framework for a broad discussion about changes in the field of librarianship, and that in turn provides a springboard for a discussion of changes in your library—and there will be changes. Neither you nor your staff can turn back the clock to the "good old days." Whether you develop a plan or not, your staff will be spending time on different activities in the future than today, and in many cases those activities will incorporate the principles of Library 2.0. The real question is how you and your colleagues will incorporate these inevitable changes into your library operations. If you have a strategic plan, you can ensure that the changes you make will support your service priorities and result in more effective library services. If you don't have a plan, the coming changes will be disruptive for staff and library users alike.

Getting Started

The two tasks in this chapter will set the stage for the successful completion of the planning process, and more important, for the implementation process that will follow. In Task 5, you will take the action necessary to prepare the library for the changes that will come with approval of the new strategic plan. In Task 6, you will work with others to define the core values of the library and to consider whether or not you need a mission statement.

TASK 5: PREPARE FOR CHANGE

The steps in Task 5 will be completed by the library director and the management team. The work in these steps can be initiated before or during Task 1 or during any task between Task 1 and Task 5. However, all the steps in Task 5 will need to be completed before you begin Task 6. The information you gather during Task 5 and the decisions you make based on that information will affect the way you complete the steps in Tasks 6, 7, 8, 9, and 10.

Step 5.1
Assess the Library's Readiness for Change

This task is about preparing the staff in your library for the changes that will be required to implement the strategic plan you are developing. Before you can consider ways to help staff adjust to those changes, you will need a clear understanding of their "change readiness." Change readiness can be defined as the current beliefs, attitudes, and expectations of staff regarding the need, value, and probable result of a change—major or minor. There are several factors that influence a library's change readiness. Some of those factors relate to any change that might be implemented, and others are influenced by the specific change under consideration.

As mentioned earlier, library staff are not generally enthusiastic about change, and in this they appear to mirror workers in other organizations and industries. The Impact Factory, a corporate consulting and training firm, notes that "staff are inclined to greet every change, no matter how minor, as a crisis. In a survey, a group of office workers were asked to list in order of severity what might cause them stress in their work environment. Top of the list was . . . 'Changing their office chair.'"[2]

The negative reaction to change can be affected by the change itself. Changes that affect others (perhaps changing someone else's chairs, but not mine) are less traumatic than changes that affect me. Changes that will alter things that have been changed recently may be harder to implement than changes in things that have been unchanged for a long time. Past experiences with similar changes will also affect the staff's attitudes about the current change.

How Can You Measure Change Readiness?

You can determine how ready your library is to make changes by gathering a variety of data, and most of the data you collect will be anecdotal rather than numeric. You will be gathering information about staff feelings, attitudes, expectations, and past reactions. This data will come from surveys, focus groups, discussions during staff meetings, and interviews with key staff. The information you gather will focus on the following issues.

Previous planning processes. The change readiness assessment is intended to provide you with the information you need to design a process to successfully complete—and begin to implement—your strategic plan. One of the most significant factors to be considered is the way any preceding planning processes were managed.

Does the library have a current strategic plan? When was it completed? A "current" plan is a plan that was developed no more than five years ago and has objectives that are still current.

Who was involved in your last planning process? A plan that was developed without any staff input is probably not well-supported by staff. In fact, some staff may not know that the plan exists.

Did the last plan focus on service priorities, or did it just address organizational structure and resource allocation issues? Many staff will not see a direct relationship between the work they do and a plan that focuses on organizational structure or resource allocation issues.

Did the past plan include a measurement and evaluation component? If so, has the data to track progress been collected? If asked, could staff point to any changes that resulted from the strategic plan? Did members of the management team refer to the past plan when they made resource allocation decisions? These questions all get to the heart of the matter. If staff members have seen no changes that can be attributed to the most recent strategic plan, they are unlikely to believe that the plan you are developing will make any difference in the future.

Recent major changes. Think about the major changes that have been made in the library in the past five years. Include such things as purchasing a new integrated library system (ILS), moving or renovating your building, hiring a new director, initiating a major new service, eliminating or significantly changing a service, or dealing with major changes in available resources (increases or decreases).

Which changes, if any, were well-received by the staff? Which changes, if any, were implemented on time and on budget? Were any frontline staff involved in the decisions to initiate the changes or in the process of implementing any of the changes? Do staff look back on the changes as being beneficial to the organization or harmful to the organization? Do staff think the results of the changes were worth the effort? If your recent change efforts have been successful, you are in a stronger position when you initiate a new change process.

Organizational culture. It can be difficult to assess the culture of a library, and this is particularly true for people who are part of that culture. One way to define the culture in your library is to look at the shared assumptions and beliefs that the staff have developed based on their past experiences and the behavior patterns they have observed. These shared assumptions and beliefs evolve over time, and they are difficult to change quickly.

New staff members are introduced to these assumptions and beliefs as "the way things are in this library." This process of acculturating new staff members explains why people who were hired two years ago can speak as though from personal experience about a divisive or controversial event that occurred years before they were hired. Figure 25 provides an example of how and why the culture in one library changed over a period of years.

One way to assess the organizational culture in your library is to commission a staff survey. This survey could include questions about staff satisfaction with their job duties and their assessment of the library environment. The library environment questions could focus on such topics as the library's formal and informal communications, the library's

FIGURE 25

How Organizational Culture Evolves

There was once a library that had been managed by the same director for thirty years. The director was competent and effective. She involved staff in decision making and was generally respected by staff and community members alike.

She retired and was replaced by a much younger director who decided that the library was behind the times, that immediate changes were necessary, and that the staff were so invested in current practice that there was no point in involving them in the change process. Her tenure was brief and turbulent. Staff were shocked, angry, and frustrated.

Another director was hired. She was not prepared to deal with the backlash from staff and the community that the previous director had caused. She stayed in the job for several years, but was widely seen as ineffective and uninterested in the staff.

Another director was hired. This director understood the problems in the organization and was ready to involve staff in resolving those problems. However, the organizational culture had shifted from one of trust and shared problem-solving to one of distrust, suspicion, and hostility. Staff who were hired after the current director began were just as distrustful and suspicious as staff who had worked in the library since the long-time director retired.

---

performance appraisal process, how comfortable staff feel about suggesting changes in the way they perform their job duties, and whether or not staff feel they are involved in the library's decision-making process. This survey could also include questions about staff reactions to the most recent strategic plan, if there is such a plan. You will find more information on staff surveys in *Human Resources for Results: The Right Person for the Right Job*.[3]

Risk-taking environment. The degree to which the library supports risk-taking is a part of the organizational culture, but it is such a critical part of your assessment of change readiness that you will want to pay special attention to it. There is an element of risk in every change, and some library managers are so risk-averse that they are unable to successfully implement any change. Symptoms of risk-averse library managers include collecting extensive data before making decisions in a futile search for the one "right answer," refusing to implement a change until another library of similar size has done so successfully, distributing both responsibility and authority so widely that no one person can be blamed for anything (of course, this means that no one can get credit for anything either), and reversing the decision to make a change at the first sign of staff dissatisfaction.

Staff morale. Staff morale will also affect the change readiness of a library. While staff morale both influences organizational culture and is affected by it, morale is more personal than institutional and is somewhat easier to modify than the library's culture. The staff in every library can be divided into at least three groups: staff who love their jobs and get a feeling of satisfaction from their work; staff who like their jobs and think they do them well; and staff who are unhappy with their jobs and think they do the jobs as well as anyone could under the circumstances.

Staff in the third group share many of the feelings listed in figure 26. Change readiness is affected by the percentage of staff who exhibit some or all of the symptoms in the figure, how strongly they exhibit those feelings, and whether or not the percentage of staff who exhibit low morale is growing, staying the same, or shrinking.

Staff reactions to change. Another way to look at the change readiness of your staff is to divide the staff into four groups:

FIGURE 26
Symptoms of Poor Staff Morale

It is relatively easy to identify staff members suffering from morale problems. These staff members are

- distrustful of top management
- angry with middle management
- unclear about library priorities
- unhappy about the library priorities they do understand
- angry about the perceived lack of support for staff during past changes
- wary of anything new
- fed up with the difference between promises and reality
- disillusioned about the effects of technology
- absent a lot and use their vacation and sick leave as it is earned

- cynical about the future
- suspicious of staff who seem to be happy in their jobs
- frustrated by changing user expectations
- sad about the erosion of public support for traditional information services
- fearful about their jobs
- considering unionizing in reaction to perceived disrespect from library management
- adhering strictly to job descriptions and often saying "that's not my job"
- critical of library management in public or online forums

- those who enthusiastically support change
- those who are relatively positive about change
- those who have reservations about change
- those who actively oppose change

Estimate what percentage of your staff fall into each category. The percentages in each category may shift somewhat based on the change under consideration, but you should be able to come up with a general assessment. Typically, 10 or 15 percent of the staff in any organization will support any change and 10 or 15 percent will oppose any change.

The change battles in most libraries are won or lost with the remaining 70 percent of the staff, those who are relatively positive about change and those who have reservations about change. The boundary between these two groups is porous and people flow back and forth between them, depending on the change under consideration and how effectively those who support the change make their case.

Some library managers want to have full support from those staff affected by a change before they initiate that change. These managers spend an inordinate amount of time trying to convert those who are most opposed to the change, which is almost always a losing battle. The managers' energies would be better spent working with those who have reservations about the change. The members of this group are more likely to be responsive.

If you wait until 100 percent of the staff affected by a change agree on something, you will never carry out that change. In fact, if you wait for 75 percent of your staff to agree on something, you are still unlikely to do it. As a general rule, if more than 50 percent of the staff who will be affected by a change are supportive, move forward. Many of the people who still have reservations will accept the change once it becomes a reality. The people who totally oppose the change will remain in opposition until the next change comes along. Then they will shift their attention to opposing the new change instead.

FIGURE 27
Workform F: Analyze Change Readiness—Example

A. **Factors That Create an Environment That Supports the Change(s)**	B. **Wt.**		C. **Factors That Create an Environment That Impedes the Change(s)**	D. **Wt.**
The library management team supports the new planning process	3		The library has been involved in selecting a new ILS for over a year and still hasn't made a decision	3
The previous plan led to positive changes in the library	3		Many first-line supervisors are skeptical of the proposed priorities	3
We have a number of new staff members who are enthusiastic about the new priorities	1		Senior managers have a tendency to collect more data than needed to make decisions	1
Staff morale is better than it was a year ago	2		In certain departments staff morale is considerably lower than the library average	2
Over 60% of the staff participated in the meetings on the preliminary service responses	2		Two senior managers and many supervisors will retire in the next two years	1
There are two new board members who are very enthusiastic about the planning process	3		Frontline staff have said that they feel out of the communication loop	3

(Center vertical label: Change(s) under Consideration)

What Do You Do with the Data You Gather?

When you have finished gathering data on some or all of the issues described above, you will have a lot of information to evaluate, and most of it will be anecdotal or narrative. One of the easiest ways to begin to make sense of all the data you have collected is to use Workform F, Analyze Change Readiness. This workform enables you to list the factors that you think help to create an environment that supports making the changes that will result from your strategic planning process, and to list the factors that you think will make it difficult for you to implement those changes. It also enables you to weigh each of the factors you list. You can see some of the strengths and weaknesses identified by the Tree County Library management team in figure 27.

Workform F should be completed by the members of the senior management team. First, ask each member of the team to consider all of the data and record their impressions on a copy of the workform. Then bring the members of the team together to share their perceptions and to create a composite workform that lists and weighs all of the factors supporting and impeding change. When the members of the group have completed their work, you will be ready to move on to Step 5.2.

Step 5.2
Plan to Create a Positive Environment for Change

There are two ways to improve the change environment in your library. You can either eliminate or minimize the factors that impede the change environment, or you can add to or enhance the factors that support creating such an environment. Managers often put more of their energies into eliminating or ameliorating the negative factors than they do into adding to or enhancing the positive factors. This is not always the most effective approach to improving your change environment. The most successful efforts may be those that accentuate the positive.

How Can You Accentuate the Positive Factors?

Start by reviewing the factors you and your colleagues listed in column A of Workform F. Look at the factors that you consider to be the most significant ones. Why do you think they are so important? What can you do to capitalize on those factors? In the example in figure 27, the Tree County Library managers agreed that one of the most significant positive factors was the success in implementing the previous plan. However, they thought it was likely that most staff were only familiar with the effect the previous plan had in their own units and not with all of the success stories from other parts of the library. The Tree County Library might decide to take full advantage of the success of the previous plan by appointing a cross-functional team to work with staff in each unit to identify the three most positive changes that occurred in that unit because of the plan. These positive results could be compiled and posted on the library intranet or sent to the staff in printed form. It won't do much good to write a dry, boring, official memo or e-mail listing accomplishments, however. Personalize the messages you send. Name the staff members responsible for the successes, give specific examples of successes, include testimonials from users, and use pictures if you can. Truly celebrate the staff members' achievements.

Another significant factor in creating a positive change environment in the example in figure 27 is that the members of the library management team support the current planning process. One way to build on this strength is to spend some time with the managers discussing why they support the process. Use this discussion to create a list of "talking points" that capture the group's positive feelings about the planning process. Encourage the library managers to use the talking points to describe the planning process when talking to other staff. The message will be much stronger if all of the senior managers are emphasizing the same benefits.

Now is also the time to identify new things you could do that would have a positive influence on your change environment. Managers in the library in the example might initiate a program that rewards staff members who propose innovative changes in programs, services, or workflow. The award would be based on the creativity of the suggested change and the work the staff member does to implement the change, and not solely on the ultimate success of the change. Staff can learn as much from a project that doesn't succeed as they can from one that does. The intent of this reward program is to help staff become more comfortable taking risks, and therefore become more comfortable in a changing environment.

What Can You Do to Eliminate or Ameliorate the Negative Factors?

It is easier to build on strength than it is to address weakness. After all, if the negative factors that are influencing the library's change environment were easy to fix, you probably would have fixed them already. It will be important that you enter into any process to address the negatives with a realistic attitude. Too many managers are inclined to apply a bandage to a problem and then either declare the problem solved or decide that it is insoluble. Neither approach will work here. It will require sustained and focused efforts to address the negative factors on your list.

Some of the items on your list of negative factors may be out of your control. In the example in figure 27, one of the negative factors is that two senior managers and many supervisors will be retiring in the near future. The Tree County Library managers can't change that factor, but they can establish a voluntary training program for staff who are interested in being considered for supervisory positions as they become open. This has the potential for turning a negative into a positive. Staff who are interested in promotions will be given the training they need to be effective supervisors. Some of the young staff who are enthusiastic about the new planning priorities will probably be in the training programs, and their enthusiasm may be contagious.

It may be difficult to turn some of the other negatives into positives. In the example in figure 27, the fact that the library has been involved in selecting a new ILS for over a year was listed as a serious negative—and it is. There is nothing anyone can do about that fact except resolve the issue as soon as possible. What can be done, however, is to acknowledge to all staff that the process was not as effective as it might have been, determine why the process is taking so long, and take visible steps to ensure that future decisions are handled more effectively. Managers should also make every effort to ensure that the migration to the new system is smooth and trouble-free. That will help staff forget about the problems during the procurement process.

Sometimes the negative factors on the list provide the first information that a problem exists. There are a number of reasons why staff morale might be lower in one department than in the rest of library. If this is a change for this department, a member of the management team should take steps to identify the source of the problem. Is there a new supervisor who is having problems relating to staff? Is there a staff member who is causing problems? Did a staff member retire from that department recently? Sometimes changing one person in a tight-knit group can destabilize the whole group. Whatever the problem is, it should be addressed as soon as possible.

Some of the negative factors will never be eliminated. Frontline staff will always feel at least a little out of the communications loop because they are. There are decisions that must be made without the input of frontline staff, and those staff will always wonder "what really happened." However, just because a problem can't be fixed doesn't mean it can't be minimized. It is impossible to overestimate the importance of open, honest, factual, and timely information in creating a library environment that is conducive to change. In Step 5.3 you will think more about how to do this, and the topic will be covered again in more detail in chapter 5.

Remember, too, that the work of the library will not stop while the members of the management team review the positive and negative factors and make plans to address them. Library managers will go right on making and implementing decisions. It will be critical for the current and ongoing actions of the members of the management team to be consistent with the efforts being made to improve the library's change readiness. It won't do any good to improve the communication with staff about the planning process if managers still keep staff in the dark about other important initiatives.

Step 5.3
Review and Revise Communication Plans

By the time you reach this step, you and your colleagues will have identified a number of projects or processes that you believe will improve the change environment in your library, and you will be ready to announce your proposed projects. If your library is like most, someone will prepare a written report that includes the results of the change readiness assessment and a list of the projects that will be initiated because of the assessment. Library managers will be asked to attend a meeting during which the report will be distributed and discussed. The managers will be encouraged to share the report with their staff members.

The managers will then go back to their units and share what they think they heard with the staff members. Some of them will route the written report to their staff, some will post it on a bulletin board, and some will file it away or discard it. Three weeks or three months later, senior staff will be shocked and amazed to learn that no one on the staff seems to know or care about their efforts to alter the library's change environment.

Telling managers things and expecting them to tell other staff what they heard is like playing an organizational version of the old game "telephone." You probably played telephone when you were a child. A group of children sit in a circle. The first child whispers a sentence into the ear of the second child, who in turn passes the sentence on to the third child, and so on. The first child might whisper "Mary has a pet dog named Red." As the phrase moves around the circle, it morphs into "Mary has a pet named Red" to "Mary has a red pet" to "Mary's pet is dead."

You may think that you can resolve the "telephone" problem by providing the managers with a written report as well as a verbal presentation. However, this assumes that managers will (a) read the report, (b) believe the report, (c) remember what they read, (d) share the written report with their staff, (e) file the report in a place from which it can be retrieved, and (f) change their attitudes or behaviors based on the report. The first five assumptions are shaky, and the sixth is just plain wrong. Things that people hear in meetings or read in general reports almost never cause them to change their attitudes or behaviors.

Real communication is a two-way process. It is not enough to simply send a message. Communication does not occur until that message has been received by the person to whom it was sent and that person has been affected by it. That effect isn't always the one you intended when you sent the message. You may send a message to staff telling them about a new service or program with the intention of creating enthusiasm for the program. It may, instead, create anxiety as overworked staff wonder how they can do more than they are already doing. The problem here isn't a lack of communication. The recipients understood the message. They just didn't like it.

Any time two people communicate, there is a potential for misunderstanding. Just think about some of the problems you have had with friends or loved ones over the years. Even with the best of intentions and good relationships, communication can be challenging. Communicating effectively in an organizational environment can be even more difficult. There are more people sending messages and more people receiving those messages than ever before. The opportunities for miscommunication, missed communication, and distorted communication increase exponentially in an organizational environment. There is more information about formal communication processes in the Library Communication tool kit in part 3.

As part of the *plan to plan* process in Step 1.4, planners were encouraged to use Workform A to develop a communication plan for each of the ten tasks in the *Planning for Results* process. In most cases, the communication plans developed during Task 1 for the later tasks in the process will be somewhat cursory.

During this step, you will revise your communication plans to reflect what you have learned about the planning process and what you learned during the assessment of the library's readiness for change. As a reminder, Workform A provides a place to answer the following six questions for each of the stakeholder groups in the planning process:

> Why do the members of the group need to know about this task?
>
> What do they know now?
>
> What will they need to know?
>
> When will they need to know it?
>
> How will you inform them?
>
> Who will be responsible for informing them?

Refer back to Step 1.4 in chapter 1 for more information on answering each of these questions.

As you and your colleagues revise Workform A for the remaining tasks, don't lose track of the fact that staff will be more likely to support a strategic plan they helped to shape than a plan that was developed for them. If you expect staff to support the final strategic plan, you will have to involve them in the planning process. This will require the active and informed support and cooperation of every library manager and supervisor.

Step 5.4
Train Supervisors and Managers

Managers and supervisors need formal training in organizational communication to be able to develop and maintain a library culture that supports change. Unfortunately, the closest thing to training of this type that most supervisors receive is the customer service training that many libraries offer. Customer service training focuses on teaching staff members to communicate effectively with irate users in one-on-one settings. While this kind of training might be helpful for supervisors when they deal with irate staff members, it does nothing to help them understand the theory or practice of organization communication, nor does it give them the skills needed to communicate effectively in an organizational setting. For this, they need specialized training.

The strategic planning process provides an excellent opportunity to enhance the skills of supervisory and management staff. The training you offer can be designed and presented by one or more library staff members or it can be provided by a professional trainer. The professional trainer you hire does not have to be a librarian, but she has to know enough about how libraries operate to use library-specific examples throughout the training program. Adult learners learn best when the concepts are presented in a familiar context.

A training program on organizational communication could be designed around the projects you identified in Step 5.1 to enhance the library's change readiness. Such a program would provide information about the principles of organizational communication, but focus on using those principles to implement or support the projects identified in Step 5.1. This will make the program appear to be pragmatic rather than theoretical and make it easy for supervisors and managers to see how the skills they are developing during the training could be applied. This will also allow the supervisors and managers to use their new skills immediately, which will reinforce the training.

Many novice trainers worry more about the content of a training program than the process, and end up presenting programs that *tell* rather than *train*. Listening is a passive activity, particularly if the listener is part of a large group that is on the receiving end of a formal presentation. It is easy for a member of an audience to get distracted by one point in the presentation, to start worrying about work or home, doing her e-mail on a Blackberry, or just start daydreaming. Effective training, on the other hand, is active. It engages the learner in the process of learning.

A group of educators from the University of Tennessee conducted research to determine the characteristics of effective training programs for adults. Among other findings, they discovered that "we often focus too much on the content of the information we provide and too little on the processes through which adults can be motivated to make life changes."[4] These educators identified four characteristics of effective adult training, which are listed in figure 28.

FIGURE 28
Effective Training

Effective training is learner-focused. It

- identifies and addresses issues important to the learner
- identifies and builds on learner strengths
- includes active participation by the learner
- recognizes and draws upon the knowledge and experience of the learner
- facilitates learning through peer exchange
- is culturally and ethically meaningful
- draws everyone into the discussion

Effective training models productive behavior and effective skills. It

- integrates decision-making, planning, organization, and implementation skill building
- models and reinforces workplace ethics and productive use of time
- provides opportunities for learners to expand social networks
- challenges learners to take responsibility for their own lifelong learning

Effective training inspires and motivates. It

- presents accurate information
- increases learner knowledge about the subject matter
- reinforces worthwhile values and principles
- provides opportunities for humor and fun during learning
- maintains a positive focus
- gives the learner a feeling of accomplishment

Effective training celebrates personal and group achievements. It

- incorporates incentives to mark learning milestones
- provides for assessment and learner-based feedback
- is acknowledged by the larger community

Source: Dena Wise and Patsy Ezell, "Characteristics of Effective Training: Developing a Model to Motivate Action," *Journal of Extension* 41, no. 2 (April 2003), available at http://www.joe.org/joe/2003april/a5.shtml.

Regardless of who develops the communication training program to be presented to supervisory staff, members of the management team should review the final agenda and handout packet. They can use the characteristics listed in figure 28 as their criteria for evaluating the program. Most trainers will welcome feedback about ways to enhance their training programs, and these criteria provide a framework for discussion.

The training program for supervisors and managers discussed in this step specifically addresses their need to understand organizational communication theory and to develop the skills required to put that theory into practice. That does not mean that this is the only management training that will be required. It is quite possible that one or more of the change issues you identify in Step 5.1 will require additional training programs. The criteria for effective training for adults shown in figure 28 will apply to any training programs you develop.

TASK 6: CONSIDER LIBRARY VALUES AND MISSION

Task 1:	Design the Planning Process
Task 2:	Start the Planning Process
Task 3:	Identify Community Needs
Task 4:	Select Service Responses
Task 5:	Prepare for Change
Task 6:	**Consider Library Values and Mission**
	Step 6.1: Define values
	Step 6.2: Consider the library mission
Task 7:	Write Goals and Objectives
Task 8:	Identify Organizational Competencies
Task 9:	Write the Strategic Plan and Obtain Approval
Task 10:	Communicate the Results of the Planning Process

In this task, you will turn your attention to library values. Values are principles or standards that library staff and board members use to guide their actions and decisions. Values express the shared beliefs that provide the foundation of the library profession, define expectations for staff work behavior and communications, and articulate the quality of services that the public can expect to receive from the library. Taken together, values provide a description of the organizational culture the staff and board want to create, if not always the actual culture of the library. In this task you will also consider the library mission statement in the context of the current planning priorities.

The steps in this task will be coordinated by members of the library management team, but will involve all staff and the members of the board. You can probably identify value statements in one or two meetings of the management team. It will take a couple of weeks for staff to review and respond to the draft value statements, but that review can happen while you are working on goals and objectives in Task 7. The discussion of mission statements and taglines may take longer, but you won't need to make any final decisions until you are ready to write the final plan in Task 9.

Step 6.1
Define Values

The identification or validation of the library's values is an important part of the planning process and one that has not received enough emphasis in the past. Over the past decade, members of community planning committees and library staff have wondered how to incorporate such basic library values as intellectual freedom and confidentiality of library records into the planning process. Some committee members have tried to select service responses that seemed to reflect specific values, but they soon realized that values apply to all service responses. Some staff have tried to write goals that reflect specific values and discovered the same problem. Values are universal and apply to all of the interactions in the library.

Library value statements can address an array of topics, from intellectual freedom and privacy issues through respect and customer service to teamwork and accountability. There are a variety of ways to frame value statements. Some libraries start each statement with the words "we value" or "we believe." Others libraries use more active verbs and write statements similar to those in figure 29. Some libraries use full sentences to describe their values and others use a list of phrases (see figure 30). There are many more examples of public library value statements on the Internet.

The format and structure of your value statements are far less important than the process used to identify them. Library values come from the staff and the board of the library, and they are unique to the library in which they were created. They describe how *we in our library* will treat our users and one another, how *we in our library* will support the principles of intellectual freedom and privacy, or how *we in our library* will manage public funds.

There is a reason why the task of defining values comes at this point in the planning process. The management team will have just completed an assessment of the change readiness of the library and will be designing ways to improve the change environment. A broad-based discussion of values can play a significant role in altering the change environment. How you go about defining your values will depend on whether or not the library has a current list of values.

What Should We Do If We Have Never Identified Values?

The process of identifying new values has eight separate phases. You will start by defining what values are and why it is important that they be identified in your library. You will then provide staff and board members with as many opportunities as possible to discuss the values in your library. When everyone has had a

FIGURE 29
Tree County Public Library Values

We defend the constitutional rights of all individuals, including children and teenagers, to use the library's resources and services.

We protect the privacy of every individual who uses the library.

We value our county's diversity and reflect that diversity in all of our services, programs, and collections.

We respect each person who uses the library and each employee of the library.

We provide friendly, knowledgeable service and work to meet the expectations of users.

We communicate effectively with the staff of the library and the residents of the community.

We encourage personal initiative, problem-solving, enthusiasm, responsible risk-taking, planning for future needs, and effective use of technology and other library resources.

We use taxpayer dollars effectively and seek to improve productivity whenever possible.

We work collaboratively within the library, with community organizations and groups, and with elected and appointed officials to achieve common goals.

We plan for the future and work to continually improve our services, programs, and collections to ensure that we meet the changing needs of our users.

We manage the resources entrusted to the library in an ethical and responsible manner.

FIGURE 30
Anytown Public Library Values

The Anytown Public Library values

- excellent customer service
- open and free access for all
- intellectual freedom and personal privacy
- collaboration with local agencies, organizations, and elected officials
- acting with initiative, creativity, and flexibility
- effective and efficient stewardship of library resources

chance to be heard, one person will take all of the suggestions from all of the sources and develop a draft set of value statements. The members of the management team will review the draft and determine the order in which the value statements will be listed. The revised draft will be made available to the staff and board for review and comment. The draft will be revised again as needed and submitted to the board for approval. Each of these phases is discussed in more detail below.

Define values and why they are important in your library. Before the staff and board members can identify possible library value statements, they will need to have a shared understanding of what values are, how they will be used, and why they are important. The library management team could identify the key concepts, and then one member of the team could create a document that includes a definition and brief descriptions of why values are being identified and how they will be used.

Provide opportunities for discussion and comment. This is similar to other parts of the planning process: the more opportunities that staff have to participate in the identification of values, the more likely they are to support the final product. You may want to use the same mechanisms you used to involve staff in the review of the preliminary service responses in Step 4.3. You may also want to ask members of the board to identify values during one of their meetings.

Designate one person to develop a draft. It is never a good idea to ask a committee to write something. The process of group writing and editing is frustrating, inefficient, and ineffective. You can almost always tell when something has been written by a committee. It is too verbose, it includes words that are too long and too formal, and it tends to be repetitive. This is because the easiest way to resolve differences of opinion among committee members is to include each member's opinion in the final product. Ask one person who writes well to develop draft value statements based on all of the input that came from the staff.

Determine the order in which the value statements will be listed. Most libraries develop multiple value statements, which means that the statements will have to be presented in some order. The members of the library management team are the logical people to determine the order of the values. Most libraries group their values into subsets (customer service, intellectual freedom, etc.) and then list the groups in priority order.

Make the draft available for review and comment. Staff and board members should have a chance to review the draft value statements before they are made final. In most libraries, this can be done electronically through the library's intranet. However, if there were disagreements among staff about the values to be included or the relative importance of various values, it might be necessary to hold another series of meetings to try to see if the staff can reach some consensus.

Revise the draft as needed. The person who wrote the original draft of the values will revise them based on comments and suggestions from the staff. If there are still substantial disagreements among staff, the members of the management team will make the final decisions.

Submit to board for approval. The members of the library board will probably be asked to approve the value statements. If they were involved in suggesting values and reviewing the draft values, this should be a simple matter.

Distribute to staff. When the values have been approved, they should be distributed to staff throughout the library. Supervisors should be encouraged to review the values with their staff and to post the value statements in a prominent place in the unit.

What Should We Do If We Have Already Identified Values?

Many libraries have developed value statements at some point in the past. If your library has value statements that were approved more than three years ago, you will probably want to go through all of the eight phases described above, with two modifications. In the first phase, you will not only define values and describe why they are important; you will also include a list of the library's current values. The meetings during the second phase will begin with a review of the current value statements before moving on to a discussion of new or revised values.

If your value statements are less than three years old, you can probably do an abbreviated review of the values and provide an opportunity for people to recommend revisions or additions. You might ask the managers in each unit to discuss the values with their staff and to send any suggested changes to a designated person who will develop a draft, post it for review, and revise the draft as necessary. If the values were changed in any meaningful way, they should be taken to the board for discussion and approval.

How Can We Use the Values to Improve the Change Culture in the Library?

The final value statements that are approved by the board describe the attributes of a library culture that both staff and board members agree is positive and supportive. Now those attributes need to move from paper to practice. The members of the management team may want to conduct an informal values audit to compare the ideals stated in the values with the reality of day-to-day life in the library. The values audit will include a review of library policies, the library's performance appraisal process, and the relations between supervisors and their employees in each unit of the library. The members of the management team will probably want to look at the library's formal and informal communication patterns. (There is more information on this in the Library Communication tool kit in part 3.) The audit might also include a review of public complaints to identify customer service problems and a customer satisfaction survey to assess the quality of current customer service. The final elements of the values audit in each library will be driven by the values identified in that library.

It is almost inevitable that the values audit will identify some problems to be addressed. The number and severity of those problems will vary depending on the library, but virtually every library will find some issues. The most effective way to address those issues is to appoint cross-functional teams to review the difference between values and practice and to develop recommendations for bringing the two into alignment. This will have two benefits. The management team will not only be sending a clear signal that values matter; they will also be addressing some of the systemic problems that can have a negative effect on the organizational culture. This reinforces the efforts that are being made to create an environment that supports change.

Step 6.2
Consider the Library Mission

A mission statement is generally defined as a statement that describes the reason an organization exists—its core purpose. Over the years, library boards have spent a great deal of time carefully crafting library mission statements that end up sounding somewhat vague and generic. Many of those mission statements are similar to this one: "The library is dedicated to meeting the educational, recreational, informational, professional, cultural, and social needs of all residents." In their desire to make it clear that the library provides materials and services to everyone, board members often create statements that mean little or nothing to anyone.

Alan Ehrenhalt wrote about his reactions to library mission statements in a column in *Governing* magazine:

> What struck me . . . was the number of government institutions that seem to be breaking away from conventional modesty and writing mission statements that could have come from the pen of Pillsbury's management consultant. For some reason I couldn't fathom at first, most of these heavy promisers seemed to be libraries and school systems. . . . At first I thought there was some law of inverse competence at work here. The worse a public institution performs, the more it seems to promise. But that is not exactly the case. It would be more accurate to say that a grandiose mission statement suggests an organization that hasn't quite figured out what it is supposed to be doing. . . . And so we come to the ultimate Catch-22 of mission statements: if you know what you are doing, you probably don't need one. And if you don't know what you are doing, a mission statement probably isn't going to help.[5]

What Is a Mission Statement?

The definition, function, and perceived value of library mission statements have evolved over the past twenty years. In 1987 in *Planning and Role-Setting for Public Libraries,* the mission statement was defined as "a concise expression of the library's purpose [that] specifies the fundamental reasons for the library's existence."[6] The 1998 version of *Planning for Results* said: "The library's mission statement tells the community what business the library is in. It says what the library does exceptionally well that is unique, or different, from what other agencies and organizations do."[7]

Using those definitions as a guideline, it is hard to think of a better mission statement than "Free Books for All," which was used by Head Librarian John Thomson when he opened the Philadelphia Free Library's first central branch at City Hall in March 1894.[8] This is clear, concise, and describes a unique service.

In 2001 *The New Planning for Results* said: "In this process, a library mission statement is a marketing tool. Its purpose is to inform the community about the library's priorities in clear and easily understood terms."[9] In today's marketing terms, "Free Books for All" would probably be considered more of a tagline than a mission. A tagline is *a statement or motto that succinctly defines or represents an organization's mission.*[10] A tagline distills the benefits of the library and its values into a short and memorable phrase that can be used to help brand the library.

To help decide if you need a tagline or mission statement or both, consider the following questions.

- Do you have a mission statement now?
  - What is its purpose?
  - Has it been an effective way to achieve its purpose?
  - If you didn't have this mission statement, what difference would it make?
- Do you have a tagline now?
  - What is its purpose?
  - Has it been an effective way to achieve its purpose?
  - If you didn't have this tagline, what difference would it make?
- If you don't have a mission statement now:
  - What would be the purpose of a mission statement?
  - Who is the target audience for the mission statement?
  - How will the mission statement be disseminated?
  - How will you know that your mission statement achieved your intended purpose?
- If you don't have a tagline now:
  - What would be the purpose of a tagline?
  - Who is the target audience for the tagline?
  - How will the tagline be disseminated?
  - How will you know that your tagline achieved your intended purpose?
  - Would a tagline supplement or replace a mission statement?

What Should Be Included in a Mission Statement?

If your answers to the preceding questions convince you or your board that you need to write a mission statement, start with service responses that have been approved for the current planning cycle. Taken together, they define the library's priorities. The titles in the service responses have two components. The phrase before the colon describes the benefits that the people in your community receive from the library. The phrase after the colon usually describes the service in more library-centric terms. For example:

> Build Successful Enterprises: Business and Nonprofit Support
>
> Discover Your Roots: Genealogy and Local History
>
> Get Facts Fast: Ready Reference
>
> Learn to Read and Write: Adult, Teen, and Family Literacy

Use the phrases before the colon as the basis of your mission statement. They are much more proactive and user-friendly than the descriptions of library services that follow the colon. For example:

The Anytown Public Library stimulates people's imaginations, satisfies their curiosity, supports parents who want their children to become readers, and helps students succeed in school.

The Tree County Library is a comfortable and welcoming place where people of all ages can express their creativity, become informed citizens, connect to the online world, and satisfy their curiosity.

There may be some people on the board and on the staff who resist this colloquial approach to mission statement writing. One librarian who read the service responses when they were being developed felt that the phrases in the titles should be switched so that the library service terminology was listed first. She said that a professional and businesslike presentation was valued by the library's funding agencies, and she seemed to believe that the focus on the community in some way diminished the library's professionalism. This feeling, of course, runs counter to everything that the *Planning for Results* process is based on. It is, however, a feeling that you may have to address among your staff and board members.

When you have completed a draft mission statement, go back to the questions that led you to decide you needed a mission statement and check to see if the draft statement does what you hoped it would. If it does, that's great. If it doesn't, you can either revise the mission statement and check it again or you can decide that what you really need is a tagline.

You will have to determine what role the board will play in all of this. In some libraries, the board members take an active part in the decision of whether you need a mission statement or a tagline. These boards will probably want to be involved in developing the mission or tagline and may expect to approve the final product. In other libraries, the mission or tagline would be presented to the board as an informational item during a regularly scheduled board meeting.

What Should Be Included in a Tagline?

Taglines are even more challenging to develop than mission statements, because they have to be short and memorable. Consider Nike's very effective tagline, "Just Do It." In three words it manages to convey commitment, determination, and action—key traits for the athletes who are Nike's customers. Libraries have also developed some memorable taglines:

> *A Great Place to Learn:* Carroll County Library (MD)
>
> *Engaging Minds, Expanding Opportunities:* District of Columbia Public Library
>
> *Your Unexpected Oasis:* Maricopa County Library District (AZ)
>
> *A City with a Great Library Is a Great City:* Nashville Public Library (TN)
>
> *Enrich Your Life:* Queens Library (NY)
>
> *Be a Reader, Be Informed:* Saxton B. Little Free Library (Columbia, CT)

Developing a tagline for your library should be a group process. Consider appointing a cross-functional team to lead the effort. Appoint your most creative staff members to the team, and be sure to appoint an effective chair. Your goal is to have a team that is both creative and productive. Encourage all staff to participate in the process. You might ask supervisors in each unit to spend twenty or thirty minutes brainstorming with their staff to answer these questions:

> What makes the library unique? How is it different from other agencies in the community?

> What do you want people to think of when the library is mentioned?

> What do you want your customers to feel when they think of the library?

You could also post the questions on the staff intranet and encourage staff to post their suggestions electronically.

The members of the team responsible for developing the tagline should develop a list of the key words from all of the staff suggestions and add to this list if they can. Then the creative part of the process begins. The members will combine the key words into phrases, looking for one combination that reflects the library. They could look for alliteration, rhymes, similes, and paradoxes. This is going to take time, but sooner or later the team will come up with some taglines that they like. This list of potential taglines should be distributed throughout the library for review and comment. Ask staff to use the following criteria to evaluate the taglines:

> Is it memorable?

> Does it communicate the message the library wants to send?

> Does it differentiate the library from other organizations?

> Does it reflect the library's personality?

> Is it believable?

> Is it original?

The team should review all of the staff feedback, make any revisions that are necessary, and submit the top two or three taglines to the management team for final selection. After the management team has selected the tagline, it should be used on everything from the library's website and official e-mail signature files to the library's stationery and printed promotional materials. The whole point of having a tagline is to tell people what the library is—it is a powerful communication tool. However, you have to send the communication before it can be received.

What's Next?

The tasks in this chapter addressed two broad issues: organizational culture and values. These issues may, at first glance, appear to be peripheral to the library's strategic planning process, but upon closer inspection it becomes clear that they provide the foundation for any successful planning effort. In the next chapter, the focus moves from these broad organizational issues back to the priorities selected by the planning committee. In Task 7, you will learn how to develop goals that reflect the service responses selected by the committee, and objectives that will measure your progress toward reaching those goals. In Task 8, you will assess the library's operational capacity to support the selected goals and objectives and identify needed changes.

Key Points to Remember

The changes in your library are not happening in a void. Public librarianship is in a state of transition and all libraries are facing new challenges.

The more things change, the more they stay the same. Ranganathan's five laws of librarianship are as valid today as they were in 1931.

Change readiness is based on the current beliefs, attitudes, and expectations of staff regarding the need, value, and probable results of a change—major or minor.

The change environment in your library will be a major factor in your ability to implement the changes that will result from your strategic plan.

It is often more effective to accentuate the positive conditions in your library than to focus solely on addressing the negative conditions.

Too many managers are inclined to apply a bandage to a problem and then either declare the problem solved or decide that it is insoluble. Neither approach works. It will take sustained and focused effort to address the factors that negatively affect your library's change readiness.

Current and ongoing actions of the management team must be consistent with the efforts being made to improve the library's change readiness.

Managers and supervisors need formal training in organizational communication to be able to develop and maintain a library culture that supports change.

The identification of the library's values is an important part of the planning process.

Think carefully about the purpose of the library mission statement. Would a tagline be more effective? Do you need either?

Communicate, communicate, communicate.

Notes

1. Ken Chad and Paul Miller, "Do Libraries Matter? The Rise of Library 2.0," November 2005, http://www.talis.com/downloads/white_papers/DoLibrariesMatter.pdf.
2. The Impact Factory, "Change Fatigue," http://www.impactfactory.com/p/change_fatigue_skills _training/snacks_1438-7105-10143.html.
3. Jeanne Goodrich and Paula Singer, *Human Resources for Results: The Right Person for the Right Job* (Chicago: American Library Association, 2007).
4. Dena Wise and Patsy Ezell, "Characteristics of Effective Training: Developing a Model to Motivate Action," *Journal of Extension* 41, no. 2 (April 2003), http://www.joe.org/joe/2003april/a5.shtml.
5. Alan Ehrenhalt, "In Search of a World-Class Mission Statement: Is Your Government Ready for the Superbowl?" *Governing,* March 1997, http://www.governing.com/archive/1997/mar/assess.txt.
6. Charles R. McClure and others, *Planning and Role-Setting for Public Libraries: A Manual of Operations and Procedures* (Chicago: American Library Association, 1987), 28.

7. Ethel Himmel and William James Wilson, *Planning for Results: A Public Library Transformation Process* (Chicago: American Library Association, 1998), 31.
8. Free Library of Philadelphia History, "Founding 1889–1898," http://libwww.library.phila.gov/75th/founding.htm?page=his.
9. Sandra Nelson, *The New Planning for Results: A Streamlined Approach* (Chicago: American Library Association, 2001), 76.
10. Johns Hopkins University, Bloomberg School of Public Health, "Identity Guidelines: Glossary of Terms," http://www.jhsph.edu/identity/glossary/glossary.shtml.

Chapter 4

Describe the Future

In the absence of clearly-defined goals, we become strangely loyal to performing daily trivia until ultimately we become enslaved by it.

—Robert Heinlein

MILESTONES

By the time you finish this chapter you will be able to

- write goals that reflect the library's service priorities and support the library's values
- write objectives that include measures of progress toward reaching each of your goals
- review the data that the library currently collects and determine what additional data will be needed to track progress toward reaching the targets in your objectives
- assist staff in library units to determine the priority of the system goals for their units
- explain the concept of organizational capacity to the board and staff
- determine the organizational competencies and initiatives needed to implement the goals and objectives

Up to now the planning process has focused on broad concepts and issues. What would the ideal community look like? What services can the library provide that will help the community residents make progress toward that ideal? What are the library's values? Does the library need a mission statement? Does it need a tagline? All of these concerns seem pretty far removed from the actual day-to-day work of a children's librarian, or an adult services library assistant, or a unit manager struggling with desk schedules.

This will change when you start to discuss goals and objectives. The *Planning for Results* process places great emphasis on using hard data to evaluate the effectiveness of programs and services. Every objective includes a specific and measurable target and the date by which the target should be met. This is a new emphasis for the staff in many libraries, who think of data collection primarily in the context of completing monthly reports and submitting statistics to the state library agency. In other words, many staff currently see data collection as a passive activity; things happen and we count them. In this planning process, the data collection environment is much more active. Staff will be expected to influence what is happening to ensure that they reach specific targets within a given time frame.

Typically, it is during the review of the draft objectives that staff start getting concerned about the implications of the planning process for their day-to-day work. The objective "During 2XXX, a minimum of 10,000 children will attend programs presented by the library staff in off-site locations" sends a powerful message to the staff in the children's area, particularly if they are currently providing most or all of their services within the library. The minute they read this objective, the strategic plan goes from being something "they" are talking about to something "I" will have to live with.

This is the point at which staff anxiety levels shoot up and the whole planning process becomes open to question. Where, staff members ask, did these goals come from? Who were those people on the planning committee, and what makes you think they know anything about library services? We have been serving our clients for a long time and we are in the best position to judge what they need. Why didn't someone tell us about this before?

While all of these questions are frustrating for managers, the last one is particularly irritating. The planning process has been going on for a couple of months. The staff attended an orientation to the planning program (Step 1.5) during which the entire process was explained. They were given an opportunity to review the preliminary service responses and provide feedback to the planning committee (Step 4.3). There may be a planning web page on the staff intranet, and if not, printed copies of planning updates have been distributed to each unit. In addition, unit managers have been encouraged to keep their staff informed about the process. What more, managers ask, could we have done to keep staff involved?

Unfortunately, the answer is probably nothing. Most people are too busy to worry much about "what if," and they only become engaged in the discussion when it moves from "if" to "when." That is why the work you do in Task 5 is so important. You and your colleagues will have to be prepared to address staff concerns in a proactive manner. You don't want to come across as combative, defensive, angry, hurt, or cranky. Any of these reactions will hinder your planning progress. Instead, you want to be ready to respond to staff concerns in a serious and professional manner. Understanding the change readiness of your library will help you prepare your responses. So will understanding the real issues that are driving most of the staff reactions.

The reasons for the staff's reactions to the new goals and the measurable objectives go back to the early days of library planning. Prior to the introduction of the *Planning for Results* process in 1998, most library planning processes were based on four interrelated assumptions:

1. Planning is about identifying new services and activities.
2. Our existing services are very good or excellent.
3. New services and activities require new resources.
4. If we don't get any new resources, we can't accomplish our plan.

These assumptions make planning a no-risk process. By starting the planning process from the premise that the library would continue to do most or all of what was currently being done, managers told staff that new people might have to do new things, but current staff wouldn't be affected. By assuming that all new services and programs would be funded with new money, managers automatically limited the number of new programs or services that could be started. There wasn't all that much new money available. Again, managers reinforced the unspoken message that the new long-range plan wasn't going to change the status quo significantly.

In 1998 *Planning for Results: A Public Library Transformation Process* was published, and it was based on a new and more realistic set of assumptions:

1. Planning is about defining organizational priorities.
2. Our current services and activities must be regularly reviewed to ensure that they are effective and efficient in relation to current priorities.
3. Many new services and programs will have to be funded from reallocated resources.
4. We will accomplish the priorities in our plan with or without new resources.

Unlike the earlier planning assumptions, these assumptions make it clear that planning is all about change. No staff member who understands these assumptions can sit back and observe the planning process with the comfortable assurance that any changes resulting from the process will be someone else's problem. It is not surprising that many staff continue to resist the new planning assumptions while clinging to the old ones.

Those who are leading the planning effort need to understand that staff bring an additional set of assumptions to the planning process:

1. Staff in this library have been assigned to do more work than they can accomplish during their regular workweek.
2. Supervisors routinely give staff new responsibilities without adjusting the level of their current responsibilities.
3. We don't have the resources we need to do our jobs effectively.
4. Changes are always decided by senior staff—who have no experience with the jobs they are changing—but implemented by frontline staff—who have experience in the job and rarely think it needs to be changed.
5. The job that I do is important, and I am doing the job as well or better than anyone else in my situation could do it.

Compare these staff assumptions with the current planning assumptions, and the most serious problem becomes evident immediately. The planning assumptions call for reallocating resources, which means doing some things *in place of* other things. The experiences that staff members have had make them believe that all of the current work of the library will continue unchanged and that new things will be done *in addition to* everything else.

The only thing the word *reallocate* means to most staff is that you won't be asking for new resources, and the resources you do have will be stretched ever more thinly to cover new services and programs. The only thing that will convince staff that *reallocate* means what it says and that staff duties will be adjusted to support the new priorities is actual experience—and that won't happen until much later, when you are implementing your plan. What you can do as you work through the tasks in this chapter is to remain aware of and sensitive to staff concerns. This will help you to find ways to keep staff engaged in developing the goals and objectives. The more involved staff are with the process at this point, the more likely they are to support the final planning document.

There is another dimension to this discussion of staff perceptions. In every library, there are organizational issues that make it difficult to accomplish any service priorities—current or new. Outdated policies can make it hard for staff to provide equitable services; poorly trained staff can't do the jobs they were hired to do; slow delivery service among the branches makes it difficult for staff to get materials to users quickly; and a web page designed five years ago may be static and difficult to use. Systemic issues such as these create another layer of anxiety for staff. They believe they will not only have to do new things with existing resources, but they will have to do them within an organizational framework that does not provide the support they need to succeed. It is no wonder they are anxious.

It is somewhat easier to help staff feel positive about the potential for resolving the library's capacity issues than it is to ease staff members' anxieties about changing their own job duties. Remember the example in chapter 3 in which the staff in one office were asked to list in order of severity what might cause them stress in their work environment, and the top choice was changing their office chair. Strong emotional reactions to change come when the change is "all about me." Organizational capacity is usually seen as "all about them." In fact, some staff wonder whether senior managers even know that the organizational capacity issues exist. Just openly acknowledging that there are problems can create a more positive change environment.

Getting Started

When you have completed the tasks in this chapter, you will have created the two main components of your strategic plan. During Task 7 you will identify the goals and objectives for the current planning cycle. This is when the generic service responses are shaped to reflect the unique needs of your community. This is also when staff will decide how to measure the progress being made toward reaching the goals you create. In Task 8, you will evaluate the current capacity of the library and identify the capacity needed to provide effective and efficient library services. You will then define the organizational competencies that will be addressed during this planning cycle.

TASK 7: WRITE GOALS AND OBJECTIVES

The steps in this task involve every member of the library staff, from the director to the maintenance people. They all work in the library, and they all need to be given the opportunity to shape the goals and objectives that will affect their jobs during the new planning cycle. This requires more than just inviting people to review a finished product. Managers will want to identify a mix of ways for staff to participate. This is all part of creating the change-friendly environment described in chapter 3.

There is no question that involving the staff in the steps in this task will take longer than it would take to have a few people do the work. The extra time is worth it, but it is a balancing act. You will need to be careful not to let this part of the process go on for too long. If you look at the suggested planning time line in figure 6 (chapter 1), you will see that both of the tasks in this chapter should be completed in about a month.

One person should be put in charge of coordinating the steps in this task. That person is normally the planning coordinator, although this is not always the case. Sometimes the planning coordinator works primarily with the community planning committee and the board, and a different person is made responsible for managing the tasks that are staff-intensive.

The first two steps in this task involve a lot of writing and editing. Although it is important to involve staff in the process of developing goals and objectives, the actual writing is not work that should be done in committee. It could take hours and perhaps days to write draft goals in that setting. Everyone is an editor, and the members of the group will cheerfully—or not so cheerfully—argue about every word that is written. It is far better to ask one or two people to develop the first draft of the goals and objectives and then involve the rest of the staff in the review and revision process.

The planning coordinator or another staff person with strong writing skills should be responsible for actually crafting the goals and objectives. However, this is not a creative writing process, and the writer will not be free to write whatever he or she wants to write. The goals must support the selected service responses and must be written in the specific style described in Step 7.1. The objectives must include measures, targets, and dates, and the measures to be included will be identified during one or more group processes. In reality, the person who writes the goals and objectives will function more as a scribe than an author.

Step 7.1
Write System Goals

Semantics can become a problem during both this step and the next one. The terms *goal* and *objective* are among the most confusing words in management. Goals have been defined as everything from a desired state to the specific tasks required to accomplish an objective. Interestingly, objectives have also been defined as everything from a desired state to the specific tasks required to accomplish a goal. One particularly puzzling definition states that an objective is "the aim or goal."[1]

Most staff have been involved in at least one planning activity at their church, in a club, as part of an organization, in a previous job, or in their current job, and virtually all of them spent part of that planning activity arguing about the difference between goals and objectives. There is no need for that to happen in this process. In *Planning for Results,* the terms *goal* and *objective* have clearly defined and distinct meanings:

> *Goal.* The benefit your community (or a target population within your community) will receive because the library provides a specific service response.
>
> *Objective.* The way the library will measure its progress toward reaching a goal.

During this step you will be creating library goals. Objectives will be discussed in detail in Step 7.2.

Notice that the definition of *goal* focuses on the services that members of the community receive from the library and not on the resources that the library needs to provide services. The intent is to give people who read the strategic plan a clear picture of the value of the library rather than a wish list of the resources the library would like to have.

Figure 31 lists the goals from the strategic planning documents of two school districts. Which school district seems to be more concerned about its students than its administrators? Which school district has a clearly defined set of expectations for student

---

FIGURE 31
Two School Districts

THE SCHOOL DISTRICT OF MENOMONEE FALLS STRATEGIC PLAN

1. Each student will apply and demonstrate proficiency in technology skills identified for his/her level in the district technology standards.

2. Throughout the educational experience, each student will seek opportunities and participate in meaningful activities that demonstrate an understanding and acceptance of individual differences.

3. Each student will demonstrate continuous individual growth in a comprehensive educational experience.

4. Throughout the educational experience, each student will understand, select, and achieve an ongoing healthy lifestyle.

5. Each student will be able to communicate effectively, resolve conflicts, and work cooperatively.

6. Each student will participate actively and demonstrate individual responsibility in school, community, nation, and the world through ethical behavior and service to others.

Available at http://www.sdmf.k12.wi.us/sdmf2/schools/plan.html

PALMYRA-EAGLE AREA SCHOOL DISTRICT STRATEGIC PLAN

1. The school district will provide the facilities and equipment necessary to support the curriculum and instruction needed to exceed specified state and local standards of achievement by the start of the 2004–2005 school year.

2. The school district will secure funding that continues and enhances the present levels of educational programming, staffing, resources, and maintenance over the next five years.

3. Beginning with the 2002–2003 school year the school district will increase levels of district-wide support for, and involvement in, our schools and unity in our community.

4. Students participating in the WKCE and WRCT will achieve at the proficient or advanced levels.

Available at http://www.palmyra.k12.wi.us/district/strategicplan.htm#goals

---

achievement? Which school district seems to spend public funds more effectively? Which school district would you select if you had a child and a choice?

Many library plans developed in the 1980s and early 1990s included goals that were similar to those from the Palmyra-Eagle Area School District in figure 31. These goals described the organizational capacity or resources the library would need to provide services to the public, but did not address the actual services to be provided. Although these plans were often distributed to the general public, they seemed more appropriate for internal audiences. As you can see in the following examples of goals of this type, the reader gets a clear picture of what the library wants, but doesn't get much information about why the library wants it.

> The Oldtown Public Library will secure sufficient funding to provide quality library services and programs.
>
> The Oldtown Public Library will develop partnerships with local organizations.
>
> The Oldtown Public Library will recruit and retain qualified staff members.
>
> The Oldtown Public Library will use technology to improve service delivery.
>
> The Oldtown Public Library will develop and maintain a library advocacy group.

The goals in the *Planning for Results* process should be similar in format to the goals in the Menomonee Falls School District plan in figure 31. These goals are intended for external audiences. They shift the emphasis from the library to the public and focus solely on the benefits the various constituencies in the community receive because the library provides a service:

> Preschool children in Anytown will enter school ready to learn.
>
> Teens in Anytown will have materials and programs that excite their imaginations and provide pleasurable reading, viewing, and listening experiences.
>
> Adults in Anytown will have the support they need to improve their literacy skills in order to meet their personal goals and fulfill their responsibilities as parents, citizens, and workers.

This does not mean that there isn't a place in the planning process for a discussion of the organizational competencies and resources that will be required to accomplish the library's goals. In fact, before you start writing and reviewing library goals, you should read the information in Step 8.1. In that step you will learn to differentiate between goals and organizational capacity issues, and you will develop the skills to explain the difference to board members and frontline staff. The actual work of identifying and writing organizational competencies will take place in Steps 8.2 and 8.3.

The issues surrounding the allocation and reallocation of resources to support the strategic plan are more complex. When you have completed the tasks and steps in this book, you will have much of the information you need to write your strategic plan: the library's value statements, goals, and objectives. Your plan may also include some examples of activities that support the goals and objectives (you will decide this in chapter 5), but the plan will not include any detailed information about your implementation strategies. The tasks and steps you will need to implement your plan are in *Implementing for Results,* the companion volume to this book.[2]

What Should Be Included in a *Planning for Results* Goal?

Each goal is derived from a specific service response, and all goals contain the same two elements: they begin by naming the audience being served, and then they describe the benefit the audience receives because the library offers a service.

TARGET AUDIENCE

The number of goals you develop to support each service response will be determined by the number of specific target audiences you want to link to that service response. This is going to be a judgment call. There is no magic number of goals that should be developed to support a single service response, nor is there a magic number of total goals that should be included in the plan. However, the general rule is that you don't want to have more goals in your plan than you can remember—and that is clearly somewhat limiting. Typically, strategic plans have a total of eight to ten goals, although the number can vary from five to twelve.

Target audiences are defined either by demographics (typically age) or by condition (student, business owner, new immigrant, etc.). Some of the service responses are designed to serve a single target audience, and that audience has been defined in the title or description (e.g., "Create Young Readers: Early Literacy," "Welcome to the United States: Services for New Immigrants"). Although the descriptions of these service responses may suggest additional audiences, most libraries will write a single goal focusing on the primary audience.

Other service responses are age- and condition-neutral (e.g., "Stimulate Imagination: Reading, Viewing, and Listening for Pleasure," "Make Informed Decisions: Health, Wealth, and Other Life Choices"). In these instances, you will have to identify the target audience or audiences for the service in your library. The best place to start is by reviewing the vision statements that the members of the planning committee developed (Step 3.2). The members of the committee were encouraged to focus on specific target audiences when developing those vision statements. If the committee identified one or more specific target audiences for a service response, give serious consideration to writing a goal (or goals) that focuses on those target audiences.

You may find that the committee did not identify target audiences for the vision statement that led to the selection of the service response, or that the link between the vision statement and the service response is somewhat tenuous. For instance, the vision statement may say, "The quality of life in Anytown will be excellent," and committee members may have selected "Stimulate Imagination" as one way to improve the quality of life. You can see how the committee made the leap from the vision to the service response, but the vision does not provide much direction for identifying a target audience.

In the absence of guidance from the planning committee, you could fall back on the generic target audience "all residents," and in some cases this might be the most effective thing to do. However, the whole point of writing goals from the user's point of view is to help people understand what they get from the library. People are more likely to see themselves as part of a narrower target audience (teens, small business owners, etc.) than as part of the very general "everybody," particularly if the service is or is perceived to be quite different depending on the audience.

Let's consider a specific example. The Anytown planning committee identified "Stimulate Imagination" as a service response, and the discussion among the members made it clear that they thought this service priority applied to all residents. The Anytown Library staff could write the following goal, which would reflect the committee's discussion:

> All residents who want materials to enhance their leisure time will find what they want when and where they want them and will have the help they need to make choices from among the options.

There is nothing wrong with this goal, but it isn't very personal, it certainly isn't exciting, and it probably doesn't reflect what the committee *meant* even if it reflects what the members *said*.

Goals are more compelling if they focus on the unique needs of specific target audiences, as you can see in the following examples, which also support the "Stimulate Imagination" service response.

> Children will discover the joy of reading and will become lifelong readers.
>
> Teens will have materials, programs, and interactive experiences that focus on their current interests and that provide satisfying recreational experiences.
>
> Adults will enjoy a wide variety of new and popular materials available when and where they want them.

These goals are written to engage the members of the target audience and make them want to take advantage of the benefits described. There is another more practical reason for writing targeted goals. Such goals reflect the organizational structure of many libraries and will make it easier to develop objectives in the next step and to identify and implement activities when the plan is complete.

THE BENEFIT THE AUDIENCE RECEIVES

There are two places to start when considering the benefit the members of the target audience(s) receive because the library provides a service. Return again to the vision statement or statements that led to the selection of the service response. If the vision statement is specific enough, it may provide the wording you need for the second part of the goal. If the vision is vague or its relationship to the service response is tenuous, consider the one-sentence description of the benefits that all or part of the community receive that is a part of each service response. (See figure 18 in chapter 2 for a complete list of the service responses and their one-sentence descriptions.) These descriptions can be edited to reflect the unique conditions in your library or your community.

When you review the descriptions of the benefits in the service responses, you will notice that each description is written as a declarative statement: residents *will* have the information they need . . . , children from birth to five *will* have programs and services . . . , and so on. None of these benefits say that residents will have *access* to information or to programs and services. *Access* is a term much loved by library staff, particularly the staff who write goals. If you look at library plans on the Web, you will find many plans with goals like this: "Residents of Mytown will have access to information on topics of interest to them." The person who wrote this goal would no doubt say that the library can provide access to information, but the staff have no control over whether or not people choose to use that access. This is a quibble. While it is true that staff can't control what users do, the actions that staff take and the decisions that staff make can significantly influence what users choose to do. By using the word *access* in the goal, staff are simply opting out of any responsibility for reaching the goal.

The person or people writing the goals can use Workform G, Goal Worksheet, to develop the goals. They will use a separate copy of the workform for each goal that is developed. Figure 32 is an example of a goal developed by the staff of the Tree County Library to support the service response "Express Creativity: Create and Share Content." Notice that the final goal includes components of both the description of the service response and the planning committee's vision statement that led to the selection of the service response. The Anytown Public Library might write a different goal for the same service response. In figure 33, you see that the vision of the Anytown planning committee that led to the selection of the "Express Creativity" service response was quite different from the vision of the Tree County committee. That difference is reflected in the final goal.

Step 7.2
Write System Objectives

Objectives are defined as "the way the library will measure its progress toward reaching a goal." Notice that the emphasis is on the library and not on the target audience. This is

---

FIGURE 32

Workform G: Goal Worksheet—Tree County Library Example

A. Service Response: Express Creativity

B. Service Response Description: Residents will have the services and support they need to express themselves by creating original print, video, audio, or visual content in a real-world or online environment.

C. Target Audience: Teens

D. Vision Statement(s), If Any: Teens will have access to group and individual activities after school and on weekends that are exciting, informative, and interactive.

E. Benefit: Services and support to create innovative and interactive media.

F. Goal Template

1. Audience	2. Benefit
Teens	Services and support to create innovative and interactive media.

G. Final Goal: Teens will have services and support to create innovative and interactive media.

FIGURE 33

Workform G: Goal Worksheet—Anytown Library Example

A. Service Response: Express Creativity

B. Service Response Description: Residents will have the services and support they need to express themselves by creating original print, video, audio, or visual content in a real-world or online environment.

C. Target Audience: Teens

D. Vision Statement(s), If Any: Teens will be comfortable with all types of technology applications and will be able to learn and use new applications easily so that they are prepared to adapt to ever-changing school and work environments.

E. Benefit: Learn to use technology to create and share audio and visual electronic content.

F. Goal Template

1. Audience	2. Benefit
Teens	Learn to use technology to create and share audio and visual electronic content.

G. Final Goal: Teens will learn to use technology to create and share audio and visual electronic content.

the point in the planning process when the focus shifts from the user to the library. This is also the point in the process where you move from open-ended statements describing long-term benefits (goals) to very specific statements that describe exactly what the library hopes to achieve during the planning cycle and how the progress being made toward those achievements will be measured (objectives). Every objective contains the same three elements: a measure, a target, and a date or time frame by which time the target should be met.

The directions for writing an objective are fairly straightforward:

1. Select one of the four *Planning for Results* measures. The four measures are listed and described in figure 34.
2. Decide on the target you hope to reach.
3. Decide when you want to reach the target.
4. Put the measure, the target, and the time frame together into a sentence that reads smoothly.

FIGURE 34
Measures

MEASURE 1: People Served

- Total number of users served

What this measures: The total number of users who used a service during a given time period.

Example: If the same 20 children attend a story hour every week, at the end of the year the total number of children served through the story hour would be 1,040 (20 children x 52 weeks)

- Number of unique individuals who use the service

What this measures: The total number of unique individuals who use the service during a given time period regardless of how many times they use the service.

Example: If the same 20 children attend a story hour every week, at the end of the year the total number of unique children served through the story hour would be 20.

MEASURE 2: How Well the Service Meets the Needs of the People Served

What this measures: The user's opinion about how well the library's service(s) met his or her needs; this opinion could be about the quality of the service, the value of the service, the user's satisfaction with the service, or the impact of the service.

Example: This data is normally gathered through user surveys and expressed as a percentage of the number of people surveyed, e.g., "During FY___, at least ___% of the high school students who use the public library for homework assistance will indicate they found what they needed."

MEASURE 3: Total Units of Service Provided by the Library

What this measures: The number of actual library service transactions that were performed to make progress toward a specific goal. This includes all of the standard library outputs such as circulation, number of reference transactions, etc.

Example: Most libraries collect these data to report annually to their state library agency, e.g., "By FY ____, the circulation of picture books and easy books will increase from ____ to ____."

MEASURE 4: Outcome Measurement

What this measures: Outcome measurement is a user-centered approach to the planning and assessment of programs and services that are provided to address particular user needs and designed to achieve a change for the user. What difference did the library program make to the participant? What changes occurred in the participant's knowledge, skill, attitude, behavior, condition, or status?

Example: "Students who attend the library's college test preparation class will improve their scores on a sample SAT test by at least 50 points from their PSAT scores by the end of the course."

Things get more complicated when you are actually selecting the most appropriate measures for the goal and deciding on targets that are both challenging and realistic. Writing objectives is not an intuitive process for most staff, many of whom have little or no training in measurement and evaluation. Some staff—both frontline and managerial—will find the whole concept of measurable objectives cumbersome, irritating, and unnecessary. After all, many say, the library has been around for X number of years and we have never done this before. People still like us and they still use us. We are too busy already, and it seems like a waste of time to collect all of the data. What difference will it really make?

The answer to this question is both clear and sobering. Now, more than ever before, libraries must be prepared to justify their existence. Just saying "We do good" is no longer adequate. Libraries are competing with other publicly funded organizations for limited funds. If library managers and board members can't prove that the library makes significant contributions to the people in the community—the people who pay the bills—they will find it hard to make a case for continued funding at any level.

Many library staff and managers have relied on anecdotal data to make their cases in the past, and there is no question that anecdotal data can be effective. Everyone loves the story about the immigrant who used information she found in the library to start a small business that grew to employ fifty people. However, anecdotal data by itself is not enough. One city council uses the following criteria, among others, to make funding decisions:

> Does the agency make a contribution to the city?
>
> Do the majority (51 percent) of the taxpayers benefit from this service?
>
> What are the structural goals and objectives of the agency?
>
> Has the documentation for the past three years, detailing how past city funds and other sources of income were spent, been received?
>
> Have these expenditures benefited the citizens of Hendersonville by furthering economic development, social welfare and the common good?[3]

These are not questions that can be answered by a story, no matter how warm and fuzzy. You will need hard data to make and substantiate your case.

MEASURES

As you see in figure 34, the data used to measure progress in *Planning for Results* are divided into four categories. Three of the four categories of measures listed in the figure relate to library users: number of users, the perceptions of users, and user outcomes. The fourth measure, units of service delivered, is the only library-driven measure, and by this time it should come as no surprise to you that it is the least effective of the four measures. Refer back to the questions the city council members considered when making funding decisions listed in the preceding paragraph. None of these questions can be answered by saying the library processed X number of books or presented Y number of programs. Even use data such as circulation are more powerful when presented from the users' point of view. "We circulate 6 items per person per year" is stronger than "We circulate 480,000 items a year."

Although there are no absolute rules about how many objectives you should include for each goal, you will probably want to include at least two objectives for most goals.

Then you can use at least two different types of measures to track your progress. If you write three objectives for a goal, each should include a different measure. This will allow you to evaluate the success of your services from several perspectives. While you are developing objectives, remember that you will have to collect all of the data that you include in all of the objectives. This suggests that you will want to limit the number of objectives for each goal to a manageable number. The typical number of objectives for each goal ranges from two to six or eight, and the average is three or four objectives per goal.

Most library staff are familiar—and comfortable—with counting the number of people who use specific services or attend specific programs and the number of units of service delivered. You may find that they are less comfortable with collecting data on the users' perceptions of the services they received, and that they are actively uncomfortable with the whole concept of measuring the changes in a specific user that occurred because of services the library provided (outcome measurement). This last issue is likely to be the most challenging one.

Outcome measurement was first used in the social service sector to measure such things as the number of teen mothers-to-be who attended prenatal programs and then delivered babies that weighed at least seven pounds. As you see in this example, the measure does not include *all* teenage mothers, only those who attend a specific series of programs. The measure of success is not how many teen mothers-to-be attended all of the programs or even how the teen mothers-to-be who attended felt about the programs. It is what the teen mothers-to-be did as a result of the program. This focus on how the user changes as a result of a service or program is in direct contradiction to one of the underlying principles of librarianship: librarians provide information; what the user does with that information is his or her business.

Obviously, outcome measurement is not an appropriate way to measure many of the programs and services that libraries offer. Reference services are offered to anyone who asks and are considered to be private and confidential. Most states have laws that mandate the confidentiality of circulation transactions. There are, however, some programs that are best measured using outcomes. To determine if a program is suitable for outcome measurement, consider the purpose and design of the program, the program's intended users, the desired impact of the program, and the management, staff, and stakeholders in the library presenting the program. Figure 35 can help you determine when to include outcome measurement in your objectives.

The complete descriptions of the library service responses in part 2 of this book include possible measures for you to consider in each of the four categories of measurement. The suggestions are just that—suggestions—but staff often find that reviewing the possible measures helps them to identify measures appropriate for their libraries and their goals.

TARGETS

It is relatively easy to identify targets if you have current data to use as a starting point. If 1,000 children enrolled in your summer reading program three years ago, 1,100 children enrolled two years ago, and 1,200 children enrolled last year, you can see that your program is increasing by about 10 percent each year. You can use census data to determine how many children there are in your service area. If there are 5,000 children under the age of 12 in your community, you are reaching 24 percent of the target audience, a higher-than-average percentage. In that case, you may decide that an annual increase of

FIGURE 35

When to Use Outcome Measurement

If you can answer "Yes" to fifteen or more of the following questions, the program is probably suitable for outcome measurement.

Purpose and Design of the Program

1. Has the program been developed in response to an identified need?

2. Can this program have a significant (not total) influence on the need?

3. Is impact on the end user a major purpose of the program?

4. Is the program more concerned with impact than with outputs?

5. Is it more concerned with public service than with internal library operations?

6. Is the program focused on effectiveness rather than efficiency?

7. Is it focused more on users' benefit than users' satisfaction?

8. Does the program—or a user's participation in it—have a distinct beginning and end?

The Program's Users

9. Are the users clearly defined?

10. Do the users participate consistently so you can track their progress?

11. Will the users be willing to participate in an evaluation?

The Desired Impact

12. Is the desired impact measurable?

13. Will the impact occur within a few years (so that it can be observed)?

Management, Staff, and Stakeholders

14. Do the management and staff have a service or user orientation?

15. Is the program stable enough to undertake this endeavor?

16. Is the library leadership commited to devote resources to outcome measurement and then to act on the results?

17. Are the program stakeholders supportive?

18. Will measuring outcomes provide useful feedback to improve the program?

19. Will measuring outcomes improve accountability to the library or stakeholders by demonstrating effectiveness?

Adapted from Workform 1, Program Suitability for Outcome Measurement, in *Demonstrating Results: Using Outcome Measurement in Your Library,* by Rhea Joyce Rubin (Chicago: American Library Association, 2006).

---

10 percent is an appropriate target. However, if there are 50,000 children in your community, you are only reaching 2.4 percent of the target audience, a much lower-than-average percentage. In that case, you would probably set a more demanding target. You might decide that you want to increase the number of children who enroll in the summer reading program by at least 500 children each year for three years, which would nearly double the percentage of the target audience you reach. You would go from reaching 2.4 percent to 5.4 percent.

Staff are often uncomfortable setting targets if there are no current data to use as a baseline. Some staff want to write objectives to collect baseline data during the first year of the plan and then use the baseline data to revise the objectives in year two. This is not acceptable. Objectives always include both a measure and a target. If you don't have the baseline data you need to establish a target, you will have to use estimates. This is not as hard as it may sound.

One of the goals from the Anytown Public Library that was included in Step 7.1 of this task was: "Teens will have materials, programs, and interactive experiences that focus on their current interests and that provide satisfying recreational experiences." Progress toward reaching this goal could be measured in a number of ways. Anytown Public Library staff might measure the increase in the number of teens in their service area who have library cards (number of users). They might measure the circulation of teen materials (number of units of service). These are both adequate measures, and the staff probably have current data on each of them. However, the best way to measure progress toward this particular goal is the perceptions of the teens themselves. It is very unlikely that the Anytown Public Library has baseline data for this measure. Therefore, the staff will have to find other ways to establish the target to include in the objective.

User perceptions are always determined by asking users what they think in a survey, and the responses are normally expressed as a percentage of the people surveyed. Knowing this, the Anytown Public Library staff could write this objective:

> Each year, X teens who use the library will say that the materials, programs, and interactive experiences in the library focus on their current interests and provide them with satisfying recreational experiences.

Now the staff need to replace the X with a percentage. Notice that the objective specifically measures the perceptions of "teens who use the library." This suggests that the Anytown Library staff will want to use a fairly high percentage as the target. There is not much point in writing an objective stating that 20 percent of the teens who use the library will say that the materials, programs, and interactive experiences in the library focus on their current interests and provide them with satisfying recreational experiences. If that is all you hope to do, then why bother doing anything at all? Don't forget that this is a public document, and one of the purposes of the plan is to make it clear that the library's services and programs make a difference to the people in the service area. The Anytown Library staff should consider using 75 or 80 percent of teen library users as the target for this objective. That target should be easily attainable if library staff provide the right materials, programs, and interactive experiences.

Not all targets have to reflect an increase. In some instances, maintaining the status quo is all that is needed. Let's go back to the summer reading program example presented earlier. During the preceding year, 1,200 children enrolled in the summer reading program. Now let's assume that there are only 3,000 children in the library's service area, and all of the library's resources were stretched to capacity during the preceding year. A large number of children were routinely turned away from programs because the meeting rooms were filled to the fire marshal's limit. The shelves in the children's room were virtually empty for most of the summer, and children were taking books from the book trucks before they could be reshelved after check-in. Both children and parents complained about the limited resources. Under these circumstances, there is not much point in setting a target to increase the number of children who enroll in the program. Staff may be able to reallocate some collection resources to buy additional materials and they may be able to find some off-site locations for programs, but those solutions will only partially address the current capacity issues. In this instance, an objective that states "Each year, at least 1,200 children will enroll in the summer reading program" is quite appropriate. An even more effective objective would be: "Each year, 40 percent of the children served by the library will enroll in the summer reading program."

You and your colleagues will be considering the best ways to measure progress toward each goal individually when you are suggesting measures, targets, and time lines. In some cases, different people may be involved in discussing the measures to include. For instance, youth services staff might focus on youth services objectives, while adult services staff work on objectives relating to their clients. This makes it imperative for the planning coordinator to review all of the targets and time lines before a final draft of the objectives is developed. Targets and time lines that seem reasonable for each goal might well be overwhelming when reviewed as an aggregate.

The person or people responsible for drafting the objectives will use Workform H, Objective Worksheet, to help them organize the information in their objectives. Figure 36 is an example of a completed copy of Workform H that was used by the staff of the Tree County Library to develop objectives for the goal they wrote in figure 32.

How Can Staff Be Involved in Developing Goals and Objectives?

When the writers/scribes have completed a draft of the goals and objectives, the planning coordinator will review the draft to make sure the goals reflect the service responses, the objectives are realistic, and both are formatted correctly. Then the draft should be sent to members of the library management team for review and discussion. After the writer or writers have made any changes requested by the management team, the draft goals and objectives should be distributed to all staff for review and comment. As you will see in the next task, the draft organizational competencies and initiatives will be distributed to the staff at the same time.

In Step 4.3 (chapter 2) you were encouraged to use a variety of means to distribute planning information to the staff. Suggestions included posting the information on the *Planning for Results* intranet site, establishing a blog or discussion list, and scheduling a series of meetings to discuss the information. These same suggestions apply to distributing the goals and objectives.

There is no need to consider all of those pros and cons again. Branch or unit meetings are by far the most effective venue in which to discuss the draft goals and objectives. Branch and unit managers should be asked to attend a preliminary meeting to review the draft goals and objectives and ask their questions. The purpose of this meeting is not to get suggestions for additions, deletions, or revisions from the branch managers. Rather, it is to be sure that all of the branch managers understand the relationship of the goals to the service responses that were approved by the board and that they understand how the objectives were developed. The branch and unit managers will submit their suggestions for changes along with the suggestions of their staff members.

When all of the branch and unit managers understand the draft goals and objectives, they should schedule meetings with their staff members. They may have to hold two meetings to ensure that all staff members—full- and part-time—can attend. During the meeting, the manager and staff should discuss each goal and its supporting objectives. Staff should be encouraged to suggest editorial changes in the goal and its objectives and to suggest additions or deletions from the list of objectives. Staff can also suggest that goals be added or deleted from the draft list.

FIGURE 36
Workform H: Objective Worksheet—Example

A. Service Response: Express Creativity

B. Goal: Teens will have services and support to create innovative and interactive media.

C. Possible Measures from Service Response Description:

Number of Users

Number of people attending a training session on the use of technologies that can be used to create and share content

Number of people who use library-provided equipment or technology to create content

Number of people who create and share content with other library users

Percentage of people who indicate on a survey that they used the library to create and share content

Number of people who attend a performance at the library

Perceptions of Users

Percentage of users surveyed who respond that:

The library-provided equipment or technology is very good or excellent

The information assistance they receive from staff when creating or sharing content is very good or excellent

User Outcomes

Number and percentage of specified users who use library resources and services to create new media

Number and percentage of specified users who produce pieces for the library e-zine

Number and percentage of specified users who contribute to wikis or blogs

Units of Service Delivered

Number of issues of e-zine published

Number of hands-on training programs presented

Number of production workshops presented

Number of performances offered

D. Objective 1

1. Selected Measure: Percentage of people who indicate on a survey that they used the library to create and share content

2. Target: 15% of the teens who use the library

3. Time Frame: By 2XXX

4. Objective Template

a. Time Frame	b. Target	c. Measure
By 2XXX	15% of the teens who use the library	Percentage of people who indicate on a survey that they used the library to create and share content

5. Objective 1: By 2XXX, 15% of the teens who use the library will indicate on a survey that they have used library resources to create and share content.

E. Objective 2

    1. Selected Measure: Percentage of users surveyed who respond that the information assistance they receive from staff when creating or sharing content is very good or excellent

    2. Target: 90% of teens

    3. Time Frame: Each year

    4. Objective Template

a. Time Frame	b. Target	c. Measure
Each year	90% of teens	Percentage of users surveyed who respond that the information assistance they receive from staff when creating or sharing content is very good or excellent

    5. Objective 2: Each year, at least 90% of teens surveyed will say that the information assistance they receive from staff when creating or sharing content is very good or excellent.

F. Objective 3

    1. Selected Measure: Number and percentage of specified users who contribute to the "Teen Zone" e-zine

    2. Target: At least 20% of the teens who attend one or more of the "Teen Zone" e-zine introductory programs

    3. Time Frame: Within six months of the month the teens attend the introductory programs

    4. Objective Template

a. Time Frame	b. Target	c. Measure
Within six months from the month they attended the introductory programs	At least 20% of the teens who attend one or more of the "Teen Zone" e-zine introductory programs	Number and percentage of specified users who contribute to the "Teen Zone" e-zine

    5. Objective 3: At least 20% of the teens who attend one or more of the "Teen Zone" e-zine introductory programs will contribute to the e-zine within six months of the month they attended the introductory program(s).

During this review, managers may find that some staff are uncomfortable with objectives that include measures they can't control. These staff prefer to measure the units of service delivered (number of programs presented) rather than the number of people who use a service (number of people who attend each program) or the users' perceptions of the service (percentage of program attendees who evaluated the program as very good or excellent). Needless to say, these staff members are particularly concerned about outcome measurement (percentage of program attendees who changed a specific attitude or behavior because they participated in a program). These staff argue that it is not fair to hold staff accountable for things over which they have no control. This is a specious argument. If these same staff members had surgery, they would measure the success of their surgeries by their physical condition after the surgery, and not by the fact that the doctor showed up and performed the operation.

Sometimes staff are concerned about the emphasis on measurement in the objectives because they are afraid that if the library does not meet or exceed every target in every objective, something awful will happen. They are not sure what they think will happen, but they are sure that it will be drastic. It is the job of branch and unit managers and the members of the library management team to reassure staff on this point, and remind them that it is all right to take risks. This is part of the planning you did in chapter 3 to create a change-friendly environment.

After all of the staff have had an opportunity to suggest changes in the draft goals and objectives, the branch manager will compile the suggestions and submit them to the person responsible for writing the goals and objectives. It is a good idea to post the suggested revisions from each unit on the *Planning for Results* intranet. This proves that the suggestions were submitted to and reviewed by the writer, even if all of the recommendations were not accepted. It is also helpful to include a brief statement explaining why each of the recommendations was rejected. This can be as simple as "these four recommendations were similar and were merged into a single objective," or "this suggested change in this goal was not consistent with the service response the goal supports."

The writer will work with the members of the library management team to incorporate the recommendations into the final draft of goals and objectives. The final draft will then be submitted to the board for review, revision, and approval. The members of the board should be asked to approve the goals and objectives in concept. During this same meeting, the members of the board will review and approve the organizational competencies and initiatives (discussed in the next task) in concept. The board members will give their final approval to everything when they have reviewed the complete strategic plan (Step 9.2). As soon as the goals and objectives and organizational competencies and initiatives have been approved, they should be made available on the staff planning site on the intranet or distributed in writing to the units.

Step 7.3
Determine the Priority of Goals and Measures of Progress for Each Unit

If you work in a library that has a single building, you will probably not complete this step, although occasionally larger libraries operating out of a single building ask unit managers to prioritize system goals. In most cases, this step will only be completed by staff in libraries that operate from more than one location: urban systems with branches in neighborhoods, and county systems with branches in communities throughout the county. This step is important for those libraries because it provides a way to tailor the systemwide goals and objectives to reflect the unique demographics of the people served by each branch or outlet.

This step occurs after the goals and objectives have been approved by the board. It is completed by branch managers working with their staff members during one or two staff meetings. Before the branch managers can complete this step, they will need to receive some training. The planning coordinator or another staff member will use the information presented in this step to design a two-hour training program for the branch managers. The training program will describe the reasons for determining branch priorities for system goals and the processes used to determine them. The planning coordinator will distribute and review copies of Workform I, Branch Goals, and Workform J, Branch Objectives, as well as any statistical data that the branch managers might use in their meetings. The planning coordinator will also discuss the process that will be used to review the branch recommendations and the deadline for completing the work.

Branch Meetings

Prior to the first staff meeting, each branch manager will distribute copies of the system goals, data about the community served by the branch, and the branch statistics for the past several years. At the beginning of the meeting, the manager will explain that staff will be ranking the system goals in priority order for the branch and that each branch might rank the goals differently. After reviewing the data distributed prior to the meeting, the manager will lead a discussion of the system goals.

It will be important for the manager to make sure that staff understand that they cannot change the wording of the final goals, nor can they add goals to the final list. Staff were given an opportunity to suggest changes in Step 7.2 of this task. Staff should also be told that the branch is not required to select all of the goals. Smaller branches will probably select fewer goals than larger branches because smaller branches have fewer resources. The manager will want to encourage all staff members to participate in the discussion and to avoid letting one or two staff members dominate the meeting. If someone feels strongly about an issue, the manager should allow a brief discussion of the issue and then move on.

When the staff have had time to discuss each of the goals, they should be asked to select the goals that apply to the people in the branch service area and to determine the relative priority of each of those goals. The manager can use one of the processes described in the Groups: Reaching Agreement tool kit in part 3 to do that. The dot exercise is particularly suitable for this purpose. Ideally, the decisions about branch goals will be made by consensus. However, the branch manager is the person who is ultimately responsible for the recommendations that are made, and she can override the staff's vote or break deadlocks if necessary. The branch goals should be listed in priority order on Workform I. The branch manager will have to provide a rationale for each selection. Figure 37 is an example of part of the workform that was completed by the Elm Branch Library manager.

Next the manager will work with the staff to determine the branch targets for each of the objectives under each of the system goals—both those selected by the branch and those that were not selected. The manager may decide to determine branch targets during the same meeting in which goals were placed in priority order, or the manager may decide to hold a second meeting.

The manager will start the discussion of the branch targets by explaining why the branch will be responsible for targets for goals that were not selected as branch priorities. At first glance, this doesn't seem reasonable or even fair, but it doesn't take long for staff to understand the rationale. Just because a goal is not a branch priority doesn't mean that branch will refuse to provide services which support that priority. A branch with a service

FIGURE 37
Workform I: Branch Goals—Example

A. Branch Name: Elm Branch

PART I: Branch Priority of Library Goals

B. Goal	C. Branch Priority	D. Rationale
1. Adults in Tree County will have materials and programs that excite their imaginations and provide pleasurable reading, viewing, and listening experiences.	1	Elm Branch has the highest circulation of adult fiction and DVDs in the system, and the circulation of these items is increasing 20% faster than circulation in other branches.
2. Seniors in Tree County will have the resources they need to explore topics of personal interest and continue to grow and learn throughout their lives.	7	Most of the areas served by the Elm Branch are "bedroom communities" that cater to young families.
3. Preschool children in Tree County will enter school ready to learn.	2	5% of the county population is under the age of five. 9% of the population in the Elm Branch service area is under five. The branch turnover rate of easy books and picture books is the highest in the system.

area that includes many retirement communities is going to provide access to children's materials—just not as many children's materials as a branch serving an area filled with young families. The branch that serves primarily seniors may not select any goals targeting children, but the circulation of the children's materials in that branch will still count toward reaching the system target. The branch manager will again stress that staff cannot change the wording of the final objectives, nor can they add objectives to the list.

There are three guidelines to follow when determining branch targets for system objectives:

> If the target for the system is expressed as a percentage increase, the target that is selected for the branch must be at least as large as the system target for that objective. For example, if the branch selected an objective that has as its target a 10 percent increase for the system, then the branch target should be at least a 10 percent increase.

> If the target is a percentage in a user survey, the target that is selected for the branch must be at least as large as the system target for that objective. For example, if the branch selected an objective that has its target that 80 percent

of users will respond to a question in a certain way, then the branch target should be at 80 percent.

If the target for the system is expressed as a number, the target for the branch will be a portion of that number. For example, if the target enrollment for the summer reading program is 1,200 children per year, the branch staff will have to determine how many of those 1,200 children will enroll in the branch. When all of the branches have selected their target numbers, someone will have to be responsible for adding all of the branch targets to be sure that the system total is at least 1,200.

Managers can be asked to use Workform J to report the proposed targets for each of the system goals. Figure 38 is an example of part of the workform that was completed by the Elm Branch manager. Workform J may not be the most effective way to report proposed branch targets for objectives. That is best done electronically, so that a running total can be maintained and progress toward reaching branch targets can be tracked. Consider asking a staff member to create a database that managers can use to record the branch targets for the objectives.

The members of the management team or a designated administrator will review the copies of Workforms I and J submitted by the branch managers, resolve any questions or problems with the branch managers, and then approve them. The final copies of Workform I should be posted on the staff intranet or be printed and sent to the units.

FIGURE 38
Workform J: Branch Objectives—Example

A. Branch Name: Elm Branch

PART I: Branch Targets for System Objectives

B. System Goal: Preschool children in Tree County will enter school ready to learn.

C. Branch Priority

D. System Objectives	E. Branch Target	F. Rationale
1. Each year, at least 10,000 preschool children will attend programs presented or sponsored by the library in non-library locations.	2,000 preschool children 20% of total, leaving 80% to be managed by the other eight branches	This is a high priority for the branch, and there are more day care facilities in the Elm Branch service area than in the rest of the county.
2. The circulation of easy books and picture books will increase by 10% each year.	14% each year	The circulation of easy books and picture books has increased 14% annually for the past two years.
3. By 2XXX, at least 75% of the parents or caregivers who bring their preschool children to the library will say that the library helps prepare preschoolers to enter school.	75%	The system figure is appropriate for all ten branches.

TASK 8: IDENTIFY ORGANIZATIONAL COMPETENCIES

Step 8.1 is the only step in the *Planning for Results* process that focuses on *understanding* rather than *doing,* and it is the only step that is slightly out of sequence. This step should be completed before you begin to write goals in Step 7.1. The decision about where to place this step in the sequence was rather like trying to decide which comes first, the chicken or the egg. On one hand, it makes sense to keep all of the information about organizational competencies together in a single task. On the other hand, as noted earlier, you will have to understand the difference between service goals and organizational competencies in order to develop your goals. In the end, it seemed more logical to cluster all of the organizational competency information in one task. The members of the library management team will complete Step 8.1 and explain the concepts in the step to the rest of the staff.

Steps 8.2 and 8.3 are completed by a designated writer or writers, the planning coordinator, and the members of the library management team with input from the staff and the board. Steps 8.2 and 8.3 are typically completed after the goals and objectives have been drafted, although, as noted earlier, organizational capacity issues are often raised during the goal-setting process. It is not that time-consuming to identify organizational capacity issues and write the organizational competencies and initiatives. The preliminary work can often be done during one meeting of the library management team, and it should not take a long time for the designated writer to create a draft document for review. The designated writer is again working as a scribe, not an author. The draft organizational competencies and initiatives are sent to the staff with the draft goals and objectives for review and discussion, and are then sent to the board with the final draft of the goals and objectives for approval in concept (see Step 7.2).

Step 8.1
Understand Organizational Competencies and Initiatives

To understand organizational competencies, you will need to know both what they are and what they are not. An *organizational competency* is defined as "the institutional capacity or efficiency that is necessary to enable the library to achieve the goals and objectives in its strategic plan." In other words, unlike goals, which describe what a target audience will receive, organizational competencies address the library's infrastructure and operations. Goals focus on the delivery of *effective* services to the public. Organizational competencies describe the conditions that the library will have to achieve or enhance in order to deliver those effective services. The focus is on ensuring that library operations are *efficient.* Each organizational competency addresses a single area of the library's

FIGURE 39

Typical Areas Addressed
by Organizational Competencies

External partnerships
Finance
Fund-raising
Governance
Marketing and public relations
Measurement and evaluation
Operational efficiencies
Organizational structure
Policies
Training and staff development

operations. The ten most common organizational competencies are listed in figure 39. You will learn more about these areas in Step 8.2.

As you can see from the list of organizational competencies, they don't have anything to do with the allocation of staff, collection, facility, or technology resources. This is an important point and one that staff sometimes find confusing. It isn't all that hard to explain the difference between external services to the public (goals) and internal operations (organizational competencies). It can be more challenging to explain the difference between organizational competencies and the resources required to provide or support activities, both of which deal with internal operations.

The easiest way to help staff understand the distinction is to explain that resource allocation—and reallocation—decisions are driven by the specific activities that a library offers to support the goals and objectives in its strategic plan. Organizational competencies, on the other hand, are more general and relate to systemic issues that would probably have to be addressed regardless of the service priorities selected for inclusion in the library strategic plan. Figure 40 illustrates the differences between resource allocation and organizational competencies. As you review the figure, you will see that the goal and objectives are the same for both of the libraries in the figure. The activities selected by each library, however, are different. As a result, the resources needed by each library are also different. The only overlap between the two sets of required resources is the need for staff who can plan and present story hours.

Now look at the organizational competencies that will be needed to complete the activities. They are the same for both libraries. In both instances there are policy issues to be addressed, both libraries will be initiating or expanding partnerships, and staff training will be required in both cases as well.

What Are Initiatives?

The actual work that needs to be done to address the organizational competencies will depend on the current conditions in the library. The staff of the Anytown Public Library might have recently updated the library policy manual and, therefore, they would only have to make minor revisions to reflect the new service priorities. The Tree County Public Library might have a policy manual that was last updated in the early 1990s. Obviously, the Tree County Library staff would have more work to do to ensure that the library's policies reflect its priorities.

These differences would be reflected in the initiatives identified to reach the desired competency in each library. In this context, an *initiative* is defined as "a temporary endeavor with a defined scope designed to produce a clearly identified product that will develop an organizational competency within a specified time frame." In most instances, initiatives will be project statements, and one or more staff will be assigned to complete the identified project by the specified date.

To continue with the policy example from the beginning of this section, the staff in the Anytown and Tree County libraries would write different initiatives for their shared organizational competency that addresses policies:

FIGURE 40
Resource Allocation and Organizational Competencies

GOAL: Preschool children will enter school ready to learn.

Objective 1: Each year, at least X preschool children will attend programs in the library and at least Y preschool children will attend programs at non-library locations.

Objective 2: By 2XXX, 75% of the parents of preschool children who attend programs sponsored by the library will say that the library plays an important role in helping children to enter school ready to learn to read, write, and listen.

Objective 3: By 2XXX, the circulation of materials for preschool children will increase from X to Y (10%).

ANYTOWN PUBLIC LIBRARY	TREE COUNTY PUBLIC LIBRARY
Activities	*Activities*
1. Use existing materials to create "Books-to-Go" bags. 2. Present eight story programs for preschool children each week in the library. 3. Add a "Read-to-Me" component to the summer reading program. 4. Present programs on early literacy for parents and caregivers. 5. Create an interactive "family place" in the children's area for preschool children and their parents. 6. Develop and present a series of holiday-themed puppet shows in neighborhood recreation centers throughout the city.	1. Schedule library staff to present monthly story programs in all county Head Start programs. 2. Place deposit collections in all of the county Head Start programs. 3. Provide interactive stories for preschool children on the library website. 4. Distribute "Born to Read" kits to the parents of newborn children. 5. Collaborate with local pediatricians to have them encourage parents to read to their children. 6. Put computers with appropriate software in the preschool area of the library.
Resources Needed	*Resources Needed*
Staff: Skills needed: puppetry; planning and presenting story programs; designing and presenting training for adults; knowledgeable about early literacy. *Collection:* Use existing resources. *Facility:* Redesign children's area to create a "family place." *Technology:* None.	*Staff:* Skills needed: planning and presenting story programs; identify potential partners and establish partnerships; early childhood computer skills. *Collection:* Resources for deposit collections and software. *Facility:* Space for computers in preschool area. *Technology:* Age-appropriate computers for the preschool area of the children's room.
Organizational Competencies	*Organizational Competencies*
The Anytown Public Library will operate within a policy framework that reflects the organization's priorities and values and promotes effective and efficient service delivery. The Anytown Public Library will collect and use data to ensure that all library programs and services are effective and meet or exceed the library's objectives. The Anytown Public Library staff will have the skills, knowledge, and abilities necessary to provide quality services to all library users.	The Tree County Public Library will operate within a policy framework that reflects the organization's priorities and values and promotes effective and efficient service delivery. The Tree County Public Library will collect and use data to ensure that library programs and services are effective and meet or exceed the library's objectives. The Tree County Public Library staff will have the skills, knowledge, and abilities to provide quality services to all library users.

Shared Organizational Competency: The library will operate within a policy framework that reflects the organization's priorities and values and promotes effective and efficient service delivery.

Anytown Public Library Initiative

Initiative 1:   By June 30, 2XXX, review the policies relating to partnerships and fund-raising to ensure that they support the priorities in the new strategic plan, and make revisions as needed.

Tree County Public Library Initiatives

Initiative 1:   By June 30, 2XXX, complete a policy audit and evaluate all existing library policies in the context of the new strategic plan.

Initiative 2:   By August 31, 2XXX, develop a time line and process to revise library policies as needed to ensure that they support the library's values and goals.

Initiative 3:   By August 31, 2XXX (one year after the date in Initiative 2), complete the revision of the library policies.

Step 8.2
Identify Organizational Issues

Even the best-run libraries may have problems in one or more of the areas listed in figure 39 or in other operational areas. These problems can make it difficult to provide services no matter what the library priorities are. One of the biggest challenges in earlier versions of the *Planning for Results* process was that there was no way to formally acknowledge and address problems such as these. Sometimes that led staff or board members to try to write goals like those in the examples in Step 7.1 and those written by the Palmyra-Eagle Area School District in figure 31. In fact, as noted earlier, staff will probably have identified some of the problem areas to be addressed through organizational competencies during the goal-setting process.

The results of the staff SWOT analysis of the preliminary service responses (Step 4.3) may also provide you with some ideas about potential organizational competencies. If one of the common themes in the weaknesses identified by staff was that staff didn't have the skills needed to provide services, this would suggest that you consider developing an organizational competency that deals with training and staff development.

It is also fairly common to find that staff identify weaknesses in the areas of marketing, partnerships, and measurement during the library SWOT analysis. In these cases, some of the organizational competencies that are articulated during the strategic planning process relate to long-standing problems that have not been successfully addressed in the past. Managers may have known for some time that the library's data collection and evaluation processes were inadequate, but they never had the time or the impetus to do something about the problem. The *Planning for Results* emphasis on measurable objectives provides the impetus needed.

Other organizational competencies will relate to the changing tools that libraries use and the changing expectations of library users. Library staff often voice concerns about organizational efficiencies during planning discussions. At one time, staff focused on streamlining the way work was completed. Now the focus is often on adopting self-service technologies. In the future, streamlining may well mean finding ways to provide off-site users with all of the services and resources that are available to on-site users.

Another way to identify areas that need to be addressed by organizational competencies in your library is to answer the questions on Workform K, Organizational Competency Issues. When you review the workform, you will see that there are three to five questions about each of the areas listed in figure 39, plus a space for you to add issues unique to your library. The workform instructs you to answer "Yes" or "No" to each of the questions under each of the ten areas. A "Yes" answer indicates that there is no problem with the specific issue addressed in the question. A "No" answer indicates that there is a problem that may need to be resolved to ensure that the library can successfully implement the new strategic plan. There is no hard-and-fast rule, but generally, if you have two or more "No" responses to the questions in one of the ten areas, you will want to consider writing an organizational competency and developing one or more initiatives in that area.

The staff of the Tree County Library completed Workform K during a meeting held to identify the organizational competencies needed to implement their new strategic plan. Their responses to the questions in the first three areas on the workform can be found in figure 41. As you can see, they answered "No" to all of the questions pertaining to external partnerships and added another issue to the mix as well. They answered "Yes" to all of the questions pertaining to finance, and they answered both "Yes" and "No" to the questions under fund-raising.

Obviously the staff at the Tree County Library will need to develop an organizational competency and write initiatives to address the problems relating to external partnerships. And obviously their financial house is in order and they have no need to do anything to change it. What is less obvious is what they need to do about fund-raising. The staff indicated that the library has a fund-raising plan, that fund-raising responsibilities are clearly defined and respected by all, that the library has attractive and up-to-date fund-raising materials, and that current fund-raising efforts were directed toward the priorities in the plan. However, the staff also noted that not all donors were promptly and appropriately acknowledged and recognized. They didn't identify any other fund-raising problems or issues.

Do you think the Tree County Library staff should write an organizational competency to resolve their fund-raising problem? The staff decided they didn't need to go through that process. Instead, they recommended that the director develop procedures to ensure that all donors were promptly and appropriately acknowledged and recognized. This was a relatively easy fix for the Tree County Library. Addressing this problem might be more challenging in another library, and if it is, staff in that library might decide that an organizational competency and initiatives are needed.

The deciding factor for the Tree County Library staff was not that they had only answered "No" to one fund-raising question. It was that the problem they identified was easily resolved in their library. If they had answered "Yes" to all of the questions pertaining to fund-raising except the first one (does the library have a fund-raising plan?), they might well have decided to develop a fund-raising organizational competency and initiatives. Creating a fund-raising plan is likely to take a significant amount of time and energy.

FIGURE 41

Workform K: Organizational Competency Issues—Example

A. **External Partnerships**. This includes formal and informal relationships with other governmental units, nonprofit agencies and organizations, and businesses.

1. Yes	2. No	
	X	Does the library maintain a comprehensive and accurate list of all organizations and agencies with which it has formal and informal partnerships?
	X	Is there a clear process that is observed when determining whether or not to partner with an organization or agency?
	X	Are all staff aware of the process to be followed when they wish to initiate a partnership agreement or respond to a request to establish a partnership?
	X	Have criteria been established that will be used when assessing existing or potential partnerships?
3. Other: Conflicts between library staff and staff in some of the organizations with whom the library has partnerships.		

B. **Finance.** This includes both operational and capital funding and addresses the allocation, expenditure, tracking, and reporting of those funds.

1. Yes	2. No	
X		Are library funds allocated in accordance with the priorities in the strategic plan?
X		Is the library's financial reporting system understood by staff and board members who have fiduciary responsibility?
X		Are board members and library management aware of their legal responsibility vis-à-vis public and donated funds?
X		Are accurate, timely, and easy-to-understand reports about library finances distributed to and discussed with library board members and the library management team on a regular basis?
3. Other: None		

C. **Fund-raising.** This includes all gift and donation programs supported by the library, the Friends of the Library, or the library foundation.

1. Yes	2. No	
X		Does the library have a fund-raising plan?
X		Are the fund-raising responsibilities of the library foundation, Library Friends, library management, and library staff clearly understood, respected, and observed by all parties?
X		Have the individuals with fund-raising responsibilities received the appropriate training to enable them to perform their assigned duties?
X		Do members of the foundation, Friends, and staff have access to attractive and up-to-date fund-raising materials?
X		Are all fund-raising efforts directed toward priorities in the strategic plan?
	X	Are donors promptly and appropriately acknowledged and recognized?
3. Other: None		

Staff in some libraries will find that they need to develop two or three organizational competencies. Staff in other libraries may find that they need to develop eight or nine—or even ten—competencies. Larger, more complex libraries are more likely to have organizational issues than smaller libraries, but this is not always true. As you go through this part of the planning process, you will find that your library is as unique as your community, and the problems you have are unique as well.

Step 8.3
Write Organizational Competencies and Initiatives

When you have identified the areas in which you will need to develop organizational competencies and initiatives, all that remains is to write them. Once again, the actual writing should be done by one person—or two at the most. As noted earlier, there are few things more frustrating than writing by committee.

All organizational competencies contain the same two elements: they begin with the library's name and then they describe the desired organizational capacity or efficiency. In a sense, organizational competencies are like goals. They both describe an ideal or unattainable state. Organizational competencies are easier to write than goals because you won't have to worry about the target audience—it is always "the library."

Each organizational competency focuses on a single area of the library's operations. You identified problems or issues to be resolved in the preceding step. Now you need to describe the desired organizational capacity or efficiency. In the Tree County Library example in Step 8.2, the staff identified problems with the way the library manages external partnerships. The staff member assigned to develop organizational competencies wrote the following competency:

> The Tree County Library will actively seek and maintain relationships with agencies, organizations, and institutions that will enable the library to enhance service to its customers.

Notice that the organizational competency doesn't specifically mention the issues that need to be resolved. Instead it describes the desired state of affairs.

When the organizational competency has been drafted, the writer will move on to writing initiatives to support that competency. Initiatives are used to make progress toward creating the institutional capacity or efficiency described in an organizational competency. Each initiative includes a brief description of the scope of the initiative and a date by which the initiative should be completed. Initiatives often relate directly to the problems or issues that led to the identification of the need for the organizational competency. It is not uncommon to find that more than one initiative will be required to create the needed organizational competency. The Tree County Library staff member responsible for drafting organizational competencies drafted the following initiatives for the external partnership competency:

> By 2XXX, identify current partnerships and the obligations that the library has as part of those partnerships.
>
> By 2XXX, establish criteria to be used to assess current and potential partnerships.

By 2XXX, initiate a review and approval process for the establishment of new partnerships.

As you can see, these initiatives are written to address the specific problems that were identified in the example in figure 41.

Initiatives are normally based on the assumption that a project committee will be appointed to do something within a specified time. Each project committee should be given a statement of project intent that describes the reason for initiating the project and the intended outcome, a statement of project scope that defines the boundaries of the project, and a project time line that includes the deadline for completing the project.

After the designated writer has completed a draft of the organizational competencies and supporting initiatives, the planning coordinator should review the dates assigned to the initiatives. Each date might seem perfectly reasonable by itself, but each project will not be completed in a void. There are a finite number of people to implement all of the initiatives, and those people have a finite amount of time. The planning coordinator and the members of the management team will want to be sure that the most important initiatives are completed first and initiatives with a lower priority are scheduled for later in the process. The priority of the initiatives is determined by the priority of the organizational competencies they support. The priority of the organizational competencies is determined by the effect the organizational competency has on accomplishing the library's goals and objectives.

As noted earlier, the final draft of the organizational competencies and initiatives will be sent to the staff for review with the draft goals and objectives. The final draft of the organizational competencies and initiatives will also be sent to the board with the final draft of goals and objectives for review and approval in concept (Step 7.2).

What's Next?

When you have completed the two tasks in this chapter, you will have finished writing the most important components of your strategic plan. In the next chapter, you will learn how to use those components to write your strategic plan and how to disseminate that plan to the stakeholders in the library and in your community. In Task 9 you will write your basic plan, present it to the members of the community planning committee for review and comment, and then present it to the board for final approval. In Task 10 you will define the stakeholder groups, identify what you want those stakeholder groups to do with the plan, and develop communications to target audiences.

Key Points to Remember

Many staff will believe that they will be assigned new responsibilities to complete in addition to their current assignment; they will be skeptical about the concept of reallocating staff resources.

Don't let semantics get in the way of developing goals and objectives. Use the *Planning for Results* definitions.

Each goal is derived from a specific service response. You may write more than one goal to support a service response, but a goal cannot support more than one service response.

Goals focus on what the community receives because the library provides a service, and not on the resources the library needs to deliver the service.

Objectives always include a measure, a target, and a date.

Anecdotal data can be effective, but it needs to be used in conjunction with quantitative data about library users and their perceptions.

Data about the number of units of service delivered is hard for nonlibrarians to understand or care about.

Not all objectives have to target an increase in use. In some cases, a target of maintaining the status quo is quite appropriate.

Goals focus on the delivery of effective services to the public. Organizational competencies focus on ensuring that library operations are efficient.

Organizational competencies do not address resource allocation issues.

Staff in some libraries may find they only need to develop two or three organizational competencies. Staff in other libraries may find that they need to develop eight or ten.

Communicate, communicate, communicate.

Notes

1. "Method Index: Method Acting for Directors," http://method.vtheatre.net/dict.html.
2. Sandra Nelson, *Implementing for Results: From Ideas to Action* (Chicago: American Library Association, forthcoming 2008).
3. *Hendersonville* [TN] *Free Press,* May 6, 1992.

Chapter 5

Communicate the Plan

The two words "information" and "communication" are often used interchangeably, but they signify quite different things. Information is giving out; communication is getting through.

—Sydney J. Harris

MILESTONES

By the time you finish this chapter you will be able to

- understand the elements of effective communication
- explain the difference between the official strategic plan and the targeted reports that are based on the plan
- identify the elements to include in your strategic plan
- determine why you are communicating about the strategic plan with specific target audiences
- develop a communication plan for each target audience

A dictionary definition of *information* is "knowledge obtained from investigation, study, or instruction." *Communication* is "a process by which information is exchanged between individuals." The eight tasks described in the first four chapters of this book produce a great deal of information. In the two tasks in this chapter, you will develop the processes needed to communicate that information to the people in your community, the library staff, and the library board.

At one time, most strategic planning efforts ended with a report that was at least fifty pages long and, in libraries with sufficient resources, printed in full-color with photographs, tables, and charts. This strategic plan usually included long descriptions of the process used to develop the plan (sometimes with the minutes of the planning meetings attached), voluminous statistical data about the community and the library, information about the planning committee, and—somewhere in the middle of all this—the goals and objectives of the new plan. Library staff distributed copies of this strategic plan to the various departments in the library, to the members of the library board and the board of the foundation or Friends group, to the city or county manager or commissioners, and to selected groups and organizations—and those staff members thought they were communicating. Unfortunately, simply distributing copies of the strategic plan did not qualify as communication. Communication is a two-way street. Communication does not occur when information is sent; it occurs when the information has been received and has had an effect on the recipient. Developing effective ways to communicate about the library's strategic planning process can be a challenge, particularly in today's communication environment.

We are all inundated with information every day. We wake up with the morning news, we turn on our personal computers and read the e-mails we received overnight, we read the morning paper, we listen to the radio or our iPods on the way to work, we read the e-mails in our work accounts, we go through in-boxes overflowing with reports, journals, and memos, we read and respond to e-mails as they come in all day, we attend meetings, we interact with our colleagues and the public, we go home, we look at our snail mail, and we watch television until it's time to go to bed—and then many of us check our e-mail one more time. In addition, sometime during the day, most of us connect to the Web to find information, read a blog, share with others on a social networking site, or just browse.

In 1990 most communications were either face-to-face, by phone, or by mail—snail mail. If there was a rush to deliver a message, people used fax machines or express shipping companies. In that environment, "immediate response" meant a week or ten days. Today we have telephones, cell phones, voice mail, e-mail, instant messages, blogs, podcasts, social networks, and face-to-face conversations. If we choose to, we can be in touch with the world twenty-four hours a day, seven days a week. Now "immediate response requested" means just that—respond immediately!

The combined effect of too many messages and too many deadlines has led to a shift in communication patterns over the past twenty years. People don't want to read long reports, long memos, long e-mails, or text-dense websites. *The New Planning for Results: A Streamlined Approach* included two rules for deciding who needs to know what when about your strategic plan. The first rule was: "The more important the individual, the less they want to know." Based on that definition, everyone is important today. Very few people have the time or the inclination to wade through pages of text before they get to the point of a communication. On the other hand, a large and growing number of people are quite comfortable with this message: "U R RIGHT. ITS LATE. GTG. TLK2UL8R." (Translation: You are right. It is late. I've got to go. Talk to you later.)

This is the environment in which you will be working to communicate the results of your planning process. You will be trying to affect people who are receiving dozens or even hundreds of other messages each day, who are continually responding to demands for immediate action, and who have no patience with long narratives of any kind. Before these people take the time to read and react to something, they will want to know why they should bother. What difference will the information being transmitted make to them or their family and friends? This means that the old-fashioned, fifty-page, printed library strategic planning report will be even less effective as a means of communication now than it was ten or twenty years ago.

If communication is "an exchange of information" and if effective communication means that you are "getting through," then you and your colleagues will have to reconsider the whole concept of strategic planning reports. Instead of automatically doing what has always been done in the past, you will want to think about the following questions.

Why are you preparing a report on the strategic planning process? Whom do you hope to communicate with? What do you want them to do as a result of the communication? What are the most effective ways to communicate with your intended audiences? How will you know your communications have been received?

The answers to these questions will probably lead you to conclude that you still need an official printed strategic plan, but that it doesn't need to have all of the bells and whistles that were included in earlier plans. You will probably also conclude that this strategic plan will not be the best way to tell specific audiences about library services that have been developed just for them. People tend to ignore communications that don't directly apply to them. To connect with members of specific audiences, you will need to tailor planning reports for each group.

You might develop a brief report for parents that highlights the portions of the plan that deal with services to children. Another report might be targeted to teens and describe the teen-related services in the plan. The information from both would come from the strategic plan. However, the two reports would contain different information, would look very different, and might be distributed through different media and at different locations.

The report for parents would highlight the goals and objectives that relate to services for children. It might be printed on a single sheet of paper or even a large bookmark. The illustrations would be of young children or families, and the intent would be to get parents to bring their children to the library. This report could be distributed through day care centers, parent-teacher organizations, and pediatricians.

The teen report might be a podcast or short video of another teen or members of the teen advisory board describing the cool stuff the library has for teens and encouraging them to come and see for themselves. The podcast or video could be made available on the library website, on school websites, and on social networking sites like MySpace.

There is one audience that is often overlooked when the members of the library management team begin to write the targeted planning reports described above. Most strategic planning reports are intended for external audiences and are written from the library users' point of view. This is important for all of the reasons listed earlier. However, it is equally important that strategic planning reports be developed for your internal audiences: the staff and members of the board. The strategic planning documents written for your internal audiences will be revised and expanded as activities are selected and implementation begins, and they will be used to report progress toward reaching the objectives each year.

Getting Started

The two tasks in this chapter are critical to the success of your overall planning process. All of the work you have done to date has produced valuable information about the future direction of the library. However, if that information isn't shared, all of your efforts have been wasted. The people in your community won't know anything about the fact that you have involved community leaders in your planning process, and they won't have any information about the library's new service priorities. Staff won't use the new goals and objectives as a framework for deciding how they should spend their time. Board members won't base their budget decisions on the priorities in the plan. The initiatives that support the desired organizational competencies will get lost in the welter of day-to-day crises, and the impetus for strengthening organizational capacity will fade.

You can make sure that none of these bleak possibilities occur by completing Tasks 9 and 10. During Task 9 you will write your strategic plan and submit it to the library board for approval. During Task 10, you will develop tools to communicate the results of your planning process to key constituencies in your community and within the library itself.

TASK 9: WRITE THE STRATEGIC PLAN AND OBTAIN APPROVAL

Task 1:   Design the Planning Process
Task 2:   Start the Planning Process
Task 3:   Identify Community Needs
Task 4:   Select Service Responses
Task 5:   Prepare for Change
Task 6:   Consider Library Values and Mission
Task 7:   Write Goals and Objectives
Task 8:   Identify Organizational Competencies
Task 9:   Write the Strategic Plan and Obtain Approval
    Step 9.1: Write and review the strategic plan
    Step 9.2: Submit the strategic plan for approval
Task 10:   Communicate the Results of the Planning Process

The steps in this task will be completed by a person designated to draft the strategic plan, the members of the library management team, and the members of the library board. During the first step, a designated editor will develop the strategic plan and the members of the management team will review it. During the second step, the members of the board will approve the strategic plan. The first step can be completed in a relatively short time. The designated editor should be able to compile the strategic plan in a day or two, and the management review will take place during a single meeting of the management team. The second step shouldn't take long either. After all, the members of the board have already reviewed and conditionally approved the major elements in the plan. The only time constraint will be the scheduling of the board meeting during which the plan will be approved.

Step 9.1
Write and Review the Strategic Plan

Most of the key elements of the strategic plan have already been written, reviewed, and approved in concept. All that is left to do is to incorporate these key elements into the final strategic plan. The strategic plan serves four functions. It is a record of all the decisions made during the planning process; it is the official report of the planning process; it is the document that is formally approved by the library board; and it is a public document that is made available to people who want to know about all of the library's priorities. If the strategic plan was only intended to fulfill the first three functions, identifying the components to include in it wouldn't be too difficult. You could just decide to include everything you can think of about the process. No one expects official documents to be all that interesting anyway. It is the fact that the strategic plan should also be suitable for public distribution that creates the challenge.

In order to serve as an official record of the planning process, the strategic plan must include the following elements.

Dates of the planning process. Each strategic plan is the result of conditions at the time the plan was developed. The plan should include the dates of the planning process and the dates covered by the goals and objectives in the plan.

A brief *description of the planning process.* The plan should include a one- or two-paragraph description of the process used to identify priorities. The key points to make are that this process included community leaders and was a collaborative effort that involved those leaders along with staff and board members in the decision-making process.

This is the section of the strategic plan that was often overemphasized in earlier strategic planning reports. Very few people are interested in a detailed description of the processes used to identify the library's service priorities, except perhaps the people who participated in that process, and they lived through it and don't need to read about it. Do not give in to the temptation to include charts, graphs, tables, and other types of data about the library or the community, unless there is a compelling reason to do so. If there is such a reason (in other words, if your governing authority insists), include all such supporting documentation as an appendix.

Names of community planning committee members. There are several reasons to include the names of the community planning committee's members in the strategic plan. The first is simple good manners. It is always important to acknowledge the contributions that people in the community make to the library. The second reason is a little more self-serving. You spent a lot of time carefully selecting people who represent the important constituencies in your community to serve on your planning committee. The fact that they were part of the process gives your strategic plan instant credibility. The third reason to include the names of the committee members is to reinforce the fact that the library's strategic planning process was an open process and that library managers and board members sincerely want the library's service priorities to reflect community needs.

Library values. The three preceding items are all introductory information. The real content of the strategic plan begins with a listing of the library's values. The value statements should be able to stand alone. There is no reason to provide any information about how they were developed or who was involved. Very few people care.

Library mission statement or tagline (if any). If you developed a mission statement as part of your planning process, you will want to include it in the strategic plan. However, if you have a mission statement that was developed prior to this planning effort, you will want to review it carefully before including it. If your mission statement seems disconnected from the priorities in your new strategic plan, the mixed message you are sending will weaken the entire document.

If you developed a tagline as part of the process, include it in the strategic plan. If your tagline was developed before you started the planning process, the cautions about mission statements apply here as well. If the tagline doesn't reflect your priorities, consider leaving it out of the strategic plan—and consider rewriting the tagline, too. It is not helpful to have "First with Facts" as your tagline if "Stimulate Imagination: Reading, Viewing, and Listening for Pleasure" is your highest service priority.

Goals, objectives, and sample activities. These items are the core of the strategic plan. You might want to list the goals first and then list each goal with its supporting objectives. There is no reason to include a list of the service responses that were selected by the planning committee in the strategic plan. The service responses describe possible priorities for all public libraries. Your goals were derived from the service responses and focus on the benefits the residents in *your* community will receive because *your* library provides a service.

You have not identified final activities yet, and so any activities you include will be illustrative. However, even examples of activities can be very helpful for people who might be unsure about what some goals mean, and you can probably make a good guess about two or three of the activities that will support each of your goals. In fact, there are activities embedded in some of the objectives in most strategic plans.

In figure 42 you can see some possible activities that were included in the Tree County Library's strategic plan to illustrate the goal pertaining to creating and sharing content. As you can see, activities 1, 3, and 4 are explicitly referenced in the objectives for the goal, and activity 2 is implied. When the staff of the Tree County Library complete the identification and evaluation of activities, they will probably select additional activities to support this goal and these objectives. They may even decide that rather than providing the software training described in activity 2, they will collaborate with a community college to have the training presented. They won't have to amend the strategic plan to reflect these changes, because the "Possible Activities" section was never intended to be absolute or inclusive.

Organizational competencies (if any) and supporting initiatives. If your library identified organizational competencies and initiatives, they should be included in the strategic plan. Again, there is no reason to provide information about how—or why—the organizational competencies were selected. This is more information than most people want or need. Most of the organizational competencies you identify will be intended to address operational problems within the library. There is little to be gained by explicitly listing those problems in a public document.

FIGURE 42

Possible Activities

GOAL: Teens in Tree County will have services and support to create innovative and interactive media.

Objective 1:   By 2XXX, 15% of the teens who use the library will indicate on a survey that they have used library resources to create and share content.

Objective 2:   Each year, at least 90% of teens surveyed will say that the information assistance they receive from staff when creating or sharing content is very good or excellent.

Objective 3:   At least 20% of the teens who attend one or more of the "Teen Zone" e-zine introductory programs will contribute to the e-zine within six months of the month they attended the introductory program(s).

Possible Activities:

1. Provide media production software programs for public use.

2. Provide hands-on classes to teach teens to use a variety of media production software.

3. Publish an e-zine with user-created content.

4. Provide "Teen Zone" e-zine introductory programs to encourage teens to contribute to the e-zine.

A strategic plan that includes the elements listed above will provide an official record of the planning process and can become the report that is approved by the board. However, just including these elements is no guarantee that the resulting strategic plan will be appropriate for general distribution. A public document may need to include more information to provide a context for the planning process and to make the information about the planning process more accessible. Many libraries will include such elements as an executive summary, a list of the members of the library board, and a short introduction by the library director or the board chair. Libraries with multiple outlets may want to include a map showing the location of each outlet.

The content and structure of each strategic plan will be unique. However, effective strategic plans will all share certain characteristics. They will be clear, concise, credible, logical, and persuasive. These terms were described in *The New Planning for Results:*

> A *clear plan* is one that is easy to read and understand. The language in the plan is simple and familiar to the reader. The layout is uncluttered and makes good use of white spaces. A clear plan never uses library jargon or acronyms.

> A *concise plan* uses the fewest words and sentences and avoids redundancy. It is short and to the point.

> A *credible plan* is both accurate and believable. It is particularly important that the members of the planning committee and the staff are able to easily identify their recommendations in the plan. The credibility of the plan will be undermined if it has numerous spelling or grammatical errors.

> A *logical plan* has been arranged in an orderly pattern that makes sense to the reader. When appropriate, supporting documentation is provided.

> A *persuasive plan* convinces people to take certain actions. You want to motivate the members of your governing authority to approve the plan. You also want to motivate the members of the planning committee to become library advocates and spread the word about the plan to the community. In addition, you want to persuade the library staff that the planning effort has been inclusive and successful . . . and that the plan is appropriate and realistic.[1]

Who Should Write the Strategic Plan?

There is a natural tendency to expect the planning coordinator to create the strategic plan. She has been involved with every step of the process, and she probably helped write the draft goals and objectives and the draft organizational competencies and initiatives. She will certainly be more familiar with the process than anyone else on the staff, and at first glance, this makes her the logical person to write the plan. However, her familiarity with the process may be the best reason to ask someone else to develop the plan. Many planning coordinators find it hard to step back from the details of the process and look with fresh eyes at the big picture. These coordinators know just how important all of those details were during the process, and they find it difficult to exclude them from the final strategic plan.

The person assigned to develop the strategic plan must have strong editorial and writing skills. She needs to be able to take the voluminous information produced during the planning process and turn it into a strategic plan that is clear, concise, credible, logical, and persuasive. The values, goals, objectives, organizational competencies, and initiatives have been approved in concept and will not need to be edited, but they can't stand alone. Look at the list of elements to be included in the strategic plan again. The editor will have to write the description of the process, find a way to acknowledge the contributions of the members of the community planning committee, organize all of the information in the plan, and present the information in a way that is clear, concise, credible, logical, and persuasive. This will require a discerning eye and a clear editorial voice. In larger libraries, the person who is responsible for marketing is sometimes asked to write the plan. In smaller libraries, the person who writes the news releases or annual report may be selected—and sometimes this is the director.

The editor may want to work with another staff member who can provide a sounding board and read the plan as it is being developed. It is helpful to be able to send a paragraph or section of the plan to someone else for a quick editorial review. It is also helpful for the writer to have someone to talk to when she has to make decisions about exactly what to include in the plan or how a section should be structured.

Who Should Review the Plan before It Is Sent to the Board?

The members of the community planning committee should be given an opportunity to review the final draft of the strategic plan before it is sent to the board. Normally, this review takes place during a one- or two-hour meeting of the committee that is facilitated by the library director or the planning coordinator. This meeting often includes a meal. Copies of the draft strategic plan should be sent to the members of the committee about ten days before the meeting in order to give them time to read the plan carefully. The actual meeting has two purposes. First, it gives the committee members a chance to see the results of their work and ask any questions they might have. Second, it allows the staff to thank the committee members again and, perhaps, to distribute small gifts to committee members (library book bags, pens, etc.).

The decision of who else should review the final draft of the strategic plan before it is sent to the board may be different in every library. Certainly, every library director will want to read the strategic plan carefully before the members of the board receive it. That is the only absolute in the review process. In some libraries, all the members of the management team will be given an opportunity to read the final draft and suggest revisions. In other libraries, all supervisors will be asked to review the document and make suggestions. In smaller libraries, the draft plan may be made available to all staff for review and comment. Needless to say, the more people who are asked to review the plan, the longer the review process will take.

Before you and your colleagues decide who should be asked to review the final draft of the strategic plan, take a few minutes to think about the purpose of the review process in your library. The review process is not an opportunity to debate the results of the planning process. Remember, staff have already had a chance to review and comment on the substantive parts of the strategic plan. The values, the mission statement or tagline, the goals and objectives, and the organizational competencies and initiatives should all have been thoroughly discussed earlier in the process. No matter who is asked to review the strategic plan, the review process has to be based on the explicit understanding that it is too late to change the decisions made throughout the process. The values have been adopted, the goals and objectives have been approved in concept, and the organizational competencies and initiatives have been endorsed by the library's management team and the members of the board.

The strategic plan is simply an official record of the decisions made about each of those elements, and the review process should focus on the key characteristics of effective strategic plans described earlier: clarity, brevity, credibility, logic, and persuasiveness. This raises the question of what is to be gained by having the draft strategic plan reviewed by all staff or even by all supervisors. After all, members of the management team can make a careful assessment of the draft and discuss possible revisions to it in a relatively brief period of time. This is probably the most efficient process, if all you want is to be sure that the strategic plan is complete and well-written. However, if you identified communication problems or trust issues during your assessment of the library's readiness for change (Step 5.1), it may be worth the extra time to give more staff a chance to read and comment on the draft. Every library director will have to make the decision about which people to include in the review based on local circumstances.

Step 9.2
Submit the Strategic Plan for Approval

This is the easiest step in the entire *Planning for Results* process—if you have kept your board informed throughout the process. Look again at figure 3 in chapter 1. If you follow the guidelines in the figure, the board will have reviewed and approved each of the main components of the strategic plan before the final draft of the plan is presented to them for approval. That should make the approval of the final draft a foregone conclusion, but you will not want to appear to take the board's review of the plan for granted.

Distribute the final draft of the strategic plan to the members of the board at least one week before the board meeting at which they will be reviewing the plan. The document you send to the board should be clearly marked "DRAFT." The director may want the person who compiled and edited the plan to attend the board meeting, both to acknowledge her work and to be available to answer questions or take notes on any changes that might be needed. If any changes are suggested, they will probably be editorial in nature and relatively minor. The board can formally approve the plan with the understanding that the agreed-upon editorial changes will be made.

In the very unlikely event that a board member raises concerns about one of the main components of the strategic plan (vision, goals, objectives, organizational competencies, initiatives), the director should be prepared to review the board discussion that took place when the component was originally presented to the board. While it is theoretically possible for a board to rescind the decisions made earlier in the planning process, it is virtually unheard of. If such a thing were to happen, it would suggest that the library and board have more substantive problems than approving the strategic plan.

When the board has approved the final strategic plan, copies should be made and distributed to each library unit, the members of the library board, the members of the board of the Friends of the Library, the members of the foundation board, appropriate city or county officials, and anyone else you think should receive a copy. You can also make the final strategic plan available on the library's website. However, the full strategic plan is probably not the document you will distribute widely to all interested people. You will learn more about how to tell specific audiences about the results of the planning process in Task 10.

TASK 10: COMMUNICATE THE RESULTS OF THE PLANNING PROCESS

In this task, you begin to move from planning to implementing. During this task, you and your colleagues will decide who needs to know about the information in the strategic plan, what they need to know, and what you expect them to do with the information you send them. This is not a one-time endeavor. You will want every public and internal message about library services to relate back to your strategic plan. In some libraries there is a full-time marketing person who manages communications with the public and the staff. In other libraries, there is no coordination at all and every staff member is free to communicate however he or she chooses, although this is not a good idea and can lead to serious problems. In most libraries, the responsibility for completing the steps in this task will be shared by a number of staff members throughout the library.

The time required to complete this task is equally amorphous. It will depend on the number of communications you develop and the sophistication of those communications. The steps in this task begin after the final draft of the strategic plan has been developed and will continue throughout the life of the plan.

It is recommended that you read the information in the Library Communication tool kit in part 3 before continuing with this task. If you and your colleagues understand the concepts presented in the tool kit, it will be easier to complete the steps in this task.

Step 10.1
Define the Target Audiences

Communication is an exchange of information. This means that there are at least two people involved, the person sending the communication and the person receiving the communication. In this task, you and your colleagues will be the people sending the information. Now you need to identify the people or groups who will be receiving the communications you send. The easy answer is to identify "all residents" as your target audience, and in a sense, this is true. You certainly do want everyone in your community and in your library to know about the strategic plan. The problem is that a single generic message is unlikely to be received by everyone, even if you can find a way to send it to all of them. In this case, the term *receive* means that the message is actively read, heard, or viewed, and not just deposited in the vicinity of the recipient.

Think about the way you react to the messages that you are exposed to throughout the day. The morning news on television may be sponsored by a local car dealer, but if you aren't in the market for a car, you probably tune the ad out completely. Of course, if you are looking for a new car, the ad is much more interesting. An informational memo in your in-basket that is addressed to "All Employees" is far less compelling than a memo addressed to you and you alone. E-mails forwarded to dozens of recipients are often discarded unopened. E-mails addressed to you that have interesting subject lines get opened. You ignore a magazine article on gardening because you live in an apartment, but you read an article on giving a wedding shower because your niece is getting married. Snail mail addressed to "Occupant" goes directly into the wastebasket. Personal letters are opened immediately. When it comes to communication, it really is "all about me."

Businesses know this, and they target their marketing efforts to reach specific audiences. Consider the Fox cable news channel. Although their tagline was "We Report, You Decide," many of their commentators were political conservatives, particularly during the early years of the station. These commentators targeted the large group of conservatives in the United States who believed that most news media reflected a liberal bias. The targeted audience received the message loud and clear, and the number of Fox subscribers went from 13 million in 1996 to over 80 million in 2003.[2]

It isn't difficult to identify the people you want to tell about your strategic plan. Start by identifying the external audiences that need to be informed. These will include the people in your city or county government who have some influence on the budget the library receives: the city or county manager; members of the city council or county board of supervisors; the city or county budget manager; and the directors of other city or county departments with whom the library has a significant relationship, such as information technology or public works. These people may receive an official copy of the complete strategic plan, but you will also want to think about more targeted communications to the people in this group.

You can identify other external target audiences by looking at the goals and objectives in your plan. Some of the goals or objectives are directed toward specific groups of people. These goals were used as examples in chapter 4, and the target audience for each is clear.

> *Preschool children* in Anytown will enter school ready to learn.
>
> *Teens* in Anytown will have materials and programs that excite their imaginations and provide pleasurable reading, viewing, and listening experiences.
>
> *Adults* in Anytown will have the support they need to improve their literacy skills in order to meet their personal goals and fulfill their responsibilities as parents, citizens, and workers.

If your plan includes more general goals, you may have identified target audiences in your objectives:

> **GOAL:** Everyone in Tree County will have materials and programs that excite their imaginations and provide pleasurable reading, viewing, and listening experiences.

> Objective 1: By 2XXX, the circulation of *adult* fiction will increase by 10 percent.
>
> Objective 2: Each year, at least 75 percent of the *teens* who use the library will say that they found something good to read, view, or listen to.
>
> Objective 3: Each year, at least X number of *children* will attend programs sponsored or cosponsored by the library.

Representatives from the media outlets in your community are another group that you will want to inform about your strategic plan. The media outlets themselves will be one of the methods you use to communicate with people in some of your target audiences. When you define the desired result of your communications with media representatives in the next step, you will want to be careful to differentiate between the people who work for the media outlets and the communication methods provided by the media outlets.

There are some target audiences that fall somewhere in the middle between external audiences (not us) and internal audiences (definitely us). The board members of the library Friends group and the library foundation fall into this category, as do the members of these organizations. The staff members from your regional library system and the state library agency may not be considered totally external, but they are not internal either. Whatever your relationship with these agencies, the staff in both should be kept informed about the plan. The members of your planning committee, who were once clearly an external audience, have become an audience that is no longer external and yet not quite internal as a result of their participation in the planning process. It will be important to keep the committee members informed about the strategic plan throughout the life of the plan.

Finally, you will identify the internal target audiences that need to have information about the strategic plan. The two primary internal audiences are the members of the library board and the staff of the library. Staff target audiences can be grouped in a number of ways. You might decide to target nonsupervisory staff, supervisory staff, and managers for some communications. For other messages, you might target staff members in the children's services, teen services, and adult services areas. In some cases, it may make sense to develop separate messages for public services staff, technical services staff, and information technology staff.

The intent of your communication will help you to identify the composition of your target audience. For example, if you will be collecting data to track progress on the objectives in the strategic plan that relate to youth services, you might develop messages for several audiences. The youth services staff and their managers will be doing the actual data collection. You will want them to know exactly what is expected of them and to have the instructions they need to fulfill those expectations. The youth services staff members would receive detailed instructions about how to collect the data. The people who manage the youth services staff members would receive these detailed instructions plus information about monitoring the data collection process. Other public services staff would receive a brief notice that the youth services staff will be collecting data. The intent of this message would be to make sure that all public services staff are aware of the data collection process and can direct users with questions to the appropriate people for answers. There wouldn't be any particular reason for managers in technical services or information technology to know about the data collection process. They could be sent the same message that was distributed to public services staff, but they probably wouldn't pay much attention to it. After all, it would have nothing to do with them or their staff members.

Step 10.2
Develop a Communication Plan

There are four things to consider when you develop your communication plan. First, you have to decide which audiences and messages should be given priority. Then you need to clearly define what you expect the members of each target audience to do as a result of

FIGURE 43

Workform L: Communicate the Results—Example

A. Target Audience	B. Priority	C. Intent of Message	D. Person Responsible	E. Date Due
Board	1	Approve plan	Director	4/1/XX
Foundation, board	2	Express support of plan to board members	Director	3/15/XX
Teen staff and IT staff	1	Develop the media production training program	Marvin Gardens	4/2/XX
Teens	3	Teens will attend media production workshop	Nancy Johnson	7/1/XX

the message you send them. Next, you have to decide who will be responsible for developing the messages to be sent. Finally, you will have to decide when you want the messages sent. There is more information on each of these decisions below. As you make your decisions, you can record them on Workform L, Communication Plan. Figure 43 is a copy of the workform that has been partially completed by the Tree County Library staff.

Which Audiences Should Have Priority?

No library has the resources to develop and send effective messages to every target audience that will be identified during Step 10.1 of this task. This may be one reason why staff in so many libraries just send a series of generic messages to everyone and hope that some people will actually pay attention to them. As we have seen earlier in this chapter, this is a hope that is unlikely to be realized. Generic messages are generally ineffective. You don't save time by doing ineffective things—you just waste that time.

Since you can't develop and send messages to every possible target audience at the same time, you will have to decide which audiences should be given priority. The following questions will help you to determine the priority of each group. The questions are listed in priority order.

Do the members of this group have to take some action before you can implement a part or all of the plan? For example, the board has to approve the strategic plan before you can begin to implement any part of it. Staff will have to take a variety of actions to translate the priorities in the plan into new services, programs, and collections. If any part of the plan is dependent on additional funding (and this is not recommended), then the people who control the funding will have to act. Communications to people in this group will be your first priority.

Can the members of this group influence the people who have to take action before you can implement a part or all of your plan? For example, the members of the community planning committee may be able to influence the board to approve the strategic plan. The attitudes that library managers and supervisors have about the strategic plan will influence the staff who have to implement the plan. People in this group will be your second priority.

Are there goals in the plan that relate to this group? If yes, what is the priority of those goals?
For example, if the top three goals in your plan address children and teens, this would suggest that you put more priority on developing communications for that age group than on developing communications for adults.

Do the members of this group have to take some action for the library to reach one or more targets in the objectives in the plan? For example, if one of your objectives states that the number of preschool children who attend programs sponsored by the library will increase by 10 percent each year, the parents or caregivers of those children are going to have to arrange for the children to attend the programs. Obviously, messages to groups that have to take action in order for you to reach your target will have a higher priority than messages to groups that are not specifically designated in your objectives.

Do you want to partner with a group to provide services? For example, you may have a goal that relates to helping preschool children enter school ready to learn, and the objectives measure the number of library presentations at day care centers or the circulation of materials in deposit collections at day centers. Communication between day care providers and library staff will be critical to the success of the objectives.

Can the members of this group influence the members of a target audience to take the action necessary for the library to reach one or more targets in the objectives in the plan? For example, day care providers might join the library in encouraging parents to take their children to library-sponsored programs. Messages to people who can influence members of a target audience have a higher priority than messages to groups who are not specifically identified in the plan.

As you can see when you review this list of questions, there is little room for generic messages, nor is there much point in communicating with people who are not targets in your plan. Don't forget that the whole purpose of your strategic planning process was to identify priorities so that you could make informed and effective resource-allocation decisions. Staff time is a critical resource. Using these questions to determine the priority of the audiences with whom you will communicate about the plan will save staff time, and that time can be allocated to other plan-related activities.

What Do You Expect the Members of the Audience to Do?

The questions that you use to determine the priority of the target audiences with whom you might communicate have one thing in common. They all assume that you are communicating with a group to encourage them to do something. There is not much point in developing communications to *inform* people about something. Remember, people receive far too many messages every day, and general messages are among the easiest to ignore.

Before you can create a message designed to encourage the members of a group to do something, you have to know *exactly* what it is you want them to do. The expectation has to be specific, and it should be easy for the recipient to understand. Don't combine several expectations in a single message. When a message starts getting too complex, recipients tend to tune out.

This can be more difficult than it sounds. Let's say two people are working together to inform seniors about the programs the library will be offering in the future to help them

"Satisfy Their Curiosity." One person may want the message to encourage seniors to attend a specific series of programs. The other person may want the message to encourage seniors to check the library website regularly to select programs they want to attend. These differences may seem minor, but they really aren't, as you can see below.

> Are you an amateur archeologist? Join others who share your interests and learn more about the current archeology projects in our state. John Jones, noted local archeologist, will be presenting a series of six programs every Thursday night from 7:30 to 9:00, starting on May 2 and ending on June 7, 2XXX. For more information, call 555-5555 or check the library's website (http://anytownlibrary.org).

> Now that you are retired, you finally have time to explore all of those topics that you've always wanted to know more about. The library program series "Satisfy Your Curiosity" was designed just for you. Check the library's website (http://anytownlibrary.org) for a list of the programs the library will be offering during the next three months and register for the program that will satisfy *your* curiosity.

You will notice that neither of these messages specifically mentions the library's strategic plan. However, both messages relate directly to this objective from the plan: "Each year, at least XXX seniors will attend programs designed to satisfy their curiosity," and they are both far more effective than this message:

> Seniors are a priority in the library's new strategic plan, and one of our objectives is to present programs for at least XXX seniors each year. Seniors are encouraged to check the library's website (http://anytownlibrary.org) for a list of the programs the library will be offering during the next three months and register for the programs of their choice.

Who Should Create the Message?

There is no standard answer to this question, but there are a couple of things to consider when making the decision. The person responsible for creating the message has to be an effective writer and must have a thorough knowledge of the target audience and the topic of the message. Unfortunately, these two things don't always go hand in hand. If that is the case, consider assigning two people to work together to develop a message. The content person can help the writer to understand the target audience and the intent of the message, and the writer can use that understanding to create an effective message.

When Should the Message Be Sent?

No library has the resources to create and send all of the messages that need to be sent about the strategic plan at the same time, and even if a library did, it wouldn't make sense to do so. There is no point in encouraging the public to participate in a new service until the service is actually available. That can't happen until the board has approved the plan and the staff have developed the service. The relative priority of the target audiences in your communication plan will help you to decide when messages should be sent. You will also want to consider sending messages several times, using different media.

Step 10.3
Develop Communications to Target Audiences

When you know who your audience is and what you want them to do as a result of your message, you are ready to begin to develop the actual message, determine the media you will use to send the message, and decide how you will know if the message was effective. The message and the medium are interconnected. The text for a brochure will be different than the script for a podcast or the text on a web page. If you really want to be sure that your message is received, you should consider sending it through several different media.

The actual media you select to send your message will depend on several things. First, and most important, is the audience. There probably isn't much point in developing a brochure for teens. They are more likely to respond to a podcast, video, or social network. On the other hand, you would reach fewer seniors with a podcast than you would with a brochure. You will also want to consider the cost of the medium you plan to use. It is relatively inexpensive to record a podcast and make it available through the library website. It is more expensive to print color brochures using the library's printer, and it can be very expensive to have a color brochure professionally printed. You will have to decide if the results you expect to get from using a given medium are worth the cost.

No matter which medium you use, your final message should be short, personal, and compelling. It is not easy to create messages that conform to any one of these criteria. Creating messages that conform to all three criteria can be very challenging.

Writers know that it is often easier to write a page about a topic than it is to write a paragraph or a sentence. There is lots of room on a page for the writer to say whatever she wishes about the topic. To write a paragraph that covers the same information, the writer will have to identify the key points about the topic and focus just on those points. To write a sentence on the topic, the writer must be able to distill everything about the topic into one statement, and this means that the writer must be very familiar with the topic.

Creating a message intended for all members of a target audience that seems personal to each person who receives the message can also be difficult. This is one of the reasons why messages intended for narrowly defined audiences are usually more successful than messages designed for broader audiences. A message to all parents would have to be more generic than a message to parents of preschool children. However, it isn't enough to narrow the audience for the message, if you don't find a way to make the message seem personal to members of that audience. Consider these two examples:

> The library offers story programs for three-year-old children on Mondays and Thursdays at 10:00. Parents are encouraged to bring their children to one of these programs.

> Is your active three-year-old curious and ready to explore the world? Bring your child to the library anytime to discover all of the wonderful things we have. There are programs designed just for your child on Mondays and Thursdays from 10:00 to 10:45.

The first example is all about the library and is addressed to any parents of any three-year-old. The second example is about the parent and the child and is addressed specifically to the recipient of the message—the mom or dad of a three-old-child who is active and curious.

A compelling message is one that persuades the recipient to do what you want her to do. Compelling messages tell the recipient what she needs to know before she can take the action described in the message. Compelling messages also appeal to the emotions of the recipient. They capture people's imaginations and paint an attractive picture of a desirable experience. The following two messages are about the same program. Which one captures your imagination?

> The library is presenting a program on astronomy on Tuesday, May 1, from 8:00 to 9:30.

> Did you ever want to be an astronaut and travel into space? Reserve a seat for your personal tour of the solar system at the library on May 1, from 8:00 to 9:30.

The first message tells the recipients what they need to know to make a decision about attending the program, but doesn't make any attempt to appeal to the recipients' emotions. The second message tries to capture the recipients' attention and make them *want* to attend the program.

It is relatively easy to determine if your message has been effective—if you have clearly identified the intent of the message. In the example above, the intent of the message is to get people to attend the astronomy program. The measure of the effectiveness of the message, then, will be the number of people who attend the program. However, as you learned when you wrote objectives in chapter 4, if you want to track progress on something, you need more than a measure. You will need to identify the target you want to reach. In the case of the astronomy program, you might decide that the program will be considered a success if 25 people attend. If 50 people attend the program, your message will have been extremely effective, and you should consider using it as a model for other messages to the target audience. If only 10 people attend the program, your message won't have been very effective, and you should try to decide what went wrong so that the next message you create for the target audience will be more effective.

You can use Workform M, Message Elements, as a framework for considering what to include in your messages. In figure 44, you can see how the staff of the Tree County Library completed the workform when they were planning the messages to be sent to teens in the county about the library's media production training programs.

How Do We Communicate about the Plan with the Staff and Board?

Most of the examples in this step have been about writing messages designed for the public about some aspect of the strategic plan. You will also be developing messages for the staff and the board about the plan. These messages should also be short, personal, and compelling. Those terms probably don't describe the messages you currently send your staff, many of which could be more accurately described as long, general, and boring.

The staff should have easy access to the entire strategic plan through the staff intranet or in hard copy. However, that is not likely to be seen as a clarion call to action by the staff. There are a number of ways you can make the plan seem more real to the staff. Help to personalize the plan by creating a series of "What Our New Plan Means for You" messages. Each of these messages would be designed for a different segment of the staff and would include the goals and objectives that relate to the work done by that segment of the staff. Youth services staff would receive a message that highlights goals and objectives for children and teens, circulation staff would receive a message highlighting the

FIGURE 44

Workform M: Message Elements—Example

A. Target audience: Teens

B. What we want them to do: Participate in training programs to learn to use the library's media production software and equipment.

C. What they need to know in order to do what we want them to do:

1. The library has a new media production center with state-of-the-art equipment and software.

2. Teens can use the library's media production center to create and share their work.

3. Teens must attend a two-hour training program before they can use the library's media production facilities.

4. Training programs are presented once a month in the media production center.

D. What they need to feel or believe in order to do what we want them to do:

1. Working in the library's media center is going to be fun.

2. Library staff have the skills needed to teach them to use the media production equipment.

3. The media production center has everything they need to create their own electronic media.

4. There will be minimal restrictions on the content of the media that they create.

E. Media to be used to deliver the message:

1. Podcasts by teens who have used the media production center

2. Brochure with teen-friendly graphics describing the media production center and announcing the workshop dates

3. Short video about the production center on YouTube

4. Links to teen-created media on library website that include information on the training programs

F. Evaluation measure and target

1. Measure: Number of teens who attend the media production training programs

2. Target: Ten teens per training program between September and May

objectives that include circulation measures, and so on. These personalized messages would also include appropriate organizational competencies and initiatives. Workform M can be used to create messages for staff as well as for the public.

Consider using the same types of personalized messages to report the progress being made to reach the targets in the objectives or to accomplish the initiatives that support the organizational competencies. These progress reports should be prepared and distributed quarterly. By using personalized reports, you are addressing two of the criteria for creating effective messages: you are making them short and personal. These personalized messages may not be compelling, but they are probably more interesting for most staff than a general report of progress would be. You will, of course, also provide access to data about the progress being made on all of the objectives in the plan on the staff intranet. Remember, you want to use several media to deliver your messages.

One way to be sure that staff actually pay attention to the messages you send about the strategic plan is to develop a template that you can use to create the messages. The template might have a graphic that represents your plan, and it might use a unique font. Perhaps it will have a border or some other eye-catching layout. If you use the special template every time you send a message to the staff about the plan in writing or electronically, the staff will be able to identify the topic at a glance. This makes it less likely that the message will be buried among all the messages that bombard the staff every day.

The most effective and efficient way to communicate with the board about the strategic plan is to organize the director's report to the board around the plan's goals and organizational competencies. This will ensure that board members remain aware of the plan, and it will encourage board members to work with the management team to make the changes needed to reach the targets in the objectives and to complete the initiatives within the scheduled time frame.

What's Next?

When you have completed the tasks in this chapter, you will have finished your strategic planning process. You will have a formal, approved strategic plan and you will have informed the key target audiences about the plan. Now you have to actually do something about implementing the plan. In the next chapter, you will learn more about the implementation process.

However, before you get too involved in thinking about implementing your strategic plan, it is a good idea to take some time to reflect on the process that you went through to develop the plan. Which parts of the process worked well for you and your colleagues? Where did you run into problems? What caused those problems? Were the problems successfully resolved? Are there still planning issues to be addressed, even though the formal planning process has been completed? What changes will you make the next time you develop a strategic plan for the library?

Your new strategic plan will probably not be the first plan ever created for your library, and it probably won't be the last either. In today's environment of constant change, planning has evolved from a major event that occurs every five or ten years to a more organic process. Staff will track progress toward the targets in the objectives monthly and adjust activities as needed to reach the targets. Objectives will be reviewed and revised annually to reflect current conditions in the library and in the community.

Most libraries will go through all of the tasks and steps of the planning process every three or four years. This will ensure that library services will continue to evolve to meet the changing needs and demographic profile of the residents of the community. It also reinforces the fact that library leaders want to develop an ongoing collaborative relationship with community leaders in order to define the library's place in the community and to refine the library's service priorities. The message is clear and powerful: This library belongs to all of us, and working together we can make it a library that we all use and are proud to support.

Key Points to Remember

Communication does not occur when information is sent; it occurs when the information has been received and has had an effect on the recipient.

Everyone receives too many communications. Before people take the time to read and react to something, they will want to know why they should bother. When it comes to communication, it really is "all about me."

Develop strategic planning reports for both external and internal audiences, and don't forget the audiences that fall in between the two.

It will be important to keep the committee members informed about the strategic plan throughout the life of the plan.

The person assigned to write the strategic plan must have strong writing skills. She needs to be able to take the voluminous information produced during the planning process and turn it into a strategic plan that is clear, concise, credible, logical, and persuasive.

The review process is not an opportunity to debate the results of the planning process.

Before you can create a message designed to encourage the members of a group to do something, you have to know *exactly* what it is you want them to do.

A compelling message is one that persuades the recipient to do what you want her to do. It captures people's imaginations and paints an attractive picture of a desirable experience.

The most effective and efficient way to communicate with the board about the plan is to organize the director's report to the board around the goals and organizational competencies.

Communicate, communicate, communicate.

Notes

1. Sandra Nelson, *The New Planning for Results: A Streamlined Approach* (Chicago: American Library Association, 2001), 120–21.
2. *The Supreme Court of the State of New York, County of New York, Fox News Network, LLC v. Penguin Group (USA), Inc. and Alan S. Franken,* available at http://fl1.findlaw.com/news.findlaw.com/hdocs/docs/ip/foxpenguin80703cmp.pdf.

Chapter 6

The Rest of the Story

The definition of insanity is doing the same thing over and over and expecting different results.

—Benjamin Franklin

MILESTONES

By the time you finish this chapter you will be able to

- understand the difference between planning and implementing
- describe the resource allocation environment in which the library operates
- list the tasks in *Implementing for Results*

This is the point in previous public library planning books when the focus shifted from planning to implementing—briefly. The average length of the four previous PLA planning books was about 250 pages, of which an average of thirteen pages was dedicated to implementation issues. In other words, about 95 percent of the content in the previous planning books addressed the process of planning, and about 5 percent of the content focused on translating the plan from ideas to action. Sadly, these percentages were probably similar to the number of libraries that used the planning books to develop plans and the number of libraries that fully implemented the plans they developed.

The truth, of course, is that planning should—and does—take only about 5 percent of your time and energy. Most of your time should be spent on implementation. Planning is simply the process you go through to be sure that your implementation efforts are both effective and efficient. The issues that you will need to resolve to translate the goals and objectives in your strategic plan into reality are more complex than the issues you faced during the planning process. To be able to manage your implementation issues, you will need more help than you can get in a few pages at the end of this book. You will need a manual that picks up where this book ends and describes the tasks and steps that will help you identify, evaluate, and select activities and then allocate the resources needed to implement the activities you selected. You will need workforms and examples to help you and your colleagues make the hard decisions that will be required to actually make the changes needed in your library. You will find all of that and more in the book *Implementing for Results: From Ideas to Action.*[1]

Implementing for Results is organized just like this book. It has been divided into tasks and steps, and workforms and figures illustrate how the staff members in the Tree County and Anytown libraries completed the workforms. In other words, the structure of the book will be familiar to people who have used this book to develop a strategic plan. In effect, *Implementing for Results* is volume 2 of a two-book set.

The core message in *Implementing for Results* is simple and is best reflected in the Benjamin Franklin quotation at the start of this chapter. The staff in too many libraries identify priorities, write goals and objectives, define organizational competencies and their supporting initiatives, write and distribute the strategic plan, and then sit back and wait for changes to happen. When things stay the same, staff are inclined to blame the planning process, the library's users, the library's funders, the Internet—anyone and anything but themselves. That is easier than doing what is necessary to transform the library.

The only way to reach the objectives in the strategic plan and complete the initiatives that support the organizational competencies is to change the way things are currently being done, and that requires resources. Library resources fall into four categories: staff, collections, facilities, and technology. On the surface these resources seem very different, but they share two common traits:

> *Library resources are finite.* No library has access to unlimited resources, and no library can expect all of the resources required to implement the plan to come from new appropriations.

> *Library resources are fully allocated to supporting current activities.* Few libraries have reservoirs of staff, space, collection dollars, or technology support stashed away to be used at some future time. The situation for most is better described as "what you see is what we have."

So you are unlikely to get new resources to implement your plan, and you are unlikely to have resources held in reserve that you can use to implement your plan. That leaves you with just one choice. You will have to reallocate the resources you have now, and this is never easy. Many staff have strong feelings about the value of various segments of the library's collections, which can make the reallocation of collection dollars challenging. Staff also develop proprietary feelings about the spaces in which they work and may resent efforts to change those spaces. Reallocating limited technology resources often seems like robbing Peter to pay Paul. The demand for technology resources always seems to be greater than the supply.

The strongest reactions come when staff members are expected to change the way they do their daily work or when they are assigned to completely different duties. Virtually every staff member cares about his or her job and believes that it is important, and they almost all believe that their job performances are above average. This means it is likely that some staff will feel hurt and even betrayed when it appears their work is not valued by others. In addition, many staff do not believe their time will really be reallocated. They think that they will be expected to perform new activities to support the new priorities and that they will also be held responsible for completing all of their current activities. In many libraries this has been the practice in the past, and staff have little reason to believe that this reality will be different in the future.

This somewhat grim but very realistic picture of the implementation environment in most libraries is not intended to discourage you from moving forward with your implementation efforts. Rather, it is intended to remind you yet again about the importance of creating a library culture that understands and supports change. The work you do during Task 5 of this planning process to create a library culture that is positive about change and supportive of risk taking will be critical to the success of your implementation efforts. It will provide the foundation for the tasks and steps in *Implementing for Results*.

What's Next?

There is a lot of uncertainty about the future of public libraries right now, but there are really only two possibilities:

> Public libraries will evolve into the models of service envisioned in Library 2.0 or into an as yet unimagined Library 3.0 or 4.0.

> Public libraries will fade away as people find other, more convenient ways to obtain the services currently offered by libraries.

We don't know which statement describes our future, but we do know that public libraries cannot stay as they are today. We can't stop time, and we can't stop the world around us from evolving. Thomas Edison said: "Good fortune is what happens when opportunity meets with planning." If change is inevitable, perhaps it is time to look at the future as an opportunity and not as a threat. If you can do that, the plan you develop using *Strategic Planning for Results* and put into action using *Implementing for Results* will result in good fortune for you, your colleagues, and most important, the people in the community you serve.

Note

1. Sandra Nelson, *Implementing for Results: From Ideas to Action* (Chicago: American Library Association, forthcoming 2008).

Part Two

Public Library Service Responses

Introduction to the Service Responses

Service responses are the links between the community's needs, interests, and priorities and the programs and services a library offers. Specifically, *a service response is what a library does for, or offers to, the public in an effort to meet a set of well-defined community needs.* Service responses serve multiple purposes in a library strategic planning process.

> Service responses describe the primary service roles or priorities of public libraries.
>
> Service responses provide a common vocabulary that can be used by librarians, trustees, and community leaders to identify service priorities for specific libraries.
>
> Service responses identify possible policy implications that library managers will need to address if the service response is selected as a priority.
>
> Service responses define the resources (staff, collections, facilities, technology) required to support specific service priorities.
>
> Service responses provide suggested measures that can be used to evaluate services in priority areas.

A Brief History

Service responses have evolved over the years. The concept was first articulated by Lowell Martin, who believed that libraries needed to focus on providing a few services well rather than providing a lot of services poorly. Martin suggested that there were a series of standardized roles from which libraries might choose their priorities. Those roles provided the philosophical framework for the original public library roles in *Planning and Role-Setting for Public Libraries,* published in 1987.[1]

The advent of the Internet and the rapid changes in information technology in the 1990s raised questions about the applicability of the public library roles developed in the mid-1980s. In 1998, the publication *Planning for Results: A Public Library Transformation Process* included thirteen service responses, which were defined as *what a library does for, or offers to, the public in an effort to meet a set of well-defined community needs.*[2]

The pace of change continued to accelerate, and in 2006 the PLA initiated a process to review and revise the 1998 service responses. The process was designed to allow all interested librarians, library staff, and library trustees to participate, either in person or via the Web. The process started with three meetings held during the 2006 ALA Annual Conference in New Orleans to discuss the current service responses and to begin to identify possible new service responses. Those who were unable to attend one of the meetings in New Orleans were given an opportunity to participate in the revision process through the PLA blog. In mid-November, June Garcia and Sandra Nelson developed a list of proposed service responses that reflected all of the suggestions and comments that had been received. On January 4, 2007, drafts of the complete descriptions of eighteen proposed service responses were posted to the PLA blog for review and discussion. The drafts were presented at an open meeting during the 2007 Midwinter Conference in Seattle and were completed in mid-February 2007. The final service responses reflect the wide array of input received.

The Service Responses

The eighteen service responses are not intended to be a comprehensive list of every service or program offered in every public library in the country. They are, however, designed to describe the most common clusters of services and programs that libraries provide. As noted in the introduction to the 1998 service responses, "The service responses . . . are not intended to make libraries more alike. Quite the contrary, the descriptions and examples offered are provided to help library planners see the many possibilities that exist for matching their services to the unique needs of their communities. The service responses are a starting, not an ending, point."[3]

Each service response contains eight sections: the title, the description, suggested target audiences, typical services and programs in libraries that select this as a priority, potential partners, policy implications, critical resources, and possible measures. These sections are described in detail below.

Title

The title includes two phrases. The first phrase describes what the user receives, and the second describes what the library offers. The titles are intended to be descriptive and easily understood by both staff and community residents.

Description

This describes the benefits that the user receives because the library provides the service. It is written in terms that lay people can understand and is intended to help library planners make the connection between identified community needs and the library's service priorities.

Suggested Target Audiences

Target audiences are defined either by demographics (typically age) or by condition (student, business owner, new immigrant). If a service is designed to serve a single target audience, that audience has been defined in the title or description (for example, "Create Young Readers"). However, if a service can be delivered effectively to multiple target audiences (for example, "Stimulate Imagination"), then the title and description are age- and condition-neutral, and library planners are encouraged to identify target audiences during the goal-setting process.

The target audiences defined by age are *children, teens, adults,* and *seniors.* In those service responses in which adults are identified as a target audience and seniors are not, the term *adult* is intended to include everyone over the age of eighteen. In several service responses, the target audiences include both adults and seniors. In those instances, seniors have unique needs or interests which are different than the needs or interests of the younger adult population. The term *seniors* includes everyone over the age of sixty-two.

Typical Services and Programs in Libraries That Select This as a Priority

These are the kinds of services and programs that libraries *that select this as a priority* might provide. This list is illustrative, not prescriptive, and is intended to describe services that go well beyond the basic level of services that a library might provide to support services that are not priorities. It is designed to help planners visualize the effect of selecting the service response as a priority.

Potential Partners

Libraries have always collaborated with other community agencies and organizations to provide services, and that collaboration has become even more important in the past several years. This section lists some of the groups that the library might partner with if the library selects the service response.

Policy Implications

All service priorities have policy implications. This section includes a list of some of the policy issues that may need to be addressed if a library selects the service response. The list of policy implications is not intended to be all-inclusive. Each library is unique, and staff will have to assess all of the policy implications of a new priority based on local conditions.

Almost all of the policy issues identified in the eighteen proposed service responses have been addressed in the policy development templates included in *Creating Policies for Results: From Chaos to Clarity.*[4] The templates include a list of questions to consider when developing and revising policy statements.

Critical Resources

These are the types of resources that libraries that select the service response will need in order to provide the service effectively. Again, the lists are simply illustrative. In most cases, the suggested critical resources are directly linked to typical services and programs listed in the service response. Obviously, the specific resources required will be driven by the programs and services that the library chooses to offer in support of that service response. The required resources are divided into four categories:

Staff (Knowledge, Skills, and Abilities)

"*Knowledge* refers to the information and concepts acquired through formal education and job experience. . . . *Skills* are the manual and mental capabilities acquired through training and work experience, the application of knowledge gained through education or training and practical experience. . . . *Abilities* are the natural talents, capacities, and aptitudes possessed by employees."[5]

There is no mention of training in any of the staff resource sections. It is assumed that library managers will provide the training needed to ensure that staff have the knowledge and skills required to provide the programs and services that support the library's priorities.

Collection (Print, Media, and Electronic Resources)

This is a list of subject areas that support the service response. There is no discussion of the level of collection development in each subject area, but it is assumed that staff in libraries that select a service response as a priority will develop collections in these subject areas in much greater depth or breadth than would be the case in libraries in which the service response was not a priority.

There is also no discussion of the language of the materials provided, even in the service response that most directly serves people who speak languages other than English ("Welcome to the United States"). Libraries are expected to provide materials in the languages spoken by the people within the target audience or audiences of the selected service responses.

In some service responses, there are no format-specific recommendations, and the expectation is that staff will purchase materials in the formats most appropriate for their community. However, in other service responses the format in which materials are made available is an important factor, and specific formats have been recommended. For example, libraries that select "Stimulate Imagination" will have to provide visual, audio, print, and electronic materials to meet user expectations and demand.

Facility (Space, Furniture, and Equipment)

Space describes an area of the library building that has a common usage or purpose.[6] *Furniture and equipment* are the physical items within the structure.

This section does not include shelving, basic furnishings (tables, chairs, etc.), or basic equipment (copy machine, etc.) It is assumed that the library will provide shelving for all materials that support the service response and that the library has appropriate furnishings and equipment for general services. Most of the items identified in this section go beyond the minimum requirements for providing general service and are unique to the service response they support.

All library facilities should be in full compliance with the provisions of the Americans with Disabilities Act.

Technology (Hardware, Software, Networks, and Telecommunication)

Hardware includes computer workstations, servers, and other technologies such as scanners, self-check machines, and printers. *Software* includes desktop operating systems and unique programs that support the service responses (for example, literacy tutoring programs for "Learn to Read and Write"). A *network* is a group of interconnected computers. *Telecommunication* refers to the transmission of data.

It is assumed that libraries provide public access to the Internet and have sufficient bandwidth to manage the online services provided. It is also assumed that the library has an existing web page and that the web pages included under "Typical Services" can be added to that web page. Finally, it is assumed that the library technology is in full compliance with the provisions of the Americans with Disabilities Act.

Possible Measures

There are four methods that can be used to measure progress toward meeting the goals that are established to support the selected service response. This section includes sample measures for some or all of the four methods. The four methods are:

Number of Users

This includes the total number of people who used a service during a given time period or the number of unique individuals who use the service during a given time.

User Perceptions

This measures the user's opinion about how well the library's service(s) met his or her needs; this opinion could be about the quality of the service, the value of the service, the user's satisfaction with the service, or the impact of the service.

User Outcomes

This is also referred to as *outcome measurement* and is "a user-centered approach to the planning and assessment of programs or services that are provided to address particular user needs and designed to achieve change for the user."[7] Outcomes typically result in changes in knowledge, skill, attitude, behavior, or condition of the end user.

User outcomes are always expressed in both number of users and percentage of users. Outcome measures can only be used with programs planned "to meet the identified needs of a clearly defined group of end-users" (library customers).[8] Each of the suggested user outcomes starts with the phrase "Number and percent of specified users . . ."

Units of Service Delivered

This is the number of actual library service transactions that were done to make progress toward a specific goal. This includes all of the standard library outputs such as circulation, number of reference transactions, number of hits on the library web page, and so on.

Notes

1. Charles R. McClure and others, *Planning and Role-Setting for Public Libraries: A Manual of Options and Procedures* (Chicago: American Library Association, 1987).

2. Ethel Himmel and William James Wilson, *Planning for Results: A Public Library Transformation Process* (Chicago: American Library Association, 1998), 54.

3. Ibid.

4. Sandra Nelson and June Garcia, *Creating Policies for Results: From Chaos to Clarity* (Chicago: American Library Association, 2003).

5. Scott B. Parry, "The Quest for Competencies," *Training* 33, no. 7 (July 1996): 50. Quoted in Jeanne Goodrich and Paula Singer, *Human Resources for Results: The Right Person for the Right Job* (Chicago: American Library Association, 2007).

6. "LIBRIS Design Glossary," available at http://www.librisdesign.org/help/glossary.html.

7. Rhea Rubin, *Demonstrating Results: Using Outcome Measurement in Your Library* (Chicago: American Library Association, 2006), 3.

8. Ibid., 15.

Be an Informed Citizen
Local, National, and World Affairs

> Residents will have the information they need to support and promote democracy, to fulfill their civic responsibilities at the local, state, and national levels, and to fully participate in community decision making.

Suggested Target Audiences

- Adults
- Teens
- New voters

Typical Services and Programs in Libraries That Select This as a Priority

- Provide information on issues of public policy.
- Convene meetings to provide an opportunity for people to discuss community issues.
- Convene meetings to provide an opportunity for people to discuss national and international issues.
- Develop and maintain a web page with links to local, state, and federal information resources.
- Host regularly scheduled open discussions with elected officials (local, state, and federal) and make the discussions available as podcasts or downloadable digital videos.
- Provide paper and electronic copies of local information such as annual reports from city agencies, environmental reports, revised population estimates from the city planning office, and the minutes of city council meetings.
- Participate in blogs that focus on local issues.
- Present programs in partnership with local and national organizations that promote democracy and civic involvement.
- Operate a community TV station and broadcast community meetings.
- Provide tax forms and volunteer tax advisers.
- Register voters or provide voter registration forms.

Potential Partners

- AARP tax advisors
- Board of elections
- Chamber of commerce
- City council
- County commission
- League of Women Voters
- Other city or county departments

Policy Implications

Meeting Rooms

- Use of meeting rooms by outside groups
- Use of meeting rooms for partisan events
- Use of meeting rooms for issue-based programs
- Use of meeting rooms after library hours
- Meeting room fees

Programs in the Library

- Cosponsorship of programs

Web Page

- Criteria for linking to sites sponsored by advocacy groups

Critical Resources

Staff (Knowledge, Skills, and Abilities)

- Staff are knowledgeable about local government structures and elected and appointed officials.
- Staff are knowledgeable about issues of local concern.
- Staff are knowledgeable about resources that provide information about local, state, national, and international public policy issues.
- Staff can facilitate meetings.
- Staff can establish partnerships with local and national organizations that promote civic engagement.
- Staff can record podcasts or digital videocasts and make them available to download.

Collection (Print, Media, and Electronic Resources)

- Constitutional law
- Current events
- Environmental issues

- Globalization
- Grassroots organizing
- Local, state, and national government
- Municipal finance
- Political ideologies
- Political process
- Politics
- Public administration
- Public policy issues

Facility (Space, Furniture, and Equipment)

- Meeting space
- Equipment to record podcasts/videocasts

Technology (Hardware, Software, Networks, and Telecommunication)

- Public access computers, audio headsets, and printers

Possible Measures

Number of Users

- Number of people attending programs on topics related to local, national, and world affairs
- Percent of people who indicate on a survey that they use the library to become an informed citizen

User Perceptions

- Percent of users surveyed who respond that:

    The library's collection of materials on local, national, and world affairs is very good or excellent.
    The information assistance they receive from staff when looking for information or asking a reference question is very good or excellent.

User Outcomes

- Number and percent of specified participants who become more actively involved as citizens
- Number and percent of specified participants who gain a sense of community

Units of Service Delivered

- Circulation of materials in subject areas associated with local, national, and world affairs

- Number of programs offered on topics related to local, national, and world affairs
- Number of hits on the library's "Be an Informed Citizen" web page
- Number of podcasts/videocasts recorded and the number of times each was downloaded

Build Successful Enterprises
Business and Nonprofit Support

Business owners and nonprofit organization directors and their managers will have the resources they need to develop and maintain strong, viable organizations.

Suggested Target Audiences

- Business owners
- People who want to start businesses
- Entrepreneurs
- Managers in businesses
- Not-for-profit organization directors and staff
- Not-for-profit organization board members

Typical Services and Programs in Libraries That Select This as a Priority

- Develop and maintain a web page with links to resources for business.
- Develop and maintain a web page with links to resources for not-for-profit managers and board members.
- Sponsor or cosponsor workshops and seminars on topics of interest to businesses or not-for-profit organizations.
- Provide podcasts, videocasts, RSS feeds, or a wiki on business-related topics.
- Provide podcasts, videocasts, RSS feeds, or a wiki on topics of interest to not-for-profit staff and boards.
- Participate in blogs for small business owners and entrepreneurs.
- Establish and maintain a business center in the library.
- Establish and maintain a grants center in the library.
- Make presentations to local business organizations about the library's business-related services and programs.
- Provide paper and electronic copies of local ordinances that affect businesses, including zoning, local census projections, development plans, etc.
- Provide SCORE (Service Core of Retired Executives) volunteers to provide assistance to business and not-for-profit managers and board members.

Potential Partners

- Chamber of commerce
- Local community foundation
- Foundations (local, regional, state, and national)
- SCORE (Service Core of Retired Executives)
- Service organizations (Rotary, Kiwanis, Lions, etc.)
- Small business centers in local community colleges or universities

Policy Implications

Circulation

- Cards for nonresidents who own businesses
- Cards for business or nonprofit organizations

Community Presentations or Programs Offered at Nonlibrary Locations

- Classification of staff who can deliver presentations or programs
- Use of volunteers
- Process that agency or organization must follow to request a presentation or program
- Minimum or maximum number of anticipated attendees
- Number of times a presentation or program will be given to the same group during a specified period of time

Fees and Fines

- Fees for videoconferencing equipment
- Fees for using equipment in the business center or grants center

Meeting Rooms

- Use of meeting rooms by outside groups
- Use of meeting rooms for fee-based programs
- Use of meeting rooms after library hours
- Meeting room fees
- Sale of items during meetings

Programs in the Library

- Cosponsorship of programs
- Programs presented by for-profit organizations or individuals

Critical Resources

Staff (Knowledge, Skills, and Abilities)

- Staff are knowledgeable about print and electronic business resources.
- Staff are knowledgeable about business structures (sole-proprietor, partnership, LLC, etc.).
- Staff are knowledgeable about the requirements for establishing a new business or not-for-profit organization.
- Staff are knowledgeable about grant sources and grant-writing.
- Staff are knowledgeable about local ordinances that affect businesses.
- Staff can plan and make presentations to community groups.
- Staff can plan and present programs on a variety of business-related topics.
- Staff can work with community agencies to plan and present collaborative programs on business topics.
- Staff can manage a blog or develop a wiki.
- Staff can record podcasts/videocasts and make them available electronically.
- Staff can recruit and manage SCORE volunteers.
- Staff may have experience in managing a business or not-for-profit organization.

Collection (Print, Media, and Electronic Resources)

- Accounting
- Commerce
- Consulting
- Customer service
- Home-based businesses
- Human resources
- Local industry related
- Management
- Marketing
- Nonprofit organizations and charities
- Organization development
- Retailing
- Small business
- Technology issues for small business

Facilities (Space, Furniture, and Equipment)

- Meeting spaces (including spaces for small meetings)
- Space for a business center or grants center
- Equipment to record podcasts and videocasts
- Electrical outlets for personal computers

Technology (Hardware, Software, Networks, and Telecommunication)

- Computers configured to allow downloading of licensed digital content to personal storage devices (PDA, MP3 player, Flash drive, etc.)
- Publication software and color printer
- Videoconferencing capability
- High-speed color copiers
- Blog or wiki software

Possible Measures

Number of Users

- Number of people attending programs or presentations on topics related to business or nonprofit organizations and issues of interest to them
- Number of people attending programs presented by library staff for businesses or nonprofit groups

User Perceptions

- Percent of people who indicate on a survey that they use the library for purposes related to a business or a nonprofit organization
- Percent of users surveyed who respond that:

    The library's collection of materials related to business is very good or excellent.

    The information assistance they receive from staff when looking for information or asking a reference question is very good or excellent.

User Outcomes

- Number and percent of specified users who use library resources and services to start a new business
- Number and percent of specified users who use library resources and services to solve a business- or work-related problem
- Number and percent of specified users who use library resources and services to solve a problem in a nonprofit organization

Units of Service Delivered

- Circulation of materials in subject areas associated with business or nonprofit organizations

- Number of programs offered on topics related to business or nonprofit organizations
- Number of presentations made by library staff to business and nonprofit organizations
- Number of hits on the library's business and nonprofit support web page
- Number of hits on licensed databases purchased to support businesses and nonprofit organizations
- Number of podcasts recorded and the number of times each was downloaded
- Number of questions answered by staff in the business or grants center

Celebrate Diversity
Cultural Awareness

Residents will have programs and services that promote appreciation and understanding of their personal heritage and the heritage of others in the community.

Suggested Target Audiences

- Adults
- Teens
- Children

Typical Services and Programs in Libraries That Select This as a Priority

- Offer programs on various aspects of the cultural heritage of community residents (art, cooking, customs, dance, drama, history, holidays, literature, music, religion, etc.).
- Work with local agencies and organizations to cosponsor programs about their cultural heritage.
- Mount exhibits and displays that reflect the cultural heritage of the community residents.
- Develop and maintain a cultural diversity web page.
- Convene meetings to provide an opportunity for people from different cultures to learn about one another.
- Host cultural fairs.

Potential Partners

- Churches, mosques, and synagogues
- Ethnic groups and organizations
- Newspapers in languages other than English
- Public and private schools
- Social service agencies
- Student exchange programs

Policy Implications

Bulletin Boards

- Eligible organizations
- Criteria for materials
- Length of time materials will be posted

Distribution of Nonlibrary Materials

- Eligible organizations
- Criteria for materials
- Length of time materials will be distributed

Exhibits and Displays

- Criteria for inclusion of items in library exhibits and displays

Library Publications

- Languages in which library publications are printed

Meeting Rooms

- Use of meeting rooms by outside groups
- Use of meeting rooms after library hours
- Meeting room fees

Programs in the Library

- Cosponsorship of programs

Special Events

- Participation criteria

Staff Participation in Community Meetings and Events on Work Time

- Approval process

Web Page

- Criteria for linking to community agencies or organizations

Critical Resources

Staff (Knowledge, Skills, and Abilities)

- Staff are knowledgeable about the cultural heritage (customs, famous people, holidays, history, etc.) of racial and ethnic groups in the community.
- Staff are knowledgeable about the beliefs, traditions, and holidays of religious groups in the community.
- Staff are knowledgeable about the agencies and organizations that provide services to various ethnic, racial, and religious groups.
- Staff are knowledgeable about the ethnic, racial, and religious organizations in the community.
- Staff can establish partnerships with the ethnic, racial, and religious organizations in the community.
- Staff can establish partnerships with agencies and organizations that provide services to various ethnic, racial, and religious groups.
- Staff can plan and make presentations to community agencies and organizations.
- Staff can plan special events such as cultural fairs.
- Staff can plan and mount exhibits.
- Staff can record podcasts or digital videocasts and make them available to download.

Collection (Print, Media, and Electronic Resources)

- Art
- Biography
- Cooking
- Customs
- Dance
- Drama
- Fiction
- History
- Holidays
- Music
- Religion

Facilities (Space, Furniture, and Equipment)

- Meeting space
- Display shelving to merchandize selected portions of the collections
- Exhibit and display space

Technology (Hardware, Software, Networks, and Telecommunication)

- Computers configured to download licensed digital content to personal storage devices (PDA, MP3 player, Flash drive, etc.)
- Software to manage program registration and reminders

Possible Measures

Number of Users

- Number of people who indicate on a survey that they use the library to learn about their cultural heritage or the heritage of others
- Number of people who attend cultural events or fairs hosted by the library

Perceptions of Users

- Percent of users surveyed who respond that:

    The library's collection of materials related to cultural heritage and diversity is very good or excellent.

    The information assistance they receive from staff when looking for information or asking about cultural heritage or diversity is very good or excellent.

User Outcomes

- Number and percent of specified users who develop a deeper understanding of their own cultural heritage as a result of attending one or more library programs
- Number and percent of specified users who develop an understanding of the cultural heritage of others as a result of attending one or more library programs
- Number and percent of specified users who feel positive about living in a diverse community

Units of Service Delivered

- Circulation of adult nonfiction in targeted subject areas
- Number of programs and demonstrations presented
- Number of exhibits presented

Connect to the Online World
Public Internet Access

Residents will have high-speed access to the digital world with no unnecessary restrictions or fees to ensure that everyone can take advantage of the ever-growing resources and services available through the Internet.

Suggested Target Audiences

- Adults
- Teens
- Children

Typical Services and Programs in Libraries That Select This as a Priority

- Provide public access computers and printers.
- Provide high-speed access to the Internet.
- Provide wireless access to the Internet.

Policy Implications

Customer Service

- Level of assistance provided

Fees and Fines

- Fees for printing

Internet Use

- Filtering
- Confidentiality
- Time limits for use of public access computers
- Use of library computers to access e-mail, discussion groups, games, etc.
- Downloading to personal storage devices from public access computers

- Use of public access computers by people without library cards
- Use of wireless Internet access by people without library cards

Critical Resources

Staff (Knowledge, Skills, and Abilities)

- Staff are knowledgeable about navigating the Internet.
- Staff are knowledgeable about portable storage devices and the library policies that pertain to their use on public access computers.
- Staff can instruct people on how to log on to a computer and to the wireless network.
- Staff can keep Internet access and networks up and running.
- Staff can help people to set up and access e-mail accounts.
- Frontline staff can do basic hardware troubleshooting.
- Frontline staff can operate, add paper, and clear jams in public printers.
- Computer staff can maintain hardware, software, and the network.
- Staff can make people feel comfortable while using the library technology.

Collection (Print, Media, and Electronic Resources)

- Materials available for in-house use in the public computer area, including

    How to use Internet browsers
    How to use web search engines
    How to use Adobe Acrobat, Media Player, etc.
    How to use software programs available on the library's
        public access computers

Facilities (Space, Furniture, and Equipment)

- Electrical outlets that can be easily accessed for use with personal computers
- Workstations that are large enough for people to work comfortably
- Ergonomic workstations and chairs
- Good wire management
- Appropriate lighting

Technology (Hardware, Software, Networks, and Telecommunication)

- Adequate number of public access computers that are configured for speed and graphics
- Adequate number of printers
- Computers configured to allow downloading of licensed digital content to personal storage devices (PDA, MP3 player, Flash drive, etc.)
- Sufficient bandwidth to manage the Internet traffic
- Current software and operating systems on all public access computers

- PC reservation system
- Privacy screens on all public access computers
- Wireless network

Possible Measures

Number of Users

- Number of people who use library-provided computers to access the Internet
- Number of hits on library portal web pages
- Number of people who use the wireless connectivity provided by the library

Perceptions of Users

- Percent of people who indicate on a survey that they use the library to access the Internet
- Percent of users surveyed who respond that:

    The assistance they receive from staff when using the Internet is very good or excellent.
    The library's Internet service is very good or excellent.

User Outcomes

- Number and percent of specified users who increase their computer/technology skills
- Number and percent of specified users who access e-mail for personal, school, or work purposes
- Number and percent of specified users who use the Internet for personal, school, or work purposes

Units of Service Delivered

- Percent of time the public access terminals are in use
- Average wait time to use a public access Internet terminal

Create Young Readers
Early Literacy

> Children from birth to age five will have programs and services designed to ensure that they will enter school ready to learn to read, write, and listen.

Suggested Target Audiences

- Children from birth to five
- Parents, caregivers, and service providers who work with children ages newborn to five

Typical Services and Programs in Libraries That Select This as a Priority

- Present regularly scheduled story programs divided by age of intended audience.
- Include interactive components such as singing, puppets, etc., in story programs.
- Present story programs in off-site locations such as day care centers, parks, hospitals, etc.
- Sponsor a "Born to Read" program.
- Participate in Dolly Parton's "Imagination Library" program (http://www.imaginationlibrary.com).
- Include a "Read to Me" component in the summer reading program, and other reading programs, with incentives for parents/caregivers and the children.
- Plan and present puppet shows.
- Develop theme packets that include books, tapes, toys, software, and games for parents and caregivers to use with their children.
- Provide "Books-to-Go" bags, each with a collection of related materials (concept books, bilingual reading kits, picture books about animals, etc.).
- Participate in blogs for new parents.
- Provide computers with appropriate programs for preschool children.
- Provide access to online e-books for preschool children.
- Provide classes, such as those outlined in Every Child Ready to Read @ your library, on early literacy for parents and caregivers.
- Produce podcasts or videocasts on early literacy for parents and caregivers.

Potential Partners

- Community colleges that offer courses for preschool providers
- Day care providers
- Head Start operators
- Hospitals
- New parent groups
- Pediatricians
- Social service agencies

Policy Implications

Circulation

- Age at which someone can get a library card
- Circulation limits by media type
- Institutional cards

Community Presentations or Programs Offered at Nonlibrary Locations

- Classification of staff who can deliver presentations or programs
- Use of volunteers
- Process that agency or organization must follow to request a presentation or program
- Minimum or maximum number of anticipated attendees
- Number of times a presentation or program will be given to the same group during a specified period of time

Critical Resources

Staff (Knowledge, Skills, and Abilities)

- Staff are knowledgeable about early childhood development.
- Staff are knowledgeable about early literacy.
- Staff are knowledgeable about materials for preschool children.
- Staff can design and deliver effective programs for preschool children.
- Staff can teach parents and caregivers the skills needed to support early literacy.
- Staff can develop or assist in the development of a website appropriate for preschool children.
- Staff can establish partnerships with parents, child care providers, and others who serve children ages birth to five.
- Staff can record podcasts or digital videocasts and make them available to download.

Collection (Print, Media, and Electronic Resources)

- Board books
- Book/media kits
- Books and media on early literacy for parents and caregivers

- Concept books
- DVDs and CDs
- E-books for children
- Educational software to encourage vocabulary development and motor skills
- I-Can-Read books
- Picture books

Facilities (Space, Furniture, and Equipment)

- Dedicated area for children ages newborn to five that is comfortable, safe, and appropriate for this age group as well as the adults with them
- Dedicated space for family use
- Space to provide preschool programs
- Family restrooms
- Family computer areas that support shared use of digital resources
- Appropriate shelving for preschool materials
- Child-friendly furniture and computer desks
- Listening and viewing stations
- Appropriate seating at computer workstations to encourage adults and young children to use the computer programs together

Technology (Hardware, Software, Networks, and Telecommunication)

- Child-friendly computers

Possible Measures

Number of Users

- Number and percent of preschoolers in the community who have a library card
- Number of preschoolers attending programs in the library
- Number of preschoolers attending programs at nonlibrary locations
- Number of preschool children participating in the "Read to Me" program
- Number of parents and caregivers trained in early literacy techniques
- Percent of people who indicate on a survey that they use the library on behalf of their preschool child or children.

Perceptions of Users

- Percent of parents and caregivers surveyed who respond that:

  The library plays an important role in helping children to develop a love of books, reading, and learning.

  The library plays an important role in helping children enter school ready to learn to read, write, and listen.

  The library's services for preschoolers are very good or excellent.

User Outcomes

- Number and percent of parents and caregivers who read to their children at least twice as often than they had before attending library training programs
- Number and percent of parents and caregivers who bring their preschool children to the library at least twice as often as they had before attending library training programs
- Number and percent of specified parents and caregivers who foster a love of reading in their children

Units of Service Delivered

- Number of presentations made by library staff at preschools, day care centers, etc.
- Circulation of materials for preschool children (see "Collection" above)
- Number of deposit collections circulated to preschools, day care centers, hospitals, etc.
- Number of preschool programs presented in the library
- Number of preschool programs presented in nonlibrary locations
- Number of hits on the library's early literacy web page
- Number of hits on the library's website designed for preschool children

Discover Your Roots
Genealogy and Local History

> Residents and visitors will have the resources they need to connect the past with the present through their family histories and to understand the history and traditions of the community.

Suggested Target Audiences

- Seniors in the community
- Seniors visiting the community
- Adults interested in local history or genealogy
- Students studying local history

Typical Services and Programs in Libraries That Select This as a Priority

- Provide access to online genealogical resources.
- Develop and maintain a web page with links to sites of interest to genealogists and people interested in local history.
- Plan and present classes on how to do genealogical research.
- Provide one-on-one genealogical tutoring.
- Index local newspapers.
- Collect and make available local family histories and genealogical records.
- Record, collect, and make available oral histories from local residents.
- Digitize and index local photographs and documents.
- Collect all books written about the community.
- Collaborate with local organizations to mount rotating exhibits on the history and traditions of the community.
- Present programs about various aspects of the community (local architecture, neighborhoods, etc.).
- Store local records and artifacts in temperature- and humidity-controlled space.

Potential Partners

- Archives (local and state)
- Chamber of commerce

- Clubs and organizations
- Daughters of American Revolution
- Historical societies (local and state)
- Museums
- Newspaper(s)
- Professional genealogists
- State library agency

Policy Implications

Fees and Fines

- Fees for providing one-on-one genealogical tutoring or research

Information Services

- Time limits on use of machines to read, print, and copy all formats in which local history and genealogical information is supplied
- Level of local history and genealogical reference assistance provided on-site
- Level of local history and genealogical reference assistance provided via e-mail and phone
- Interlibrary loan of local history and genealogical materials
- Restrictions on access to items in the local history collection

Critical Resources

Staff (Knowledge, Skills, and Abilities)

- Staff are knowledgeable about print and electronic genealogical resources.
- Staff are knowledgeable about print and electronic local history resources.
- Staff are knowledgeable about basic archival and preservation practices.
- Staff are knowledgeable about digitization methods and techniques.
- Staff are knowledgeable about adult education and training design.
- Staff are knowledgeable about American studies, museum studies, or folklore.
- Staff can design effective training materials.
- Staff can teach people in class settings and provide one-on-one tutoring.
- Staff are skilled at doing genealogical research.
- Staff are skilled at collecting oral histories.
- Staff are skilled at organizing local records, photographs, and ephemeral materials.
- Staff are familiar with local school curriculum requirements related to local history.

Collection (Print, Media, and Electronic Resources)

- Artifacts
- Biographies of local people
- Cemetery records
- Census data

- Local records
- Family histories
- Full run of local newspapers
- Local history materials
- Local maps, past and current
- Military records
- Old city directories and phone books
- Online genealogical databases
- Oral histories
- Organizational records
- Photographs
- Research guides
- Vernacular architecture

Facilities (Space, Furniture, and Equipment)

- Equipment required to read, print, and copy all formats in which the information is supplied, including microfilm and microform
- Shelving and storage appropriate for all formats in which the information is supplied
- Exhibit and display space
- Ample work space at tables and workstations
- Ergonomic workstations and chairs
- Exhibit and display furniture and equipment
- Conveniently located copy machines
- Electrical outlets for personal computers
- Temperature- and humidity-controlled storage
- Secure storage for irreplaceable items in collection

Technology (Hardware, Software, Networks, and Telecommunication)

- Computers configured to allow downloading of licensed digital content to personal storage devices (PDA, MP3 player, Flash drive, etc.)
- Digital asset management software

Possible Measures

Number of Users

- Number of people attending genealogy or local history classes and programs
- Number of people who receive one-on-one genealogical tutoring
- Percent of people who indicate on a survey that they use the library for genealogy or local history information and services

Perceptions of Users

- Percent of users surveyed who respond that:

    The library's collection of materials on genealogy and local history is very good or excellent.

    The information assistance they receive from staff when looking for information or asking a reference question on local history or genealogy is very good or excellent.

    The library programs increase their understanding and appreciation of community traditions.

User Outcomes

- Number and percent of specified users who learn to access genealogical databases
- Number and percent of specified users who make progress creating a family history
- Number and percent of specified users who find a "lost" relative

Units of Service Delivered

- In-house circulation of genealogy and local history materials
- Number of genealogy or local history reference questions
- Number of classes presented on how to do genealogical research
- Number of rotating exhibits on history and traditions of the community that are developed
- Number of genealogy and local history programs presented
- Number of hits on the library's genealogy and local history web page
- Number of hits on genealogy and local history databases

Express Creativity
Create and Share Content

Residents will have the services and support they need to express themselves by creating original print, video, audio, or visual content in a real-world or online environment.

Suggested Target Audiences

- Children
- Teens
- Adults

Typical Services and Programs in Libraries That Select This as a Priority

- Provide a multimedia production studio with the tools needed to create animated and live-action videos, record music and audio, etc.
- Provide hands-on classes to teach people to use a variety of media production tools.
- Sponsor writers' workshops and publish the results.
- Present concerts, plays, and other performing arts.
- Provide access to blogging software for users to create their own blogs.
- Host one or more library blogs to encourage users to discuss library-related issues.
- Create one or more library wikis to encourage users to create library-related content.
- Publish an e-zine with user-created content.
- Support collaborative cataloging efforts to expand the descriptions of items.
- Allow users to attach reviews to title records in the library database (as with Amazon.com) or find some other way to make user-contributed book reviews easily accessible.
- Provide media production software programs for public use.

Potential Partners

- Arts organizations
- Community colleges, technical schools, vocational schools, and universities
- Galleries

- Humanities Council
- Museums
- Newspapers
- Performing arts centers
- Public and private schools
- Senior centers
- Teen centers
- Theater groups
- Writers' workshops

Policy Implications

Exhibits and Displays

- Criteria for inclusion of items in library exhibits and displays

Fees and Fines

- Fees for the use of media production equipment

Intellectual Property Rights

- Copyright
- Fair use

Library Publications

- Editorial policy for writers' workshop publications and e-zines

Meeting Rooms

- Use of meeting rooms by outside groups
- Use of meeting rooms for fee-based programs
- Use of meeting rooms after library hours
- Meeting room fees
- Sale of items during meetings

Use of Media Production Equipment

- Age or other restrictions for use of media production equipment

Critical Resources

Staff (Knowledge, Skills, and Abilities)

- Staff are knowledgeable about all of the production equipment.
- Staff are knowledgeable about media production software.

- Staff are knowledgeable about training design and can design effective training materials.
- Staff are knowledgeable about copyright and fair use.
- Staff can teach groups in class settings and provide one-on-one tutoring.
- Staff can teach others to use the production equipment.
- Staff can mount exhibits and displays.
- Staff can create and maintain blogs and wikis.
- Staff can work with groups of children, teens, or adults to coordinate content development.

Collection (Print, Media, and Electronic Resources)

- How-to materials to support the production of content (computer animation, poetry writing, etc.)

Facilities (Space, Furniture, and Equipment)

- Media production space
- Media production equipment
- Meeting space
- Exhibit and display space
- Music practice rooms
- Performance space

Technology (Hardware, Software, Networks, and Telecommunication)

- Computers configured to support all types of media production
- Computers configured to allow downloading of licensed digital content to personal storage devices (PDA, MP3 player, Flash drive, etc.)

Possible Measures

Number of Users

- Number of people attending a training session on the use of technologies that can be used to create and share content
- Number of people who use library-provided equipment or technology to create content
- Number of people who create and share content with other library users
- Percent of people who indicate on a survey that they used the library to create and share content
- Number of people who attend a performance at the library

Perceptions of Users

- Percent of users surveyed who respond that:

    The library-provided equipment or technology is very good or excellent.
    The information assistance they receive from staff when creating or sharing content is very good or excellent.

User Outcomes

- Number and percent of specified users who use library resources and services to create new media
- Number and percent of specified users who produce pieces for the library e-zine
- Number and percent of specified users who contribute to wikis or blogs

Units of Service Delivered

- Number of issues of e-zine published
- Number of hands-on training programs presented
- Number of production workshops presented
- Number of performances offered

Get Facts Fast
Ready Reference

Residents will have someone to answer their questions on a wide array of topics of personal interest.

Suggested Target Audiences

- Adults
- Teens
- Children

Typical Services and Programs in Libraries That Select This as a Priority

- Provide a dedicated telephone reference center to triage all reference calls.
- Provide 24/7 chat-based reference services.
- Provide answers to questions submitted by e-mail and text messaging.
- Develop and maintain a virtual reference library with links to online resources that provide quick answers to common questions.

Potential Partners

- Other libraries

Policy Implications

Information Services

- Limits on the type and quantity of reference services provided
- Limits on subject areas in which questions will be answered
- Classification of staff who can provide reference service

Critical Resources

Staff (Knowledge, Skills, and Abilities)

- Staff are knowledgeable about print and electronic reference resources.
- Staff are knowledgeable about search strategies for print and electronic resources.
- Staff can conduct effective reference interviews.
- Staff can find needed information quickly using print and electronic information resources.

Collection (Print, Media, and Electronic Resources)

- Almanacs
- Consumer guides
- Dictionaries
- Directories
- Encyclopedia
- Etiquette
- Price guides
- Quotations
- Thesaurus
- Trivia

Facilities (Space, Furniture, and Equipment)

- Space for a telephone reference center
- Tables for users of print reference resources
- Adequate telephone lines

Technology (Hardware, Software, Networks, and Telecommunication)

- Telephone call queuing software
- Chat software
- Text messaging software

Possible Measures

Number of Users

- Number of people who indicate on a survey that they use the library to get fast facts

Perceptions of Users

- Percent of users surveyed who respond that:

  Ready reference service is provided in a timely manner.
  The information assistance they receive from staff is very good or excellent.

User Outcomes

- Number and percent of specified users who use the information obtained for a specified personal, school, or work purpose

Units of Service Delivered

- Number of ready reference questions answered on-site
- Number of e-mail reference questions answered
- Number of text message reference questions answered
- Number of questions answered by the 24/7 chat reference provider
- Number of hits on the library's fast facts web page

Know Your Community
Community Resources and Services

Residents will have a central source for information about the wide variety of programs, services, and activities provided by community agencies and organizations.

Suggested Target Audiences

- Seniors
- Adults
- Teens
- New residents

Typical Services and Programs in Libraries That Select This as a Priority

- Maintain an online community calendar.
- Maintain a community events bulletin board and distribute publications from community organizations.
- Develop and maintain a searchable community information database.
- Develop and maintain a web page with links to agencies and organizations.
- Host and maintain web pages for local organizations and agencies.
- Support e-government use.
- Host a community information blog.
- Serve as the local 2-1-1 provider.
- Make presentations in the community about the library's community information services.
- Participate on community task forces and committees involved in human services planning for the community.
- Participate in local blogs.
- Maintain a wish list of items needed by not-for-profit agencies for their clients or their offices.
- Maintain a wish list of volunteers needed by not-for-profit agencies for their clients or their offices.
- Develop and maintain an information packet for new community residents.

Potential Partners

- City or county departments
- Chamber of commerce
- Clubs and organizations
- Newcomers association
- Not-for-profit agencies
- Red Cross
- Social service agencies
- Service organizations (Rotary, Kiwanis, Lions, etc.)
- United Way

Policy Implications

Bulletin Boards

- Eligible organizations
- Criteria for materials
- Length of time materials will be posted

Community Presentations or Programs Offered at Nonlibrary Locations

- Classification of staff who can deliver presentations or programs
- Use of volunteers
- Process that agency or organization must follow to request a presentation or program
- Minimum or maximum number of anticipated attendees
- Number of times a presentation or program will be given to the same group during a specified period of time

Distribution of Nonlibrary Materials

- Eligible organizations
- Criteria for materials
- Length of time materials will be distributed

Staff Participation in Community Meetings and Events on Work Time

- Approval process

Critical Resources

Staff (Knowledge, Skills, and Abilities)

- Staff are knowledgeable about community agencies and organizations.
- Staff can establish and maintain a searchable community information database.
- Staff can make presentations in the community.
- Staff can develop and maintain relationships with representatives of community agencies and organizations.
- Staff can help users to identify the community agencies and organizations that can address the user's needs.

Collection (Print, Media, and Electronic Resources)

- Community information database
- Handbooks, guides, brochures, and pamphlets from local agencies and organizations

Facilities (Space, Furniture, and Equipment)

- Community events bulletin board in easily accessible site
- Information rack for free materials made available for distribution by local agencies and organizations

Technology (Hardware, Software, Networks, and Telecommunication)

- Database or content management software

Possible Measures

Number of Users

- Percent of people who indicate on a survey that they use the library to obtain information about the programs, services, and activities provided by community agencies and organizations

Perceptions of Users

- Percent of users surveyed who respond that:

    The information provided by the library about community resources and services is very good or excellent.

    The information assistance they receive from staff is very good or excellent.

User Outcomes

- Number and percent of specified users who contact an organization or agency they learned about at the library for assistance
- Number and percent of specified users who use the services of a community organization or agency new to them.

Units of Service Delivered

- Number of reference questions answered about the programs, services, and activities provided by community agencies and organizations
- Number of hits on the library's community resources and services web page
- Number of presentations made by library staff describing community information services
- Number of information packets distributed to new residents

Learn to Read and Write
Adult, Teen, and Family Literacy

Adults and teens will have the support they need to improve their literacy skills in order to meet their personal goals and fulfill their responsibilities as parents, citizens, and workers.

Suggested Target Audiences

- Adults
- Teens

Typical Services and Programs in Libraries That Select This as a Priority

- Provide self-guided programs that use books and media to help adults and teens reach their personal literacy goals.
- Provide self-guided programs that use books and media to help adults and teens with limited English skills become proficient in English.
- Provide private space for tutors to work one-on-one with literacy students.
- Recruit, train, and schedule tutors to work one-on-one with literacy students.
- Provide literacy classes.
- Provide small-group literacy training.
- Provide free children's books to parents enrolled in adult or family literacy classes.
- Provide programs to tutor learners preparing to take the GED test.
- Establish a literacy helpline and provide referral services for persons looking for literacy services.
- Provide deposit collections of materials for new readers to organizations that tutor literacy students.
- Collaborate with all organizations that provide literacy services in the community or county in order to promote and publicize literacy services.

Potential Partners

- Adult Education Department of the school district
- Churches, mosques, and synagogues
- Community colleges

- Literacy council
- Literacy Volunteers of America
- Private literacy providers
- United Way

Policy Implications

Community Presentations or Programs Offered at Nonlibrary Locations

- Classification of staff who can deliver presentations or programs
- Use of volunteers
- Process that agency or organization must follow to request a presentation or program
- Minimum or maximum number of anticipated attendees
- Number of times a presentation or program will be given to the same group during a specified period of time

Gifts and Donations

- Restrictions on donations of cash, equipment, materials, etc.

Information Services

- Time limits on use of literacy computers

Meeting Room

- Scheduling events that occur frequently on a regular basis
- Fees for meeting room use

Programs in the Library

- Cosponsorship of programs and services

Volunteers

- Screening procedures
- Qualifications for literacy volunteers

Critical Resources

Staff (Knowledge, Skills, and Abilities)

- Staff are knowledgeable about adult, teen, and family literacy issues.
- Staff are knowledgeable about unique needs of literacy students.
- Staff are knowledgeable about adult education and training design.

- Staff are trained literacy providers.
- Staff can establish partnerships with literacy providers.
- Staff can recruit and train literacy tutors.
- Staff can teach in both one-on-one and classroom environments.

Collection (Print, Media, and Electronic Resources)

- Basic life skills
- GED preparation guides
- High interest/low vocabulary materials for teens
- Materials for new adult readers
- Parenting skills
- Reading and writing skills enhancement

Facilities (Space, Furniture, and Equipment)

- Small study rooms for tutoring

Technology (Hardware, Software, Networks, and Telecommunication)

- Computer-assisted instructional self-guided literacy tutorials
- Dedicated literacy computers with sound cards and audio headsets

Possible Measures

Number of Users

- Number of people who attend tutoring sessions
- Number of people enrolled in a literacy class
- Number of people who use computer-based literacy programs
- Number of people who indicate on a survey that they use the library to improve their literacy skills

Perceptions of Users

- Percent of users surveyed who respond that:

    The library literacy programs are very good or excellent.
    They have been assigned a tutor or placed in a class in a timely manner.

User Outcomes

- Number and percent of specified literacy students who improve their reading level by at least one step
- Number and percent of specified literacy students who take the GED preparation test and pass the GED test

- Number and percent of specified literacy students who met a personal literacy goal
- Number and percent of specified literacy students who read to their children a specific amount of time or frequency
- Number and percent of specified literacy students who get a new job or a job promotion

Units of Service Delivered

- Number of volunteer literacy tutors
- Number of literacy volunteer hours
- Number of tutoring sessions held
- Number of deposit collections distributed
- Circulation of literacy-related or adult basic education materials
- Turnover rate of literacy-related or adult basic education materials

Make Career Choices
Job and Career Development

Adults and teens will have the skills and resources they need to identify career opportunities that suit their individual strengths and interests.

Suggested Target Audiences

- Adults who need a job or want to change jobs
- Teens who are making college or vocational school choices
- Teens who are making career decisions

Typical Services and Programs in Libraries That Select This as a Priority

- Provide a job and career center to offer one-stop shopping for job hunters.
- Develop and maintain a job and career web page that includes links to listings of available jobs, training centers, and local employer information.
- Provide a mobile job and career center to help job seekers locate employment by providing on-site assistance in housing projects, parks, schools, etc.
- Provide one-on-one assistance to help job seekers develop resumes, conduct job searches, and prepare for interviews.
- Present regularly scheduled programs on topics of interest to job seekers, including information about local employers, job search skills, etc.
- Provide regularly scheduled programs designed to help people use the Internet to find jobs.
- Provide self-guided programs to help students prepare to take the SAT or ACT test.
- Host a job fair.
- Host a college fair.
- Cosponsor programs to tutor learners preparing to take the SAT or ACT test.
- Cosponsor programs and services with local employment organizations.
- Cosponsor programs with high school counselors to help students understand their career choices.

Potential Partners

- Chamber of commerce
- Community colleges, technical schools, vocational schools, and universities
- High school guidance counselors
- Service organizations (Rotary, Kiwanis, Lions, etc.)
- Teen centers

Policy Implications

Web Page

- Criteria for jobs to be listed on the job and career web page

Critical Resources

Staff (Knowledge, Skills, and Abilities)

- Staff are knowledgeable about print and electronic sources of information about jobs and career development.
- Staff are knowledgeable about print and electronic career resources pertaining to career counseling and assessment testing.
- Staff can assist people one-on-one to develop resumes, conduct job searches, and prepare for interviews.
- Staff can plan and present programs on a variety of job and career topics.
- Staff can work with community agencies to plan and present collaborative programs on job and career options.

Collection (Print, Media, and Electronic Resources)

- Armed Forces study guide
- Careers
- Civil Service study guide
- College guides
- Financial aid for college or vocational schools
- Interviewing
- Job hunting
- Occupational outlook information
- Resumes
- SAT test and ACT test study guides
- Vocational study guides

Facilities (Space, Furniture, and Equipment)

- Dedicated space for a job and career center
- Private spaces for volunteers to meet with job seekers
- Meeting space for programs

Technology (Hardware, Software, Networks, and Telecommunication)

- Computers configured to allow downloading of licensed digital content to personal storage devices (PDA, MP3 player, Flash drive, etc.)
- Resume-writing software
- Office software
- Computers configured to support uploading resumes and applications to web job sites

Possible Measures

Number of Users

- Number of people who attend a job or career development program
- Number of people who indicate on a survey that they use the library for job or career development reasons
- Number of people who use the mobile job and career center

Perceptions of Users

- Percent of users surveyed who respond that:

   The library's collection of job and career development resources is very good or excellent.

   The information assistance they receive when looking for information or asking a job or career development question is very good or excellent.

   The information assistance they receive when looking for information about college or vocational schools is very good or excellent.

User Outcomes

- Number and percent of specified users who find a new job after using the library's resources and services
- Number and percent of specified users who use the library's resources and services to develop career-related skills
- Number and percent of specified users who get a promotion after using the library's resources and services
- Number and percent of specified users who pass a job-related exam

Units of Service Delivered

- Circulation of job and career development materials
- Number of job and career development reference questions answered
- Number of job or career development programs presented
- Number of hits on the library's job and career development web page

Make Informed Decisions
Health, Wealth, and Other Life Choices

Residents will have the resources they need to identify and analyze risks, benefits, and alternatives before making decisions that affect their lives.

Suggested Target Audiences

- Seniors
- Adults
- Teens

Typical Services and Programs in Libraries That Select This as a Priority

- Develop and maintain web pages that provide information to help make life decisions.
- Create electronic pathfinders or wikis to help users find resources to help make informed life decisions.
- Create displays of information resources that could be used to make life decisions.
- Present a series of programs on topics of interest to people making life decisions.
- Make presentations to community organizations about library resources that help people make informed decisions.
- Create or provide access to electronic programs that help users to assess risks, benefits, and alternatives when making life decisions.

Potential Partners

- AARP
- County extension service
- Financial planners
- Fitness centers
- Health department
- Hospitals
- Parks and recreation department
- Senior centers
- Service organizations (Rotary, Kiwanis, Lions, etc.)

- Social service agencies
- Teen centers
- YMCA/YWCA

Policy Implications

Community Presentations or Programs Offered at Nonlibrary Locations

- Classification of staff who can deliver presentations or programs
- Use of volunteers
- Process that agency or organization must follow to request a presentation or program
- Minimum or maximum number of anticipated attendees
- Number of times a presentation or program will be given to the same group during a specified period of time

Meeting Rooms

- Use of meeting rooms by outside groups
- Use of meeting rooms for product- or service-based programs
- Use of meeting rooms after library hours
- Selling items in library meeting rooms
- Meeting room fees

Programs in the Library

- Cosponsorship of programs

Web Page

- Criteria for linking to products and services

Critical Resources

Staff (Knowledge, Skills, and Abilities)

- Staff is knowledgeable about print and electronic resources.
- Staff can create electronic pathfinders or wikis.
- Staff can plan and present programs on a variety of life choice topics.
- Staff can plan and make presentations to community groups.
- Staff can plan and mount exhibits.

Collection (Print, Media, and Electronic Resources)

- Diets
- Diseases
- Drug and alcohol treatment

- Exercise
- Health and fitness
- Health care issues
- Insurance
- Investing
- Marriage/divorce guides
- Mental health issues
- Money management
- Personal finance
- Pregnancy and child care
- Retirement
- Retirement planning
- Sexuality

Facilities (Space, Furniture, and Equipment)

- Meeting space
- Display shelving to merchandize selected portions of the collections

Technology (Hardware, Software, Networks, and Telecommunication)

- Computers configured to allow downloading of licensed digital content to personal storage devices (PDA, MP3 player, Flash drive, etc.)
- Software to manage program registration and reminders

Possible Measures

Number of Users

- Number of people who attend a library program on a life choice topic
- Percent of people who indicate on a survey that they use the library to help them make an informed decision

Perceptions of Users

- Percent of users surveyed who respond that:

    The library's collection of materials related to health, wealth, and other life choices is very good or excellent.

    The information assistance they receive when looking for information or asking about a life choice issue is very good or excellent.

User Outcomes

- Number and percent of specified users who make an informed retirement decision

- Number and percent of specified users who make an informed investment decision
- Number and percent of specified users who make an informed health care decision

Units of Service Delivered

- Circulation of health-related materials
- Circulation of wealth-related materials
- Circulation of materials on designated life choice topics
- Number of life choice programs presented
- Number of hits on the library's "Make Informed Choices" web page

Satisfy Curiosity
Lifelong Learning

Residents will have the resources they need to explore topics of personal interest and continue to learn throughout their lives.

Suggested Target Audiences

- Seniors
- Adults
- Teens
- Children

Typical Services and Programs in Libraries That Select This as a Priority

- Provide programs on a variety of topics of interest to various age groups in the community (cooking, quilting, Civil War, travel, animation, dinosaurs, etc.).
- Work with local organizations to cosponsor demonstrations on topics of interest to various age groups.
- Display items created by local residents or items from personal collections.
- Mount rotating exhibits from museums and organizations such as local museums, National Endowment for the Humanities, Library of Congress, National Aeronautics and Space Administration, etc.
- Provide access to adult education courses through distance learning or video-on-demand.
- Develop and maintain a "Satisfy Your Curiosity" web page with links to topics of interest to various age groups in the community.
- Sponsor "Let's Talk about It" programs.
- Collaborate with the local Humanities Council to present programs.
- Create and support wikis or blogs in areas of special interest to local residents.
- Develop electronic pathfinders to help people find information on topics of interest to them.

Potential Partners

- Clubs and organizations
- Community colleges and universities
- County extension service
- Humanities Council
- Library of Congress
- Museums
- National Aeronautics and Space Administration
- National Endowment for the Humanities
- Parks and recreation department
- Senior centers
- Teen centers

Policy Implications

Circulation

- Circulation limits by subject

Exhibits and Displays

- Criteria for inclusion of items in library displays

Gifts and Donations

- Restrictions on donations of cash, equipment, materials, etc.

Programs in the Library

- Cosponsorship of programs

Critical Resources

Staff (Knowledge, Skills, and Abilities)

- Staff is knowledgeable about print and electronic resources.
- Staff can create electronic pathfinders.
- Staff can plan and present programs on a variety of lifelong learning topics.
- Staff can plan and make presentations to community groups.
- Staff can manage a blog and wikis.
- Staff can plan and mount exhibits.

Collection (Print, Media, and Electronic Resources)

- Antiques and collectibles
- Architecture

- Art
- Biography and autobiography
- Computers
- Cooking
- Crafts and hobbies
- Games
- Gardening
- History
- House and home
- Music
- Nature
- Performing arts
- Pets
- Philosophy
- Photography
- Psychology
- Religion
- Science
- Self-help
- Social science
- Sports and recreation
- Technology
- Transportation
- True crime

Facilities (Space, Furniture, and Equipment)

- Small-group meeting rooms
- Display shelving to merchandize selected portions of the collections
- Secure display space for rotating collections
- Comfortable seating

Technology (Hardware, Software, Networks, and Telecommunication)

- Computers configured to allow downloading of licensed digital content to personal storage devices (PDA, MP3 player, Flash drive, etc.)
- Blog and wiki software
- Software to manage program registration and reminders

Possible Measures

Number of Users

- Number of people who indicate on a survey that they use the library for lifelong learning

Perceptions of Users

- Percent of users surveyed who respond that:

    The library's collection of materials for lifelong interest purposes is very good or excellent.

    The information assistance they receive when looking for information or asking about a topic of personal interest is very good or excellent.

User Outcomes

- Number and percent of specified users who learn a new skill as a result of attending one or more library programs
- Number and percent of specified users who meet a personal learning goal
- Number and percent of specified users who learn about a topic of personal interest

Units of Service Delivered

- Circulation of adult nonfiction
- Circulation of adult nonfiction in targeted subject areas
- Number of programs and demonstrations presented
- Number of exhibits presented

Stimulate Imagination
Reading, Viewing, and Listening for Pleasure

> Residents who want materials to enhance their leisure time will find what they want when and where they want them and will have the help they need to make choices from among the options.

Suggested Target Audiences

- Adults
- Teens
- Children

Typical Services and Programs in Libraries That Select This as a Priority

- Provide readers' advisory services to assist users to locate materials of interest.
- Display new materials in a prominent location.
- Allow users to place holds on materials online.
- Mail items on hold to users when they become available.
- Provide an online reading club.
- Provide listening and viewing stations to allow users to preview materials.
- Present a summer reading program for children.
- Present a teen reading program in the summer.
- Present several adult reading programs throughout the year.
- Coordinate a "One Book, One City" program.
- Ensure that users receive reserved items within thirty days of placing the hold.
- Host gaming tournaments.
- Develop and maintain a readers' advisory web page.
- Make user-contributed book reviews easily accessible.
- Provide downloadable books, music, and videos for circulation.
- Present programs on new books and particular genres and sponsor author visits.

Potential Partners

- Authors (local, regional, state, and national)
- Book clubs

- Book stores
- Comic book and gaming stores
- Gaming groups
- Music stores
- Newspaper book and media reviewers
- Senior centers
- Teen centers
- Theaters

Policy Implications

Circulation

- Circulation limits by subject
- Circulation limits by format
- Loan periods by format

Gifts and Donations

- Restrictions on donations of cash, equipment, materials, etc.

Information Service

- Time limits on use of listening and viewing stations

Programs in the Library

- Cosponsorship of programs

Critical Resources

Staff (Knowledge, Skills, and Abilities)

- Staff is knowledgeable about classic and current fiction.
- Staff is knowledgeable about genre fiction.
- Staff is knowledgeable about classic and current music.
- Staff is knowledgeable about classic and current films.
- Staff is knowledgeable about games and graphic novels.
- Staff can provide reader/viewer/listener advisory services to users looking for recommendations.
- Staff can plan and present programs.

Collection (Print, Media, and Electronic)

- Action and adventure films
- Animated films

- Best sellers, new books, and new media
- Christian fiction
- Classic books, films, and music
- Comedy films
- Country and bluegrass music
- Drama
- Fantasy books and films
- Foreign films
- Games (electronic)
- General fiction
- Graphic novels
- Hip-hop music
- Historical fiction
- Horror fictions and films
- Jazz music
- Latin music
- Metal music
- Musical films
- Mystery
- New Age music
- Poetry
- Pop music
- Reggae music
- Religious music
- Rhythm and blues music
- Rock music
- Romance books and films
- Science fiction films
- Short stories
- Sound tracks
- Street/urban literature
- Suspense and thriller books and films
- Western books and films

Facilities (Space, Furniture, and Equipment)

- Meeting space
- Display shelving to merchandise selected portions of the collections
- Space to display new books and media
- Appropriate shelving for media
- Ergonomic workstations and seating
- Listening and viewing stations
- Identifiable readers' advisory services station or roving personnel

Technology (Hardware, Software, Networks, and Telecommunication)

- Computers configured to allow downloading of licensed digital content to personal storage devices (PDA, MP3 player, Flash drive, etc.)

Possible Measures

Number of Users

- Number of people who indicate on a survey that they use the library to find something to read, view, or listen to for pleasure

Perceptions of Users

- Percent of users surveyed who respond that:

  They find something to read, view, or listen to for pleasure.
  The collection of materials to enhance their leisure time is very good or excellent.
  The assistance they receive from staff when requesting help to locate an item to read, view, or listen to for pleasure is very good or excellent.
  The items they place on reserve are available in a timely manner.

User Outcomes

- Number and percent of specified users who increased their enjoyment of reading
- Number and percent of specified users who discussed a book with a stranger, person of a different ethnicity, or person of a different age for the first time
- Number and percent of specified users who read and enjoyed a book by a new author or on a new topic for the first time
- Number and percent of specified users who experience an alternative world

Units of Service Delivered

- Circulation of:

  New books
  CDs
  DVDs

- Turnover of items in the new book collection
- Average number of days between placing an item on reserve and notification that the item is available for pickup

Succeed in School
Homework Help

Students will have the resources they need to succeed in school.

Suggested Target Audiences

- Elementary school students
- Middle school students
- High school students
- Homeschooled students
- Parents and caregivers of students

Typical Services and Programs in Libraries That Select This as a Priority

- Provide staff or volunteers to assist students with their homework.
- Develop and maintain a homework help web page.
- Provide homework assistance using text messaging.
- Subscribe to an online interactive homework help service.
- Provide study rooms for students.
- Provide classroom collections for teachers.
- Coordinate with school media center specialists to identify materials that support the school curriculum.
- Coordinate with school media center specialists to set up a school assignment alert program.
- Provide access to courses for students through distance learning or video-on-demand.
- Make presentations about the library in the local schools.
- Provide tours of the library to classes of students.
- Develop and maintain a web page that provides links to homeschooling resources for homeschooled students and their parents.
- Provide circulating collections of materials selected to support homeschooling curricula.
- Provide orientation programs for homeschooled students and their parents.

Potential Partners

- Board of education
- Homeschooling organizations
- Library of Congress
- National Education Association and local chapters
- Parent-teacher organizations
- Public and private school media center specialists, teachers, and administrators
- Student councils
- Teen centers

Policy Implications

Circulation

- Circulation limits by subject

Community Presentations or Programs Offered at Nonlibrary Locations

- Classification of staff who can deliver presentations or programs
- Use of volunteers
- Process that agency or organization must follow to request a presentation or program
- Minimum or maximum number of anticipated attendees
- Number of times a presentation or program will be given to the same group during a specified period of time

Information Services

- Level of homework help provided
- Rules for students working in groups

Volunteers

- Screening procedures
- Qualifications for volunteers who provide homework assistance

Critical Resources

Staff (Knowledge, Skills, and Abilities)

- Staff are knowledgeable about the curricula in local schools.
- Staff are knowledgeable about how children and teens learn.
- Staff are knowledgeable about homework help resources.
- Staff are knowledgeable about search strategies for print and electronic homework help resources.

- Staff can find needed information quickly using print and electronic information resources.
- Staff can teach in both one-on-one and classroom environments.
- Staff can develop and maintain relationships with representatives from the public, private, and parochial schools served by the library.
- Staff can conduct effective reference interviews.
- Staff can recruit and train homework help volunteers.
- Staff can establish and maintain homework help and homeschooling web pages.

Collection (Print, Media, and Electronic Resources)

- Materials that support the curricula of the local schools
- Online homework help databases
- Textbooks used in local schools

Facilities (Space, Furniture, and Equipment)

- Space for homework center
- Study rooms or other space for students to work
- Workstations that are large enough to allow several students to work together
- Ergonomic workstations and chairs

Technology (Hardware, Software, Networks, and Telecommunication)

- Computers configured to allow downloading of licensed digital content to personal storage devices (PDA, MP3 player, Flash drive, etc.)
- Computers that support the upload of electronic files for assignments
- Publication software for homework projects
- Color printers for homework projects

Possible Measures

Number of Users

- Number of students who participate in a library-sponsored homework help program
- Number of people who indicate on a survey that they use the library to help them with their homework

Perceptions of Users

- Percent of students surveyed who respond that:

    They use the library for homework help.
    The library's homework help services and materials meet their needs.
    The training session offered or cosponsored by the library is very good or excellent.

- Percent of parents of school-age children surveyed who respond that the library's homework help services and materials meet the needs of their children

User Outcomes

- Number and percent of specified students who improve their reading skills
- Number and percent of specified students who improve their writing skills
- Number and percent of specified students who improve their math skills
- Number and percent of specified students who improve their grades
- Number and percent of specified students who increase their enjoyment of learning
- Number and percent of specified students who complete their year/ graduate from school
- Number and percent of specified students who achieve a personal goal associated with success in school

Units of Service Delivered

- Circulation of juvenile nonfiction
- Number of times the library's homework help web page was accessed
- Number of online tutoring sessions held
- Number of presentations made in schools to describe and promote the library's homework help services

Understand How to Find, Evaluate, and Use Information
Information Fluency

Residents will know when they need information to resolve an issue or answer a question and will have the skills to search for, locate, evaluate, and effectively use information to meet their needs.

Suggested Target Audiences

- Seniors
- Adults
- Teens
- Children

Typical Services and Programs in Libraries That Select This as a Priority

- Provide basic, intermediate, and advanced classes on how to use the Internet and proprietary databases.
- Offer classes on new technologies and web trends as they happen.
- Sponsor or cosponsor hands-on classes on various software applications (Word, Access, etc.).
- Present a regular series of short programs that focus on using both print and electronic resources to find information on a variety of topics.
- Create online tutorials to help users navigate library technology and the Web.
- Partner with local middle and high schools to provide programs to ensure that teens know how to find, evaluate, and use information.
- Partner with local senior centers to provide programs to ensure that seniors know how to find, evaluate, and use information.
- Take advantage of "teaching moments" when helping users to find information.

Potential Partners

- Community colleges, technical schools, vocational schools, and universities
- Computer clubs

- Public and private schools
- Senior centers
- Teen centers

Policy Implications

Fees and Fines

- Fees for training

Intellectual Property Rights

- Copyright
- Fair use

Programs in the Library

- Cosponsorship of programs

Critical Resources

Staff (Knowledge, Skills, and Abilities)

- Staff are knowledgeable about technology trends and new products.
- Staff are knowledgeable about the software applications they are expected to teach.
- Staff are knowledgeable about adult education and training design.
- Staff are knowledgeable about copyright and fair use.
- Staff can find and evaluate information.
- Staff can design effective training materials.
- Staff can teach people in class settings and provide one-on-one training.

Collection (Print, Media, and Electronic Resources)

- Circulating software manuals
- Online tutorials

Facilities (Space, Furniture, and Equipment)

- Computer lab
- Mobile computer lab
- Data projector

Technology (Hardware, Software, Networks, and Telecommunication)

- Portable wireless computer lab
- Wireless network

- Multiple computers dedicated to training
- Variety of software applications for training and subsequent use

Possible Measures

Number of Users

- Number of people who attend an information literacy class
- Number of people who receive one-on-one information literacy assistance
- Number of people who access computer-based training modules
- Number of people who indicate on a survey that they use the library to learn how to find, evaluate, and use information

Perceptions of Users

- Percent of users surveyed who respond that:

    The training session sponsored or cosponsored by the library is very good or excellent.
    The assistance they receive from staff is very good or excellent.

User Outcomes

- Number and percent of specified users who know how to learn to find information in the library catalog, reference books, online databases, or the Internet
- Number and percent of specified users who learn to use a computer to meet their personal needs
- Number and percent of specified users who know how to learn to use software applications such as word processing or a spreadsheet
- Number and percent of specified users who create and manage an e-mail account
- Number and percent of specified users who create and maintain a website
- Number and percent of specified students who use library resources to write a research paper
- Number and percent of specified users who know how to evaluate information found on a website

Units of Service Delivered

- Number of information literacy classes offered
- Number of computer training classes offered
- Number of programs cosponsored with middle and high schools
- Number of programs cosponsored with senior centers

Visit a Comfortable Place
Physical and Virtual Spaces

Residents will have safe and welcoming physical places to meet and interact with others or to sit quietly and read and will have open and accessible virtual spaces that support networking.

Suggested Target Audiences

- Adults
- Teens
- Children
- Local organizations and clubs

Typical Services and Programs in Libraries That Select This as a Priority

- Provide meeting rooms for public use.
- Provide comfortable seating throughout the library.
- Provide a café for the public.
- Provide a gallery or exhibit space.
- Provide performance space.
- Provide a wide range of electronic gaming opportunities.
- Develop and maintain a library events web page.
- Provide a variety of blogs, wikis, and other opportunities for social networking.

Potential Partners

- City or county departments
- Clubs and organizations

Policy Implications

Customer Behavior

- Expectations for customer behavior
- Food and drink in the library
- Process to address inappropriate behavior

Exhibits and Displays

- Criteria for inclusion of items in library exhibits and displays

Intellectual Property Rights

- Copyright
- Fair use

Internet Use

- Filtering
- Confidentiality
- Time limits for use of public access computers
- Use of library computers to play games
- Age restrictions on the use of public access computers for gaming or social networking
- Downloading to and uploading from personal storage devices on public access computers
- Use of public access computers by people without library cards
- Use of wireless Internet access by people without library cards

Meeting Rooms

- Use of meeting rooms by outside groups
- Use of meeting rooms after library hours
- Meeting room fees

Programs in the Library

- Cosponsorship of programs

Social Networking

- Types of social networking environments that are supported
- Criteria for participation in social networks (age, library card holder, etc.)
- Editorial control of social networks

Critical Resources

Staff (Knowledge, Skills, and Abilities)

- Staff are knowledgeable about a variety of electronic games.
- Staff are knowledgeable about copyright and fair use.
- Staff can create and maintain a warm, comfortable, and inviting environment in all of the public areas of the library's building or buildings.
- Staff can create easy-to-use library web pages that provide rich user experiences.
- Staff can mount exhibits and displays.

- Staff can manage galleries, performance spaces, and meeting rooms.
- Staff can create and maintain wikis and blogs.

Collection (Print, Media, and Electronic Resources)

- Games (electronic)

Facilities (Space, Furniture, and Equipment)

- Meeting rooms of various sizes
- Space for people to collaborate on projects
- Comfortable seating in busy and quiet areas
- Ergonomic workstations and chairs
- Accessible electrical outlets for personal computers
- Good wire management
- Café
- Gallery space
- Exhibit space
- Performance space

Technology (Hardware, Software, Networks, and Telecommunication)

- Adequate number of public access computers that are configured for speed and graphics
- Sufficient bandwidth to manage the Internet traffic
- Wireless network
- Software to manage reservations for meeting rooms, galleries, and performance spaces

Possible Measures

Number of Users

- Number of people who have library cards
- Number of people who attend programs in the library
- Number of people who attend exhibits in the library
- Number of community organizations that hold meetings or events in the library
- Number of people participating in library-sponsored blogs or wikis
- Library door-count

Perceptions of Users

- Percent of people who indicate on a survey that they used the library as a comfortable public or virtual space

- Percent of organizations surveyed who indicate that:

    The library meeting rooms and other public spaces meet their needs.

- Percent of people surveyed who indicate that:

    The library is a safe place to visit.
    The library is a welcoming, attractive, and comfortable place to visit.
    The library website is easy or very easy to use.

User Outcomes

- Number and percent of specified users who broaden their social network
- Number and percent of specified users who expand their worldview through cross-cultural experiences
- Number and percent of specified users who increase their sense of community

Units of Service Delivered

- Number of public service hours per week
- Number of library visits or library attendance
- Library visits per capita
- Number of shows mounted in the gallery

Welcome to the United States
Services for New Immigrants

> New immigrants will have information on citizenship, English Language Learning (ELL), employment, public schooling, health and safety, available social services, and any other topics they need to participate successfully in American life.

Suggested Target Audiences

- New immigrants
- Refugees

Typical Services and Programs in Libraries That Select This as a Priority

- Develop a comprehensive web page with links to a wide variety of resources for new immigrants.
- Present citizenship classes.
- Distribute materials developed by community organizations for new immigrants.
- Make presentations to groups of new immigrants in off-site locations.
- Provide self-guided programs that use books and media to help adults and teens with limited English skills become proficient in English.
- Provide private space for tutors to work one-on-one with ELL literacy students.
- Provide ELL literacy classes.
- Establish a literacy helpline and provide referral services for persons looking for ELL literacy services.
- Provide programs to tutor learners preparing to take the GED test.
- Host ELL conversational meetings to help learners practice speaking English.
- Provide deposit collections of materials for new readers to organizations that tutor ELL students.
- Collaborate with all organizations that provide ELL services in the community or county to promote and publicize literacy services.

Potential Partners

- Churches, mosques, and synagogues
- Ethnic grocery stores and restaurants
- Ethnic groups and organizations
- Immigration and Naturalization Service
- Literacy council
- Literacy Volunteers of America
- Newspapers in languages other than English
- Public and private schools
- Social service agencies
- Student exchange programs

Policy Implications

Bulletin Boards

- Eligible organizations
- Criteria for materials
- Length of time materials will be posted

Community Presentations or Programs Offered at Nonlibrary Locations

- Classification of staff who can deliver presentations or programs
- Use of volunteers
- Process that agency or organization must follow to request a presentation or program
- Minimum or maximum number of anticipated attendees
- Number of times a presentation or program will be given to the same group during a specified period of time

Distribution of Nonlibrary Materials

- Eligible organizations
- Criteria for materials
- Length of time materials will be distributed

Library Publications

- Languages in which library publications are printed

Meeting Rooms

- Use of meeting rooms by outside groups
- Use of meeting rooms after library hours
- Meeting room fees

Programs in the Library

- Cosponsorship of programs

Web Page

- Languages in which web pages are produced
- Criteria for linking to services

Critical Resources

Staff (Knowledge, Skills, and Abilities)

- Staff speak the languages of immigrant groups.
- Staff are knowledgeable about the unique needs of new immigrants.
- Staff are knowledgeable about the culture from which the new immigrants come.
- Staff are knowledgeable about the agencies and organizations that provide services to new immigrants.
- Staff can establish partnerships with agencies and organizations that provide services to new immigrants.
- Staff can help new immigrants determine what services they need from community agencies and organizations.
- Staff can make presentations to groups of new immigrants.

Collection (Print, Media, and Electronic Resources)

- Citizenship
- English Language Learning materials
- Handbooks, guides, brochures, and pamphlets from local agencies and organizations that serve new immigrants
- TOEFL (Test of English as a Foreign Language) preparation materials

Facilities (Space, Furniture, and Equipment)

- Meeting rooms
- Study rooms
- Multilingual signage
- Information rack for free materials made available for distribution by agencies and organizations serving new immigrants

Technology (Hardware, Software, Networks, and Telecommunication)

- Unicode-compliant integrated library system capable of displaying multiple languages simultaneously
- Computer-assisted self-guided ELL tutorials
- Dedicated ELL computers with sound cards and headsets

Possible Measures

Number of Users

- Number of people who indicate on a survey that they use the library to help them gain information or skills that help them adapt to life in the United States
- Number of people who attend ELL classes
- Number of people who attend citizenship classes

Perceptions of Users

- Percent of new immigrants surveyed in their native language who indicate that:

  They are able to find the information and services they need.
  The assistance they receive from staff is very good or excellent.
  The information on the library's website is useful or very useful to them.

User Outcomes

- Number and percent of specified new immigrants who increase their skill and self-confidence in conversing in English
- Number and percent of specified new immigrants who become citizens
- Number and percent of specified new immigrants who improve their English-reading level by at least one step
- Number and percent of new immigrants who take the GED preparation test and pass the GED test
- Number and percent of new immigrants who meet a personal literacy goal
- Number and percent of new immigrants who read to their children a specific amount of time or frequency
- Number and percent of new immigrants who get a job or a job promotion

Units of Service Delivered

- Number of ELL classes offered
- Number of citizenship classes offered
- Number of ELL volunteer tutor hours
- Number of ELL volunteer tutors
- Number of ELL tutoring sessions held

Part Three

Tool Kits

Groups
Identifying Options

Issues

Library managers must make decisions every day. Sometimes they make those decisions alone; sometimes they give the responsibility for making a decision to a committee or task force. In either case, the first step in any decision-making process is to identify the options to be considered. Regardless of whether the ultimate decision will be made by a single person or a group, it is usually more effective to involve a number of people in the process of identifying options. The greater the number of viable options that decision makers have to consider, the more likely they are to make effective decisions.

At first glance, it would seem that identifying options would be fairly easy. After all, almost everyone seems to have opinions about almost everything. In reality, when you begin to work with groups to help them identify options, you discover that people's preconceived ideas make it more difficult, not easier, to identify a range of options. Other problems include the tendency to think there is only one right answer to every question, the difficulty in identifying new options for old problems, the dominance of the group by one or more members, and the effect of peer pressure on group activities that results in a tendency among group members to minimize the appearance of conflict. Finally, it is important to remember the old computer acronym GIGO (garbage in–garbage out). It applies here, too. You need to have the right people involved in the process to identify effective options. The right people, in this instance, include people with some understanding of the problem and some experience or knowledge that provides them with a basis for suggesting solutions. Each of these issues is discussed in greater detail in the following sections.

Searching for the One Right Answer

It is important for the group leader to lay the groundwork carefully for the process to be used to identify options, stressing the need to look at a variety of points of view. Many people are uncomfortable with ambiguity and find the concept of multiple, valid options difficult to understand. Instead they search for the absolute answer to any question. They are inclined to make premature decisions to avoid having to deal with uncomfortable choices. Most groups need periodic reminders that the purpose of this part of the decision-making process is to identify as many options as possible, and that even ideas that seem wildly unrealistic at first glance may lead to new insights or choices.

Thinking "Inside the Box"

In general, the more familiar people are with a situation, the more difficult they find it to consider the situation objectively or creatively. This can be a particular problem in libraries because so many staff members have worked in the same system for decades. The group leader will want to encourage people to look with new eyes at the issues under consideration. This might be done in at least three ways.

Move from the specific to the general. Encourage group members to broaden their frames of reference. For instance, instead of thinking about the public library as an institution, broaden the definition to include all libraries, and then broaden it again to include all information providers. Remind the participants of the story of the railroad company executives who defined their business as "railroading." Not much later the competition from trucking and airfreight had pushed them close to bankruptcy. If the executives had understood that they were in the transportation business and not just the railroad business, they might well have been able to identify alternative options.

Look at what is happening beyond our own field. We can learn a lot from other organizations, both profit and nonprofit ones. For instance, many library managers have benefited from management books written by such authors as Stephen Covey and Peter Drucker, even though their books were intended primarily for businesspeople. The United Way has been very involved in helping nonprofit organizations define the results of the services they provide, and the United Way manual *Measuring Program Outcomes: A Practical Approach* would be a valuable tool for any library manager.[1]

Question everything. James Thurber once said, "It is better to ask some of the questions than to know all of the answers." When someone says, "We've always done it this way," ask "Why?" When someone says, "We can't do that" ask "Why not?" Why can't we provide off-site access to information? Why can't we let users access their e-mail accounts on library equipment? Why can't we use e-book technology to deliver current materials more quickly and cost-effectively? Why can't we use wireless technology? Why can't we collaborate with another organization to provide a service?

Dealing with Dominant Behaviors

Every group has one or more dominant members. The source of their dominance varies: some people control a group by sheer force of personality. Others are dominant because of their positions. Yet others use their expertise (real or perceived) to control a group.

Finally, some people dominate groups because they are bullies and attack anyone who disagrees with them or tries to express an alternative point of view.

It is critical for the group leader to make it clear to all group members that each person's opinion is important. This message may have to be repeated several times during the process. Then the group leader must control the behavior of the dominant members in the group. This can be done by waiting until others have spoken before asking the dominant members for their opinions. Another possibility is to divide the group into smaller subgroups, which has the effect of minimizing the impact of the dominant members. These techniques will work in many situations but may not be effective with bullies. It is possible that the group leader will have to talk to the bully privately during a break or after the meeting to ask him or her to respect the opinions of the others in the group. If this direct intervention doesn't work, the leader should consider asking the person who made the appointments to the committee to talk to the bully about his or her disruptive behavior.

Dealing with Peer Pressure

Most people are more comfortable if they feel they are part of a group and not an outsider. Therefore, people have a tendency to go along with what they think the group believes or values, even if they don't necessarily agree. This can lead to "groupthink," in which the members place a higher value on agreement than on identifying multiple options. This problem is easiest to deal with at the very beginning of the process by making it clear that the group's task is to identify multiple options. The leader should assure the group that the purpose is not to make the final decision, and that success will be defined by the number and creativity of the options identified. This in turn creates a group norm that supports and encourages diverse points of view.

Involving the Right People

Several things should be considered when determining whom to involve in the identification of options. First, of course, you want to include people who have something to contribute to the discussion. Their contributions may be based on specialized skills or expertise, on background or experience, or on position or authority. Second, you want to include people who care about the issue being considered. Third, you want to include people who will be affected by whatever option is ultimately selected. Finally, you want people who are reasonably open to change and willing to consider a variety of points of view. If you are careful in your selections (and lucky), most of the participants in whatever process you use to identify options could be included in at least three of these four categories.

Evaluating Methods of Identifying Options

Four methods you might use to help a group identify options are general group discussion, brainstorming, Nominal Group Technique, and the Delphi Method. Each of these methods can be used effectively in certain situations. The important thing is to match the method and the situation. Four measures that can be used to help you decide which method will be most effective for a given situation include the desired

> level of participation from the group
>
> range of the options identified
>
> skill required of the facilitator/leader
>
> time it takes to make the decision

Level of Participation

The first measure to use when deciding which method to use for identifying options is how much participation you need to identify the options for a specific decision. If the options you are to consider relate to a significant change in policy, you will probably want to use a process that encourages the maximum level of participation. On the other hand, if you are developing options for dealing with a situation in a single unit or dealing with a relatively minor change, you may not want or need extensive participation.

Range of Options Identified

The second measure is the range and creativity of the options that are identified. Some problems are intrinsically more difficult to address than others. Consider two committees: one responsible for identifying options for ways to integrate a new technology into the ongoing operations of the library, and the second responsible for options for improving the activities in the annual staff-day training event. Both are important, but the first will require considerably more flexibility and creativity than the second.

Leadership Skill Required

The third measure is the skill required to develop and lead the process to be used to identify the options. Some of the methods described in this chapter are relatively easy to manage; others require more specialized skills or knowledge.

Time Required

The final measure is the length of time it will take to identify options. The identification of options is just the first step in the decision-making process. There is not much point in expending so much effort on this part of the process that there is no time left to reach agreement on the most effective option to select before the deadline for implementation. Furthermore, some decisions are fairly simple or can only be addressed in a limited number of ways. As a general rule, select the easiest and quickest process that will produce the level of participation and range of options you need.

Methods for Identifying Options

General Group Discussion

Level of participation:
    Varies, often low
 	
Range of options identified:
    Low to moderate
 	
Leadership skill required:
    Low
 	
Time required:
    Low

General group discussion is probably the most common method used for identifying options in libraries. Group discussions often occur during meetings that have multiple agenda items. Someone will raise an issue, someone else will suggest a solution, there may or may not be a little discussion, and the suggestion is adopted. The other common setting for group discussion is a special committee meeting called to review a problem and to identify possible solutions.

General group discussions present a number of problems when used as the means to identify options. Because general group discussions often occur extemporaneously, people don't have time to think about the problem and bring suggestions to the meeting. Instead, they are expected to think of options very quickly. The negative effects of peer pressure and the dominance of one or more members of the group are most likely to occur in this situation. Furthermore, the process of identifying options tends to end the first time someone suggests a solution that sounds reasonable to the other members of the group. There is no reward for prolonging the identification process, and there is often considerable pressure to move on to the next item on the agenda.

When to Use

Generally, library managers overuse group discussion. However, group discussion can be an effective way to identify options in several circumstances. The first is when the decision to be made is confidential and the number of people involved in the process of identifying options is small. Two or three people would probably find it difficult and obtrusive to use any of the other methods to identify options. It is also appropriate to use general group discussions to identify options when the group is one that meets regularly and has a shared knowledge base. Branch managers, for instance, often identify options for addressing common problems during their monthly meetings. However, in both instances, the people responsible for leading the process need to be very aware of the problems presented in the preceding paragraph and work with the members of the group to avoid them.

What to Do

1. Identify the issue or question to be addressed.
2. Select the group to address the question. It may be an existing group or committee, or it may be a group convened specifically for this process.
3. Prepare a brief (one-page) description of the issue to be addressed and send it to the members of the group at least one week prior to the meeting at which it will be discussed. Ask the participants to come to the meeting ready to suggest ways to address the issue.
4. At the meeting, briefly review the issue and ask the members to suggest options. Write the options on flip-chart paper as they are presented. Encourage the group to provide as many suggestions as possible. Ask participants to clarify any options

that seem ambiguous. Encourage people to combine options that are similar. Do not evaluate the suggestions as they are proposed.

5. When it becomes clear that everyone is finished presenting options, review the list and ask if there are questions or additions. Make needed changes and develop a final list of options.

6. Use the options as the starting point for making a decision about the issue under review.

Brainstorming

Level of participation:
    Moderate to high

Range of options identified:
    Moderate

Leadership skill required:
    Moderate

Time required:
    Low to moderate

Brainstorming is a method used to identify multiple options by generating a large number of ideas through interaction among team members. The intent is to break free of preconceived ideas by exploring as many alternatives as possible and building on each other's ideas.

As shown in figure 45, in this process a group of people creates a list of ideas by having each member make a suggestion in turn, and the suggestions are recorded with no comment or discussion. Members are encouraged to build on each other's ideas. The actual brainstorming is best done in groups with six to eight members, but large groups can be divided into smaller groups for the initial brainstorming activity, and then the suggestions from all of the small groups can be combined.

This is a relatively easy process to manage and, by its very nature, makes it difficult for a few people to dominate the discussion. It is a process that many people enjoy; participants often find the fast-paced generation of ideas by a variety of people stimulating. However, the fast pace of the process can be a problem too. Brainstorming doesn't provide much opportunity for reflection. Participants are encouraged to think of options very quickly, which may mean that more complex or unusual options are never identified. Participants may also hesitate to make an unusual or creative suggestion for fear that others will laugh at them or think they are strange. There may be a tendency to follow the lead of the first two or three people who offer options rather than suggesting alternate ones that may be perceived as being in conflict with earlier recommendations.

FIGURE 45
Rules for Brainstorming

1. Be creative; push the limits.

2. Never criticize anyone's ideas. There are no right answers or wrong answers.

3. The more ideas you contribute the better. Quantity is more important than quality.

4. Free-associate ideas; build on the ideas of others.

5. Don't discuss ideas or stop for explanations.

6. Record all ideas exactly as they are stated.

7. Take turns making suggestions. Contribute one idea each time it is your turn.

8. Pass your turn if you have no further suggestions.

When to Use

Brainstorming is a good method to use to generate a lot of ideas from a group in a fairly short period of time. It works best when it is used to consider a single, focused topic. For example, brainstorming can be an excellent way to identify a list of possible activities to achieve a predetermined goal and objective. However, it is probably not the best way to identify the options for addressing the myriad of issues surrounding access to pornographic sites on the Internet. In the first case, the staff of the library probably have all the information they need to make suggestions, and any grouping of several dozen possible activities could be used to accomplish the goal and objective. In the second case, there aren't dozens of good answers. In fact, there aren't any answers that satisfy everyone involved. Having people with little knowledge of the legal issues or the political environment make suggestions is probably not going to be useful.

What to Do

1. Identify the issue or question to be addressed.
2. Decide whom to include in the process. This may be an existing group or committee or it may be a group convened specifically for this process.
3. Decide if you want to have official recorders for each group or if you want to ask the participants to share the responsibility for recording.
4. Write a short issue or problem statement. This should be specific enough to help participants focus on the issue but open-ended enough to encourage creativity. The statement could include a list of questions that would encourage exploration of the topic.
5. At the beginning of the brainstorming session, review the problem statement with the participants.
6. Prepare a handout with the rules for brainstorming (see figure 45), and distribute it to all the participants.
7. If the group has more than eight people, divide it into smaller groups.
8. Establish a specific period of time for the initial brainstorming activity, usually around twenty minutes.
9. If there is more than one group working on the problem, combine their suggestions into a master list on a flip-chart.
10. Review and discuss the items on the master list, clarifying when necessary and combining when possible.
11. Use the options on the master list as the starting point for making a decision about the issue under review.

Nominal Group Technique

> **Level of participation:**
> Moderate to high
>
> **Range of options identified:**
> Moderate to high
>
> **Leadership skill required:**
> Moderate
>
> **Time required:**
> Moderate

The Nominal Group Technique is used to generate a large number of ideas through the contributions of members working individually. Research suggests that more ideas are generated by individuals working alone but in a group environment than by individuals engaged in group discussions.[2] In this process, group members start by writing down their ideas on note cards and posting them for others to read. Members get an opportunity to ask questions to clarify other members' ideas, and then they participate in group discussions about all of the ideas presented. Finally, each group member reassesses the ideas presented and selects those that seem most effective. These conclusions are then posted for a final discussion.

The Nominal Group Technique is both more time-consuming and more structured than brainstorming. The investment in time is often repaid because this process generally produces a greater number of more developed and creative ideas than are produced in a group discussion or brainstorming process. However, people generally feel more comfortable with the fast-paced and open brainstorming process than with the Nominal Group Technique, at least partly because people are more familiar with brainstorming. The Nominal Group Technique structure can be perceived by group members as artificial and restrictive. Participants may feel that the process drives the content, rather than the other way around, and as a result, they may question the validity of the final list of options.

When to Use

The Nominal Group Technique is a good method to use with a group that has some very strong or opinionated members. Because each participant writes down his or her ideas privately before any discussion begins, the responses are less likely to be driven by the dominant members of the group. Because the facilitator reads the suggestions aloud, the process allows suggestions to be evaluated on their own merits rather than being prejudged based on who made them. The Nominal Group Technique also can be used effectively to identify options for addressing issues that are potentially controversial. For instance, you may be considering how to revise your circulation policies so they support the goal of meeting the public's demand for materials on current topics and titles. This opens up some interesting possibilities, including extending your loan period, allowing patron reserves, and so on. Each of these possibilities has proponents and opponents. Using this process, you can develop a comprehensive list of options without a lot of arguments. You can also get a sense of which options are perceived as having the potential to be the most effective ones.

What to Do

1. Identify the issue or question to be addressed.
2. Decide whom to include in the process. This may be an existing group or committee or it may be a group convened specifically for this process.
3. Write a short problem statement. This should be specific enough to help participants focus on the issue but open-ended enough to encourage creativity. The statement could include a list of questions that would encourage exploration of the topic.
4. At the beginning of the session, describe the process to be used and review the problem statement with the participants.
5. Give the participants five to ten minutes to write down their ideas on note cards without any discussion with others. Ask participants to use a new card for each idea.
6. Collect the cards and read the ideas, one at a time. Write the ideas on flip-chart paper as they are read, so that everyone can see them. There is no discussion during this part of the process.
7. After all of the ideas have been recorded, encourage participants to discuss them. Participants may be asked to clarify their suggestions. They can express agreement or disagreement with any suggestion.
8. Give participants several minutes to select the five options they think are the most effective.

9. Tabulate the choices and indicate which options received the most votes. One quick way to tabulate the choices is to use the dot exercise, described in the Groups: Reaching Agreement tool kit.
10. Discuss the final list of options.
11. Use the options as the starting point for making a decision about the issue under review.

Delphi Method

Level of participation:

   High

Range of options identified:

   Moderate to high

Leadership skill required:

   High

Time required:

   High

The Delphi Method was developed by the RAND Corporation as a way of eliminating the problems of generating ideas in groups: dominant behaviors, peer pressure, and so on. In this process the participants never meet face-to-face, and they normally don't even know who the other members of the group are. The participants are presented with a list of general questions about a specific topic and asked to prepare a written response. The responses are sent to a coordinator who edits and summarizes them into a single report. This report is returned to the participants with a second list of questions intended to clarify differences, and participants are again asked to respond. The responses from the second round are edited and summarized and sent to the participants one final time. In this third round, participants are provided with statistical feedback about how the group responded to particular questions, as well as a summary of the group's comments. This makes the participants aware of the range of opinions and the reasons for those opinions. The group is then asked to rank the responses one final time. A final report is developed and sent to all participants.

This is by far the most complex of the methods for identifying options, and most library staff members have never participated in a process that used the Delphi Method. The drawbacks are obvious. The method is quite time-consuming for the participants and extremely time-consuming for the coordinator. Furthermore, this method, more than any of the others, can be seriously compromised if the wrong people are included as participants because their involvement is so much more intensive. However, real benefits can be gained from using the Delphi Method as well. It can be used to gather options from people with significant subject expertise regardless of where they live. It can also be used to facilitate communication among individuals who disagree strongly about the issue being discussed.

When to Use

The Delphi Method is a process that library managers should use sparingly. It is simply too complex and too expensive to be used as a regular tool. However, in some circumstances the effort might well be worth the time and energy invested. For instance, let's say you are the director of a library in a community with a growing Hispanic population. You want to provide services for this new population group, but you don't know where to start. Some board and staff members feel that you don't have the resources to provide quality services to your "regular" client groups already, and it would be foolish to reach out to new groups. In this instance, using the Delphi Method to generate options from board members, staff members, members of the Hispanic community, and librarians in other communities with established service programs for Hispanics might be quite effective. It would minimize the potential for open conflict and maximize the number of options that could be considered. All points of view would be presented, and everyone involved would have a chance to respond. Because the responses are anonymous, participants might be more responsive to other points of view and more open to revising their initial suggestions.

What to Do

1. Identify the issue or question to be addressed.
2. Select a coordinator to manage the Delphi Method, preferably one who has coordinated a similar process before or at least participated in such a process.
3. Select the people to be involved in the process. The majority of Delphi studies have used between fifteen and twenty respondents.[3]
4. Send the participants a description of the process, and include the time frame. Participants have to agree to respond to three sets of questions.
5. Prepare a brief description of the issue or problem to be addressed and develop a short list of questions to be answered. Send both to each of the members. The initial questions will probably be general and open-ended.
6. Edit the responses and develop a set of follow-up questions based on the answers to the first questions. These follow-up questions will be more specific than the first open-ended questions. Send the edited responses and the second questions to the participants.
7. Tabulate the responses to each question, edit the comments, and prepare a third report. Send this to the participants for review, and ask them to answer the questions one final time.
8. Tabulate the responses into a final report. Send copies to all participants. Use the information in the report as the starting point for making a decision about the issue under review.

Notes

1. United Way, *Measuring Program Outcomes* (Alexandria, VA: United Way of America, 1996).
2. Center for Rural Studies, "Guidelines for Using the Nominal Group Technique," http://crs.uvm.edu/gopher/nerl/group/a/meet/Exercise7/b.html.
3. Barbara Ludwig, "Predicting the Future: Have You Considered Using the Delphi Methodology?" *Journal of Extension* (October 1997), available at http://www.joe.org/joe/1997october/tt2.html.

Groups
Reaching Agreement

Issues

Most public libraries make extensive use of committees and teams to explore options, make recommendations about future services, and review and evaluate existing programs. No matter what their purpose, all committees and teams have one thing in common: to be successful, their members must be able to reach agreement on the issues under consideration. As anyone who has ever served on a committee knows, this isn't easy. Problems include lack of a clear committee or team charge, groups that are too large or too small, group leaders with poor facilitation skills, group members with competing agendas, lack of accountability, and the absence of official action on committee recommendations. These issues are discussed in more detail in the following sections.

The Charge

Every committee or team should have a clearly stated charge, and every member of the committee should understand that charge. The charge should include

> an explicit description of what the committee is expected to accomplish
>
> the time frame for the committee's deliberations
>
> the person or group that will receive the committee's report
>
> the process that will be used to review and act upon the committee's work
>
> the time frame for that review and action

Group Size

Committees and teams can range in size from two or three people to as many as twenty or thirty people. The decision concerning the size of the group is a trade-off. Smaller committees are usually easier to work with because fewer people are involved. Communication is quicker, orientation takes less time, discussion and consensus may move more quickly, and smaller committees are less expensive to support. However, smaller groups may be open to potential criticism of narrow thinking or elitism. If the workload you envision for committee members is heavy, a small group may be overwhelmed and burn out before the committee completes its work.

231

Larger committees usually reflect a wider range of interests and can include people with a variety of expertise. Because the interests of the members may be more diverse, a wider scope of issues might be addressed. On the other hand, meetings will require more time for discussion and reaching consensus. Some committee members may feel lost in the crowd and lose enthusiasm. Large groups are also more difficult to lead. If the group will have more than twelve members, it is advisable to make arrangements for a trained facilitator to be the leader.

Leadership

Committees and teams are most effective when they are led by people who understand how groups work and have strong facilitation skills. Most library committees and teams are responsible for problem solving or information gathering. In these types of group activities, leaders are responsible for involving all members of the group in the work and ensuring that everyone has a say in the group's decisions. Generally, group members participate more and take a greater level of responsibility for the group's decisions if the leader focuses his or her energies on *facilitating participation* rather than on providing answers. See figure 46 for more information on group leaders' roles.

FIGURE 46
Leader's Role in Facilitating Group Participation

	Information-Giving	Instructional	Problem-Solving	Information-Gathering
Leader's Role	1. Present information so that it can be clearly understood. 2. Answer questions from the group. 3. Test to be sure that the group understands the information presented.	1. Identify learning outcomes. 2. Design training to ensure that all learning styles are accommodated. 3. Present training using a variety of training techniques. 4. Test to be sure that participants learned the key points.	1. Define the problem to be solved. 2. Establish processes to ensure full group participation. 3. Encourage group to identify all possible options. 4. Record possible solutions. 5. Facilitate group decision making.	1. Define the issue to be discussed. 2. Establish process for brainstorming. 3. Record results of brainstorming activities.

Membership

A committee or team is only as strong as its members. Group members normally play one of three roles:

> *Builders.* These people are interested in the work of the committee and focus their energies on the successful completion of the group's charge.

> *Blockers.* These people get in the way of the work of the committee by behaving in ways that block progress. There are dozens of behaviors that can derail an effective meeting. See figure 47 for more information on blockers.

FIGURE 47
Problem Behaviors in Meetings

Problem	Behavior	Suggested Solution
Latecomer	Always late	Start meetings on time—don't wait for stragglers. Do not recap meeting when Latecomer arrives, but offer to provide a recap during the first break.
Early Leaver	Never stays until meeting is adjourned	Set a time for adjournment and get a commitment from all members at the beginning of the meeting to stay until that time.
Clown	Always telling jokes; deflects group from task at hand	Laugh at the joke and then ask the Clown to comment on the topic under discussion. If the Clown responds with another joke, again ask for a comment on the topic.
Broken Record	Brings up same point over and over again	Write the Broken Record's concern on a flip-chart sheet and post it to provide assurance that the concern has been heard.
Doubting Thomas	Reacts negatively to most ideas	Encourage all group members to wait to make decisions until all points of view have been heard. Let Doubting Thomas express his concerns, but do not let him argue with others who do not share his negativity.
Dropout	Nonparticipant	Try asking Dropout's opinion during meeting or at break. Break group into groups of two or three to encourage everyone to participate.
Whisperer	Members having private conversations	Make eye contact with Whisperers. Pause briefly until you have their attention and then begin to speak again.
Loudmouth	Must be center of attention; talks constantly	Acknowledge the Loudmouth when he begins to talk and let him have his say. Then, if Loudmouth interrupts others, remind him that he has had his say.
Attacker	Makes very critical comments, often directed at leader	Thank the Attacker for his/her observation, and then ask other group members what they think. If attacks are directed at another group member, the leader has a responsibility to intervene. It is best to resolve these conflicts privately and not in front of the whole group.
Interpreter	Often says "In other words" or "What she really means"	Check this in public with the original speaker.
Know-It-All	Always has the answer	Remind the group that all members have expertise; that's the reason for meeting. Ask others to respond to Know-It-All's comments.
Teacher's Pet	Tries to monopolize the leader's attention	Be encouraging, but break eye contact. Get group members to talk to one another. Lessen your omnipotence by reflecting "What do you think?" back to the Teacher's Pet.

Maintainers. These people are more interested in maintaining relationships than in the work of the committee. They are the bridge between the builders and blockers.

Every committee needs builders and maintainers, and unfortunately almost all committees have at least one blocker. It is the leader's responsibility to see to it that the members of the group, no matter what their primary motivation, work together effectively.

Accountability

Committees and teams should be held accountable for their actions, just as individuals are. All too often the old saying, "When everyone is responsible, no one is responsible" comes into play with committees. It is not only possible but desirable to make it clear to a group that they are collectively responsible for specific results.

Action on Recommendations

If you ask any committee or group member what was the most frustrating thing about the group experience, far too many of them will say that they never saw any results from all of their work. Submitting a group report is often likened to Henry Wadsworth Longfellow's words: "I shot an arrow into the air, it fell to earth, I know not where." Library managers who appoint committees or teams to make recommendations have to establish processes for reviewing and acting on those recommendations. All group members should be aware of the review process and be kept informed of the status of the review from the beginning to the point at which a final decision has been made.

Evaluating Methods of Reaching Decisions

Three general approaches to reaching agreement in groups are consensus building, voting, and the forced-choice process. Each of these decision-making approaches can be used effectively to lead the group to a decision. The important thing is to match the approach to the situation. Four measures can be used to help you decide which approach will be most effective for the situation: the importance of the quality of the decision made; the time it takes to make the decision; the level of support the members of the group have for the decision; and the learning that takes place while the members make the decision.

Quality of the Decision

The first measure is the importance of the quality of the decision that is produced. For example, a group that decides very quickly to vote to select priorities may not make as informed a decision as a group that spends the time needed to explore all of the options in detail before making a decision. On the other hand, not all situations are equally critical. Decisions such as where the group will eat lunch or when the next meeting will be held don't require extensive discussion.

Time Required

The second measure is the time it takes to reach the decision. To continue with the preceding example, the group that voted quickly obviously made a decision in less time than the group that explored options more fully. There is often a trade-off between the length of time a group spends on a decision and the quality of the final decision. However, that is not always true: at times groups get stuck in a seemingly endless process of data collection and discussion and never do make any decision—good or bad.

Level of Support

The third measure is the desired level of support the group will have for the decision that has been made. Consensus building, by its very nature, creates the highest level of group support for the decisions being made because everyone has to agree with the decisions before they become final. On the other hand, the forced-choice process, which averages the choices made by group members in order to determine priorities, has the potential to result in decisions that none of the group supports wholeheartedly.

Development of Expertise

In some cases, it is important that the group members be given an opportunity to develop expertise in the area under consideration. For instance, if a team is going to be involved in making decisions about technology issues for the library for the next year, it is clearly important that the members of the team become knowledgeable about technology options and stay aware of changes in the field. In other cases, there is no need to support the development of such expertise. A committee of children's librarians who are responsible for developing and presenting a puppet show to publicize the summer reading program will probably have the expertise they need to accomplish their charge.

Methods for Reaching Agreement

Consensus Building

Quality of decision:
Normally very good
Time required:
Time-intensive
Group support for decision:
High
Development of expertise:
High

Consensus building is a process by which group members seek a mutually acceptable resolution to the issue under discussion. Note that *consensus* does not mean that everyone agrees that the solution is the best of all possible answers. A group has reached consensus when everyone can and will support the decision.

When to Use

This approach is best suited for making important decisions. Consensus promotes hard thinking that really gets at the issues. It can be slow, and it is occasionally painful; however, when a group finally reaches consensus, it has developed a solution that will have the support needed for implementation. Since consensus requires so much energy, the group should agree that the outcome of the decision is worth the effort. Such outcomes might include long-range planning, the development of a new program or service, or the revision of the library's job descriptions. In each of these situations, people probably care deeply about the outcome, and their support will be required to successfully implement the decision.

What to Do

People reach consensus by talking about issues in a fair and open environment. This means that the group leader will have to ensure that each member of the group has an opportunity to be heard, that no idea is discarded without a thorough review and discussion, and that all members of the group take responsibility for finding a mutually agreeable decision.

The national best seller *Getting to Yes: Negotiating Agreement without Giving In* identifies four steps to reaching consensus.[1]

> *Separate people from the problem.* People often feel strongly about issues under discussion, and discussions can shift quickly from issues to personalities. It is important to keep the discussion firmly focused on the problem under review.
>
> *Focus on interests, not positions.* Positions are the opinions that each group member brings to the discussion before the discussion begins. These positions get in the way of reaching consensus because they tend to be "all or nothing." To reach consensus, group members will have to focus on the problem and their mutual interest in resolving it, and not on their preconceived positions.
>
> *Generate a variety of options before deciding what to do.* There is no one right way to do anything. Consensus building involves identifying and discussing all of the ways the problem might be resolved. This is surprisingly difficult. Most people see problem solving as narrowing the options, not expanding them.
>
> *Base decisions on objective criteria.* This is a critical step in the consensus-building process. The group members must be able to define the criteria they will use to evaluate the options they have identified. If they can't agree on criteria, the group members are likely to revert to their positions when reviewing the options.

Voting

Quality of decision:
Varies
Time required:
Low to moderate
Group support for decision:
Moderate
Development of expertise:
Low to moderate

When people think about group decision-making processes, the first process that comes to mind is voting. Our whole society is based on the premise that the majority rules. We have all been voting on things since we were children. Voting is democratic, it's generally fair, and it's always quick and easy. However, there are some potential problems with voting. It can short-circuit consideration of all of the options, and if the issue is particularly contentious, it can split the group into winners and losers.

When to Use

If the decision under discussion is not critical and not worth a lot of discussion, it may be easiest to vote with a simple hand count. It is perfectly acceptable to take a hand count to decide where the group will have lunch. Hand counts can be used to make procedural decisions (how long the meetings will last, when the next meeting will be held, etc.).

If the decision is important, the dot-exercise voting process is more flexible and allows group members to express their opinions in more detail. It also provides a visual summary of the group members' preferred choices. The dot exercise might be used to identify activities that would help the library achieve the goals and objectives in the long-range plan, or to identify the topics for a staff-day program.

What to Do: Dot Exercise

The basic dot exercise process is quite straightforward. The process allows a large number of people to vote on a variety of options in a short period of time.

1. The leader first lists all of the options on flip-chart paper with enough space next to or between the items to allow committee members to place adhesive dots.
2. Each participant is given five self-adhesive colored dots.
3. The group members vote by putting dots on the flip-chart sheets next to their choices. Members may vote for five separate items, or they may load their vote, or "bullet vote," by giving an item more than one dot.
4. Count the votes by totaling the number of dots by each item.
5. Share and discuss the outcome of the voting exercise. Does the outcome seem to reflect the earlier discussions? Are clear priorities and a consensus emerging? Ask those who voted for items under discussion that received few votes to talk about their reasons for selecting those items.

A variation on the basic dot exercise helps to balance the effect of "bullet voting," which occurs when members place more than one of their dots by a single option. If the group is large, the bullet votes of one or two people will not have much impact, but if the group is small, those one or two people can essentially set priorities for the entire committee. With a small group, you might consider avoiding the impact of bullet voting by asking that committee members use a star to indicate their top priority. Then count votes by totaling the number of dots by each item and the number of stars by each item. Next, they share and discuss the outcome of the voting exercise. What is the difference, if any, between the priorities reflected by the dots and the stars? Does the outcome seem to reflect the earlier discussions? Are clear priorities and a consensus emerging?

Forced Choice

Quality of decision:
Varies
Time required:
Low
Group support for decision:
Low to moderate
Development of expertise:
Low

Most people find it virtually impossible to compare the relative merits of more than three or four items. The forced-choice process allows people to compare any number of items, each against the other, to determine which are the most important.

When to Use

The forced-choice process is an effective way of helping groups that have become mired in discussion to look at the options under review in a different way. The process does just what its name says: it forces people to make decisions from among a number of competing possibilities. The process also provides the information needed to place the options in priority order, based on the average ranking by each group member. That, however, is also the main weakness in the process. Because the priority of the options is determined by averaging, it is quite possible that the final list will not reflect the opinions of any single individual in the group. However, the process does identify items with little support. These can be excluded from the discussion, and one of the other processes discussed in this chapter can be used to allow the group to move forward to reach final agreement on the remaining options.

What to Do

1. List the options under review and number each. It is easier for the group members to vote if each of them has a copy of the options.
2. Prepare a forced-choice workform (see figure 48) and make a copy for each group member.
3. Each of the group members will complete the forced-choice process. (See Workform N, Forced-Choice Process, for directions.)
4. After each group member totals the number of times each option was circled, the option with the highest total is the one with the highest priority for that person.
5. The leader will help the group to see how the group members' selections compare with one another. This may be done in one of two ways:

   - Total the points for each choice from all of the group members. The choice with the highest total score is the most important; the next is the second most important, and so on.
   - Determine where each of the group members ranked each option by asking how many ranked a given option as the highest priority, how many ranked it as the second-highest priority, and so on. In this case, the option with the highest average ranking becomes the highest priority

FIGURE 48
Workform N: Forced-Choice Process—Example

Instructions

Assign a number to each of the items you are prioritizing. This worksheet will help you evaluate up to 15 items against every other item on list, each time determining which of your choices is the more important. Begin in Column A below. Compare the first and second items and circle the number of the one you think is more important (1 or 2). Continuing in Column A, compare the first item and the third item, again circling the service response you think is more important (1 or 3). Continue through all of the columns.

A	B	C	D	E	F	G	H	I	J	K	L	M	N
1 2													
1 3	2 3												
1 4	2 4	3 4											
1 5	2 5	3 5	4 5										
1 6	2 6	3 6	4 6	5 6									
1 7	2 7	3 7	4 7	5 7	6 7								
1 8	2 8	3 8	4 8	5 8	6 8	7 8							
1 9	2 9	3 9	4 9	5 9	6 9	7 9	8 9						
1 10	2 10	3 10	4 10	5 10	6 10	7 10	8 10	9 10					
1 11	2 11	3 11	4 11	5 11	6 11	7 11	8 11	9 11	10 11				
1 12	2 12	3 12	4 12	5 12	6 12	7 12	8 12	9 12	10 12	11 12			
1 13	2 13	3 13	4 13	5 13	6 13	7 13	8 13	9 13	10 13	11 13	12 13		
1 14	2 14	3 14	4 14	5 14	6 14	7 14	8 14	9 14	10 14	11 14	12 14	13 14	
1 15	2 15	3 15	4 15	5 15	6 15	7 15	8 15	9 15	10 15	11 15	12 15	13 15	14 15

To score your ratings, add the number of times you circled each number and place the total by the appropriate line below. Note that you must add vertically and horizontally to be sure that you include all circled choices. The service response with the highest number is the one you think is most important.

1. _____   4. _____   7. _____   10. _____   13. _____

2. _____   5. _____   8. _____   11. _____   14. _____

3. _____   6. _____   9. _____   12. _____   15. _____

Note

1. Roger Fisher, William Ury, and Bruce Patton, *Getting to Yes: Negotiating Agreement without Giving In,* 2nd ed. (New York: Penguin Books, 1991), 10–11.

Library Communication

Issues

If practice really did make things perfect, we would all be master communicators. We certainly spend a large part of every day communicating, both as senders and receivers: we chat, write, advise, and phone; we leave and receive voice mail, and send and receive e-mail; we remind, read, page, meet, listen, lecture—and on and on. In spite of all this communication, many people still feel uninformed, out of the loop, and misunderstood, particularly in their work environments. There are many reasons for this apparent dichotomy.

Some of the reasons are quite basic. Many people don't fully understand the communication process itself. They are also unclear about the differences between personal and organizational communication and about the functions of communication in a work environment. Even people who are familiar with communication theory can have problems putting it into practice. Most people deal with dozens or hundreds of messages every day and find it increasingly difficult to process all of the information they receive. Furthermore, there are more ways than ever to transmit information, and people don't always choose the best medium for the messages they are sending. The medium is not the only thing that can get in the way of successful communication. The message itself can be distorted by either the sender or the receiver—or by both. Sometimes the problem is not communication but the lack of communication or having the wrong people involved in the communication loop. These issues are discussed in more detail in the sections that follow.

Defining Communication

Many people think of communication as sending a message. In fact, that is only the first part of the communication process, and even that is not as simple as it might appear on the surface. As shown in figure 49, before a person can send an effective message, he or she has to *understand* the message. That should go without saying, but unfortunately it does not. Think about the number of times you have listened to a speaker who seemed to be confused or unsure of his or her message. If the sender doesn't understand the message, it is virtually impossible for the receiver to understand and act on it.

FIGURE 49
Effective Communication

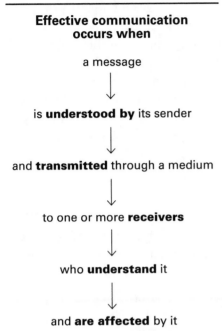

Effective communication occurs when

a message

↓

is **understood by** its sender

↓

and **transmitted** through a medium

↓

to one or more **receivers**

↓

who **understand** it

↓

and **are affected** by it

Once the sender understands the message, he or she has to transmit it through some medium. People can't read our minds (and it is just as well they can't), so we have to tell them what we are thinking. The medium we choose to transmit our message will affect how the message is received. (There is more information on matching the medium and the message later in this tool kit.) The communication process does not end when a message is sent. For effective communication to occur, there must be one or more receivers who understand the message and are affected by it. Philosophers have long debated the question, "If a tree falls in a forest and no one hears it, does it make a sound?" There is no such debate about communication. If you send a message and no one receives and understands it, you have not communicated.

People sending messages tend to blame the receivers when a message isn't understood or acted upon. However, that's not entirely fair. The responsibility for ensuring that the communication is completed rests with the sender. The person who initiates the communication has a reason for the communication and expects something to occur as a result of the communication. The receiver, who did not initiate the communication, must understand and accept the message in order to provide the expected response. While this is true in both formal and informal communications, it is more often a problem in the formal communication environment. Informal communications usually occur between two people or in small groups where it is easier to provide feedback and evaluate whether the message has been received. Formal communications, on the other hand, are often third-party communications that go through several layers of the organization. Therefore, there is less opportunity for feedback, and it may take longer to see if the message has been received, understood, and acted upon.

There are two main types of formal communication used in public libraries. One type includes all of the communications the library has with the public. The second type includes all internal communications among library staff members. It is this second type of formal communication that is the focus of this chapter.

Internal communications in public libraries have five main functions. They are used to

obtain information to make decisions

clarify job duties and provide feedback to staff

evaluate services and programs

maintain control (both formal and informal) by defining values
and sharing the expected norms

meet the social and emotional needs of the staff

When any of these functions are not addressed adequately, library managers and staff find it difficult to provide quality library services.

Managers can do several things to help staff understand the importance of communication within the library. The most obvious is to provide training at all levels. Most staff have attended one or more programs on customer service, and as a part of that training they have received some basic information about communicating, particularly with difficult library users. However, it is also very helpful for all staff to attend at least one training program that focuses on the specific elements of effective communication. A program like this can provide tools to help staff develop messages that are clear and appropriate to the intended receiver, select the best medium for the message, and identify ways to get feedback to ensure that the message was received and understood.

All library managers and supervisors should also receive training in the functions of formal communication, including discussions of how well each function is being addressed in the library. Follow up this training with meetings among managers to identify ways to improve formal communication in the library. Finally, the library director should include an ongoing review of the status of formal communication in the library as a part of regularly scheduled management meetings. This will help to identify problems early and to resolve them before there are serious consequences.

Sorting through the Cacophony

One of the biggest problems that we all have in receiving, understanding, and acting on incoming communications is that we receive so *many* messages. The sheer volume of information makes it difficult to sort out the messages that are important or urgent from those that are trivial or irrelevant. As already noted, it is up to the sender to help the receiver make these distinctions. The sender can do several things to help the receiver. By far the most important is to select the right medium for the message.

The Message and the Medium

Today there are more ways than ever before to "reach out and touch someone," and most of us haven't given a lot of thought to which way is the most effective in a given circumstance. Consider several things as you match the message and medium:

> Does the intended receiver have easy access to the medium being considered?
>
> Is the message complex, or is it fairly straightforward?
>
> Is the message important, or is it routine?
>
> Is the content ephemeral, or does it need to be maintained as a permanent record for documentation purposes?
>
> Is the message confidential?
>
> How soon does the message need to be received?

Think about these issues in relation to e-mail communications. Many library managers use e-mail as their prime method of communicating with library staff members—regardless of the message. There are several problems with this, not the least of which is that only in rare libraries do all staff members have personal e-mail accounts. Staff do not think of messages sent to a generic agency or unit e-mail address as personal messages. E-mail is also not a good medium to send long messages. As one staff member said, "I hit page down, page down, delete no matter how long the message is. I am not going to read a ten-page memo one screen at a time." E-mail is an ephemeral medium. Most people don't print out e-mail messages, and they don't file them electronically either. Therefore, it is difficult to refer back to an e-mail message if questions arise later. Finally, e-mail isn't a good medium to use for private or confidential messages. It is far too easy to hit the wrong button and send the message to a group instead of a single person, or for one person to forward the message to another with a single keystroke.

Figure 50 lists ten common media used to transmit messages in public libraries in the left column and six criteria to consider when matching the message and the medium across the top of the table. Some of the decisions about matching the medium to the message are based on local conditions or the message itself, and they are labeled with a question mark. For instance, someone wanting to deliver a message to a library director and using a phone as the medium has every reason to assume that the director has easy access to a private phone. However, there is no reason to assume that a page or a part-time circulation attendant has that same easy access. As another example, a complex message could be delivered effectively to a small meeting of people who are directly affected by the message, particularly if the meeting is long enough to allow for thorough discussion. The same complex message could not be delivered as effectively to a large group of people consisting of some who are affected by it and others who are not.

It can be helpful for library managers to develop general guidelines concerning the media to be used to transmit certain types of messages. For instance, managers might decide that all messages dealing with human resource issues should be transmitted in

FIGURE 50
Match the Message and the Medium

Medium	Access	Message				
	Receiver has easy access	Message is complex	Message is important	Permanent record is required	Message is confidential	Message is urgent
Face-to-face conversation	✓	✓	✓		✓	✓
Telephone conversation	?		✓		✓	✓
Meeting	?	?	✓	?		?
E-mail	?	?		?		✓
Individual letter or memo	✓	✓	✓	✓	✓	✓
Videotape or audiotape	?	?	?	✓		
Group letter or memo	?	?	?	✓		?
Policy and procedure manual	?	✓	✓	✓		
Web page	?			?		
Notice on a staff bulletin board	✓					

written form, either through personal or group memoranda. Sometimes the guidelines will be more general. The managers in one library developed the following preliminary guidelines for the types of messages that should be sent using e-mail:

- general information that can be sent quickly and easily
- nonconfidential messages
- short and concise messages (simple, ephemeral)
- messages that serve as means to send attachments
- scheduling for collaborative projects or meetings
- messages that don't require immediate feedback
- follow-ups to other communications
- reminders

These might not be the guidelines that you would develop in your library, but they can provide a starting place for discussion. The point is that library managers and staff should talk about how communication works in your library environment and what would make it more effective.

Repetition Works

Most experienced public speakers follow this traditional rule: tell the audience what you are going to say, say it, and then tell the audience what you said. Many speakers also provide the content of their presentation in multiple formats, using both verbal messages (the presentation) and written messages (handouts, overheads, or PowerPoint presentations). These speakers have learned that people need to hear and see information several times before they can fully understand or accept it. This is particularly true if the message contains information that is completely new to the receivers or if the message contains information that the receivers aren't particularly pleased to hear.

It will be worth your time and energy to follow the example set by these speakers. Send important messages several times using several different media. No matter what media you use, remember to rephrase the key points several times and summarize the message in the final paragraph. This improves the odds that the receiver will not only get the message but will understand it and be affected by it. It also provides an opportunity for receivers to verify the information being transmitted. They can check the different versions of the messages they receive to be sure they understand what is being said. One caveat: don't rephrase so much that receivers look for differences, thinking they're getting a new message.

Dealing with Distortion

A message can be distorted by the sender or by the receiver or by both. The sender can distort a message by deliberately filtering the content. For example, a staff member who is unhappy about a new policy might send her supervisor a memorandum describing in detail the complaints she received from two library users about the policy but not mentioning the positive comments she received from ten other users. The sender can also accidentally distort the message in a number of ways. The sender might assume incorrectly that the receiver has certain background information and thus not provide needed data, or the sender might not understand the content clearly and therefore highlight the wrong data. Finally, there is the message's language itself. Because most words have several meanings, some people will interpret a message one way and some another. The easiest way to avoid misinterpretation is to keep professional messages clear, complete, and concise. Use short words and short sentences. Ask several people to review important messages before they are transmitted to the receivers to be sure that the main points are unambiguous.

Receivers can also distort messages. Everyone perceives things a little differently based on their own experiences, needs, and interests. Emotional reactions may be the most common reason that messages are distorted by receivers. When people are involved in personal crises, they are less likely to pay attention to messages that don't deal directly with the crisis at hand. When people are angry or frustrated, they are often not responsive to messages from the people or groups that they blame for their anger or frustration. What this means, among other things, is that messages that are likely to evoke strong emotions—especially messages that deal with significant change—have to be even more carefully written and broadly disseminated than other messages.

Lack of Communication

Not all communication problems deal with how a message is framed and delivered. Many staff members say that the biggest problem with communication in their libraries is too *little* communication. Perhaps the most common reason for lack of communication is simple oversight. We are all busy, and most of us feel overwhelmed on occasion. It takes time to communicate, and time is one of our most precious commodities. We also have a tendency to think, "If I know it, everyone must know it." The corollary to that is, "I don't know it, but everyone else must know it because no one else is asking." These two assumptions keep us from transmitting important information to others and from asking for the information that we need to do our jobs.

Sent but Not Received

Sometimes "lack of communication" doesn't mean the message wasn't sent; it may mean that an important message was sent once through a single medium. The sender may feel that the message has been delivered, but, as noted previously, the intended receivers may not have actually received the message. Perhaps the message was sent to branch or department managers who were instructed to pass the message on to their subordinates. If there is no requirement for feedback built into the process, there is no way for the original sender to know if all of the managers in the middle transmitted the message as instructed. It is not uncommon for a branch manager to return to the branch from a meeting with information that is to be passed on to all employees. Too often this is what happens:

The manager sees employee 1 and gives her the complete message. The manager sees employee 2 ten or fifteen minutes later and gives him most of the message. Employees 3 and 4 run into the manager in the break room and get an abbreviated version of the message. Employee 5 doesn't see the manager at all that day and is given a very brief summary the next morning. Employee 6, who is out sick all week, never gets the message.

It is clear that employee 6 has been completely cut out of the communication loop, but even employee 1, who received the whole message, has no way of validating what she was told. Everyone but employees 3 and 4 was told something slightly different.

Sent Too Late

Sometimes information is disseminated too late to be useful to a specific audience. Consider this scenario:

January 15	The administrative team considers a policy change, and an individual, committee, or task force is asked to develop a draft of the new policy.
March 1	The draft policy is reviewed by the administrative team.
March 15	The draft policy is sent to senior managers for review and comment.
April 15	The administrative team discusses reactions from the senior managers and makes changes in the draft as needed.
May 15	The draft of the policy is sent to branch/department managers for review and comment without explicit instructions that they should share the draft with staff. Consequently some managers share it, and some don't.
July 1	The administrative team discusses reactions from branch/department managers and makes changes in the draft as needed.
August 1	The policy is officially approved by the chief administrator and sent to all units.
August 15	The policy is officially scheduled to be implemented.
August 16	Frontline staff, who actually have to implement the policy, complain that they were not informed. Managers can't understand what the staff are talking about. After all, the new policy has been under discussion for more than nine months.

Variations on this scenario are played out in libraries across the country over and over again. It is critical to involve the staff who will be affected by a new policy in discussions about that policy early in the planning stages and to be sure that the staff who have to implement policies and procedures are fully trained before the implementation process begins.

Library Intranets

Some library managers are using the library's intranet to provide staff with the information they need to do their jobs more effectively. The intranet can be used to provide access to a broad array of information, including policies and procedures, committee or task force information (membership, agendas, minutes, reports), staff directories, training schedules, job postings, public relations announcements, and so on. The most important benefit to providing information through the intranet is that all staff have access to it, and they can access it whenever it is convenient. The second benefit is that information can be loaded on the intranet fairly easily and can be updated without a lot of trouble. This is particularly important for library policies and procedures, which are very difficult to keep current at the unit level in paper formats. A third benefit is that, with proper design, most information on the intranet can be searched by keyword. This makes finding and using the information much easier.

Evaluating Communication Processes

Four general models that describe the way information is transmitted in libraries are downward communication, downward-and-upward communication, horizontal communication, and diagonal communication. None of these models is intrinsically superior to the others. At times each is appropriate to use. The important thing to remember is that in libraries with effective communication, all four of these models are used regularly. Four measures can be used to help you decide which model will be most effective for a given situation: distribution of information, ability to verify information, need for acceptance from the receiver, and time required for the transmission.

Distribution of Information

The first measure to use when deciding which model is appropriate is how widely the information needs to be distributed. Does everyone in the organization need to know? Do you need to have some verification that the message has been received? Remember, the more ways you send a message, the more likely it is that the people you are targeting will actually receive, understand, and be affected by the information in the message.

The Ability to Validate Information

The second measure to use when deciding which model is appropriate is the need for the receiver to validate the information being received. Most people have no desire to validate simple messages or messages of little importance. However, people often need to be able to corroborate messages that are complex or messages that contain information they are unfamiliar with or unhappy about.

Need for Acceptance from the Receiver

The third thing to consider when selecting a communication model is the degree to which it is important that the receiver accept the information in the message. Some messages are purely informational, and it doesn't matter a lot to the sender if the receivers accept or reject the information. The announcement that the library board will be holding its regularly scheduled meeting on July 21 is an example of such a message. However, in some instances it is critical to the sender that the receivers not only understand the message but that they accept the information in the message as accurate and valid and act upon the information in a specific way. Suppose a message is disseminated announcing a new policy and procedures for managing patron reserve requests. Staff who receive the message must not only understand the new policy and procedures, they must also put them into practice on a specified date. This is far more likely to occur if staff are familiar with the changes, understand why the changes are being made, and agree that the changes are reasonable and necessary. In general, the more involvement the staff have in the decision-making process, the more accepting they are of the final decision. Therefore, communication models that allow for discussion and interaction are the most effective ways to deal with issues that require staff acceptance.

Time Required

The fourth thing to consider when selecting a communication model is time. If there is only one way to do something or if a decision has already been made, then it makes sense to transmit the message in the fastest way possible. Communication processes that allow for staff feedback and staff involvement in decision making are time-intensive. The more participation you allow, the more time-intensive the process becomes. If the issue under consideration is important and staff involvement is critical, then invest the time needed to resolve it effectively. You will probably find that the initial investment in time pays off in significant time savings during the implementation phase

Methods for Communicating in Your Library

Downward Communication

Distribution of information:
 Moderate

Ability to verify information:
 Low

Acceptance of receiver:
 Low

Time required:
 Low

Downward communication is also known as "bureaucratic" communication. Messages are sent down the chain of command throughout the library. In many libraries, this is the most frequently used communication model. Downward communication often reflects a centralized managerial style in which decisions are made by senior managers; middle managers and staff are expected to implement those decisions with little or no input. It is rare for centralized decisions that were communicated downward to have a high level of staff acceptance.

The most significant benefit of downward communication is efficiency. It is by far the fastest and easiest of the four communication models. However, this efficiency has a price. There is no way for the sender to be sure that the message was distributed throughout the library, nor is there a way for the intended receiver to know that he or she didn't receive the message. This is important because there are often breaks in the bureaucratic delivery chain. Some of these breaks are accidental—a manager might be out sick for several days and unable to send the message—but others are deliberate—a manager might disagree with the information in the message and not pass it on. Part-time workers are often unintentionally excluded from the downward communication chain because they aren't at work when messages are being delivered to the rest of the staff. Even messages that are delivered to all intended recipients may be garbled as they move from one level in the organization to the next. Remember the game of "Telephone" in which a message that is passed through a chain of ten people is changed completely by the end of the chain?

When to Use

Downward communication can be used effectively to send simple messages that are intended to distribute general information that requires little or no action on the part of the receiver.

What to Do

1. Make it explicitly clear to managers that they are responsible for ensuring that all downward communications reach all employees.
2. Put all messages to be sent throughout the library in writing.
3. Number each message consecutively, and keep a copy for reference.
4. Clearly label all messages sent downward through the library as "For Your Information."
5. Check periodically to see if messages are being transmitted throughout the library by asking a sampling of people at all levels if they received a given message.
6. Keep each message brief.
7. Start the message with the most important information and then provide supporting data, if needed.
8. Focus on a single topic in each message. If you have several different kinds of information to share, send several separate messages.
9. Post copies of all messages sent downward through the library on the library's intranet so that employees can refer to them easily.

Downward-and-Upward Communication

Distribution of information:
Moderate to high

Ability to verify information:
Moderate

Acceptance of receiver:
Moderate

Time required:
Low to moderate

Downward-and-upward communication is also known as "two-way" communication. It follows the chain of command in the library but includes formal processes for ensuring that information flows in both directions. General staff meetings in which downward communications are presented and discussed are one common example of two-way communication.

The most important benefit of two-way communication is that it gives the receivers a chance to verify the data in the message to be sure that they understand it. Downward-and-upward communication provides a mechanism for receivers to formally express their opinions about the information in a message to the people who sent the original message. If the receivers believe that their opinions are taken seriously, they are more likely to accept the content of the message.

There are, however, a number of drawbacks to downward-and-upward communications. Because the process usually follows the structure of the library bureaucracy, the successful transmission of the communication in both directions is dependent on individual managers to provide a conduit for two-way information. Unfortunately, most libraries have at least one manager who blocks the flow of information rather than facilitating it. Even managers who make a good-faith effort to promote two-way communication have differing communication skills and attitudes. As a result, the staff in each unit of the library probably get slightly different messages. This model provides no way for staff to validate information among units.

When to Use

Three main categories of messages can be effectively disseminated using two-way communication processes. First, all formal employee-supervisor communications should be both downward and upward. One example is the performance appraisal process, in which employees and their supervisors discuss goals and objectives at the beginning of the year and then evaluate progress at the end of the year. Another example is the formal grievance process.

The second category includes all messages that transmit decisions that will affect staff duties and responsibilities. Some of these decisions, such as city or county policies or information about the library budget, will have been made without significant staff input. Other decisions will have been made after extensive discussion using horizontal and diagonal communication processes. Sometimes the participants in committee and task force meetings forget that not everyone has been as involved in the decision-making process as they have. As a result, decisions are made but not formally shared with the entire staff. It is appropriate to share these final decisions using a downward-and-upward communication process. Be sure to include a brief description of the participative process used to reach the decisions in your message.

The final category of messages that can be delivered using downward-and-upward communication are messages containing suggestions from staff and the public for improving services or changing policies. These are messages that originate with staff and are passed up through the chain of command for action. When the recommendations have been acted upon, messages are sent back to the originating staff to inform them of the action taken.

What to Do

1. Personnel communications
   a. Review your performance appraisal process to be sure that it provides a mechanism for two-way communication.
   b. Require supervisors to communicate with employees about their performance regularly throughout the year.
   c. Ensure that all staff are aware of the grievance process.
2. Disseminating decisions
   a. Make it explicitly clear to managers that they are expected to serve as conduits for information—both downward and upward.
   b. Provide training to help managers improve their communication skills and learn to facilitate group discussions.
   c. Clearly label messages that are intended to be discussed by managers and staff as "For Discussion."

d. Include a date by which feedback and questions about the information in the message are due to be submitted to a single person.

e. Develop a specific format for managers to use to submit feedback, and use it consistently. For example:

> Issue discussed
> Date discussed
> With whom
> General reaction
> Questions
> Suggestions

f. Prepare and distribute a final message that summarizes the feedback and describes what actions, if any, have been taken to respond to the feedback.

g. Monitor the feedback that is received over a period of time. If you notice that some managers rarely provide feedback, speak to them to determine why.

3. Suggestions from the staff and the public

a. Develop specific forms for staff and for public suggestions and make the suggestion forms readily available.

b. Provide a link on the library website to a public suggestion form and make sure someone is assigned to retrieve and process the suggestions.

c. Provide an electronic version of the staff suggestion form on the library intranet.

d. Consider posting selected staff and public suggestions on the intranet for staff to review. Include some indication of the disposition of the suggestion.

e. Make sure that staff and the public know when actions are taken as a result of a suggestion.

Horizontal Communication

Distribution of information:
  Low to moderate

Ability to verify information:
  High

Acceptance of receiver:
  High

Time required:
  Moderate to high

Horizontal communications in libraries normally take place in regularly scheduled meetings of people with similar positions who work in different units of the library. Common examples include children's librarian meetings, circulation attendant meetings, branch manager meetings, and main library unit manager meetings.

Horizontal groups provide peer support for their members and can significantly improve staff morale. They are the ideal forum for developing new and innovative services or programs and for solving problems in specialty areas that affect more than one library unit. Horizontal groups also provide a mechanism for staff in various library units to verify all kinds of messages that have been distributed downward through the organization.

However, horizontal groups are not always the best way to disseminate information to other staff members in the library. Often the members of the group place far more value on communicating with each other than on communicating with non-group members. This can cause real problems for library managers who expect horizontal group members to share information with other staff in their units. If a library manager announces a change in circulation policy to the members of the circulation attendant group and asks them to pass the word, that manager cannot assume that everyone who needs to know about the change will be informed. In fact, it is highly probable that some group members will not pass on the message and that some unit managers will be irritated (to say the least) that they were not informed directly.

The primary drawback with horizontal groups is the *time* they take staff from other activities. Horizontal meetings usually occur monthly. Someone has to plan the meeting, and participants have to travel to a single location for their meeting and then spend one to three hours in the meeting before traveling back to their library units. Next, someone has to write the minutes from the meeting and pass on any recommendations from the group to the managers who can act on the recommendations. Many library managers resent the scheduling problems that result from staff participation in horizontal meetings.

When to Use

Most participants of horizontal groups benefit from their participation in those groups and use their meetings to discuss ways to improve the services they offer. However, many libraries offer the opportunity to participate in a horizontal group only to selected staff members, generally children's staff and unit managers. Library managers should discuss the benefits that would result from encouraging members of other horizontal groups to meet regularly. Some possibilities to consider are reference staff, staff who serve people with special needs, technical support staff (formal or informal) in each unit, paraprofessional staff, and staff with materials selection responsibilities.

What to Do

1. Provide an opportunity for members of any horizontal group in the library to meet if they wish to and if they can explain the benefits that will result from their meetings.
2. Make sure that all members of a horizontal group are given equal opportunity to meet with the group.
3. Establish a regular schedule for each group to meet.
4. Identify a group leader. This can be an appointed or elected position and can remain the same year after year or change annually.
5. Develop a standard format for horizontal group agendas and minutes, and expect all groups to use it.
6. Ask each group to prepare an agenda (using the standard format) for each meeting and distribute it to all participants and all managers at least one week before the meeting. If you have a library intranet, post all agendas there.
7. Ask each group to have someone responsible for preparing minutes from each meeting (using the standard format) and distributing them to all participants and all managers within one week of the meeting. If you have a library intranet, post all minutes there.
8. Establish a formal process for reviewing the recommendations received from horizontal groups and for acting on those recommendations.
9. Disseminate the final actions taken on recommendations from horizontal groups to all staff members using the downward-and-upward communication model. If for some reason a decision is made not to implement one or more of the recommendations, be sure to explain why.

Diagonal Communication

Distribution of information:
    Moderate to high

Ability to verify information:
    High

Acceptance of receiver:
    High

Time required:
    High

The most common diagonal communication models in libraries are cross-functional work groups that include people with different job classifications who work in different units of the library. The two types of cross-functional groups are task forces and teams. Cross-functional task forces are normally convened for a specific purpose; when the task is completed, the task force is disbanded. Cross-functional teams, on the other hand, generally have continuing responsibilities. For example, a task force might be appointed to coordinate the selection of a new automation system for the library. When the system has been selected, the task force will have completed its work. On the other hand, a cross-functional team might be appointed to monitor library safety issues. The members of the team might change, but the team itself would be ongoing.

Cross-functional teams and task forces are the most open of the communication models. They encourage communication among all staff at all levels. This in turn allows staff to verify messages received through any of the other models. Cross-functional teams and task forces also give staff members a very real voice in the decision-making process, which significantly increases staff acceptance of the final decisions.

While cross-functional groups have strengths, they also have some drawbacks. The most obvious drawback is the time it takes to bring disparate people from all over the library system together to discuss a problem and identify possible solutions. In addition, some members of these groups might find it difficult to remember they were appointed to represent a specific constituency and instead promote their personal views. The reverse can be true as well. Sometimes the members of a constituent group don't trust the person selected to represent them. Furthermore, some task forces do not include people with the skills and knowledge required to accomplish the task. Others include people with diametrically opposed positions who refuse to consider compromise. Teams and task forces function most effectively if they are led by an experienced facilitator who has credibility with the members of the team and other stakeholders.

When to Use

Most libraries use cross-functional teams and task forces differently. Cross-functional teams are appointed to discuss ongoing issues that affect all staff and to make recommendations when appropriate. Different libraries will have different teams, depending on local conditions. Examples of teams include the safety team mentioned previously and staff development teams. Generally the membership of a team changes each year, but the team charge remains the same. Teams give staff members a forum to discuss issues of ongoing interest or concern and provide managers with recommendations for action and with feedback about staff attitudes.

Almost all task forces address some aspect of decision making. Some task forces provide the information needed to reach a decision. Other task forces are responsible for determining how to implement a decision that has been made. Still other task forces are responsible for actually implementing a decision. The members of each task force must understand both their responsibility and their authority clearly.

Task forces should be used when the decision under consideration or being implemented will have a significant effect on the way most or all staff members do their jobs. Never appoint a task force to consider an issue that you, as a manager, know how you want to handle. More than one library manager has appointed a task force firmly believing the task force would recommend a specific action. When the task force made a different recommendation (and they almost always do), the manager had a serious problem: He could either adopt the task force recommendation even though it was not at all the way he wanted to solve the problem, or he could do what he intended to do all along and alienate the members of the task force and the rest of the staff. Neither option is attractive.

What to Do

1. Identify a clear charge for each task force or team that is appointed.
2. Determine which library constituencies should be represented on the task force or team. Make it clear to everyone that the people asked to be members of the task force or team are expected to represent their specific constituencies and not their own personal points of view.
3. Require task force and team members to report regularly to the constituent groups they represent.
4. Establish a time line for each task force that includes a deadline for the receipt of recommendations and a deadline for taking action on those recommendations.
5. Disseminate the charge and membership of every team and task force to all staff. Include information on the time lines for all task forces. If any of this information changes, notify all staff that the changes have occurred. If you have a library intranet, this information can be posted there.
6. Develop a standard format for task force and team agendas and minutes, and expect all groups to use it. Consider using the same form used for horizontal groups.
7. Ask each task force and team to prepare an agenda (using the standard format) for each meeting and distribute it to all participants and all managers in the library at least one week before the meeting. If you have a library intranet, post all agendas there.
8. Ask each task force and team to have someone responsible for preparing minutes from each meeting (using the standard format) and distributing them to all participants and all managers within one week of the meeting. If you have a library intranet, post all minutes there.
9. Establish a formal process for reviewing the recommendations received from task forces and teams and for acting on those recommendations.
10. Disseminate the final actions taken on task force and team recommendations to all staff members using the downward-and-upward communication model. If for some reason a decision is made not to implement one or more of the recommendations, be sure to explain why.

Presenting Data

Issues

Public library staff and managers collect a wide variety of information about library services and programs. In theory, five main reasons for collecting all of this data are to

> measure progress toward accomplishing the goals and
> objectives in the library's strategic plan
>
> document the value of library services
>
> make resource allocation decisions
>
> meet the requirements of a grant project
>
> meet state library data-collection requirements

In practice, much of the information that is collected in libraries is never used at all, and when managers attempt to use the information they collected, they often have problems presenting the information effectively.

The first and most basic problem with presenting data concerns the selection of which data elements to use to support the intended outcomes. This is trickier than it appears. Too little data is unhelpful; too much data is overwhelming; and the wrong data is misleading. The second problem is the difficulty some people have in organizing data. This was a more serious problem when we had to use adding machines and ledgers to analyze data; today we have a variety of computer software programs that help to manipulate and organize data. However, we still have to have a coherent reason for the organizational decisions that we make; otherwise, the data won't make sense. The third problem has to do with the layout and design of the data. It doesn't do any good to select the right data elements and organize the data elements in a logical pattern if you don't present them in a clear and attractive manner. These issues will be discussed in more detail in the following sections.

Selecting the Right Data

Before you can begin to select data for any purpose, you have to know who your audience is and what that audience needs to see in order to make a decision or reach a conclusion. If you are making a presentation intended to encourage seventh-grade students to use the library, there isn't much point in telling them about the increase in the number of senior citizens who use the library for personal development and ongoing learning. If you are making a presentation to senior citizens about the opportunities for lifelong learning at the library, they probably won't be interested in the number of hits on your homework help web page or the rapidly increasing circulation of game cartridges.

Knowing your audience goes beyond understanding their interests. You also have to have some idea of what they already know and what they don't know. If you present information on document delivery to library managers, you can reasonably assume they will know you are talking about interlibrary loan, reserves, and the delivery of requested items among the various units in the library. If you present information on document delivery to the members of the city council, they may well assume you are talking about services to the homebound.

There are two kinds of data: quantitative and qualitative. Quantitative data is numeric and measures how much of something there is or how often something happens. Most library data is quantitative (circulation figures, number of reference questions, number of users who log on to the Internet, number of online searches, etc.). Qualitative data comes from observations or interviews and results in patterns or generalizations about why something occurs. The information obtained from a series of focus groups on business services is qualitative data. Both types of data can be effective. Figure 51 lists nine common purposes for collecting data and suggests which type of data would be most effective in each case.

FIGURE 51

Quantitative and Qualitative Data

Reason	Quantitative Data	Qualitative Data
Measure number of people who use a service or program	✓	
Show reasons for current use		✓
Show trends in the numbers of people who use a service or program	✓	
Show relations between trends in current use	✓	
Show reasons for trends in current use		✓
Measure user satisfaction		✓
Measure units of library service delivered	✓	
Show trends in units of library service delivered	✓	
Measure cost per unit of service delivered	✓	

No matter which types of data you decide best meet your needs, be selective about the specific data elements to include. Too much data is worse than too little. However, once you select the data elements you want to use, be sure to include the entire data set for each element. Let's say you want to explain to the members of the library board the relation between increased use of electronic resources and decreased print and media circulation. After reviewing all of the possible data elements, you might select circulation figures and number of electronic searches as the two data elements that would best illustrate what is happening. The data set for circulation includes all of the different categories of circulation you count. You may not want the board to focus on the increase in the circulation of media items, but once you decide to use circulation figures you have to include them all. In the same way, to present an accurate picture of the number of electronic searches, you will have to include all electronic searches that take place using library equipment, both on- and off-site, and both CD-ROM and Internet. It is equally important to include the full set of data elements when you use qualitative data. If you decide to report on public reaction to a new service, you have to report all of the reactions, not just the positive ones.

The key to all this is to be as honest as you can with the statistics you select and present. You will want to be able to explain why you chose the data elements you are using and the source of each. It is also important that you check and double-check your numbers. If one number is inaccurate, it doesn't matter how carefully you selected the data elements you included or how accurate the rest of the numbers are: the single inaccurate number will taint the entire report.

Organizing the Data

Once you have selected the data elements to use, you have to decide how to organize the information so that it is clear and easily understood. Three basic organizational models that you might want to consider are historical order, priority order, and narrative logic. Your choice from among these three options depends on what you are trying to accomplish, what data elements are available, and which of the three options seems most logical to you.

What you want to avoid is the fourth option—no particular order. This is just what it sounds like—data elements are arranged without pattern and in no conscious order. This makes it difficult for the person using the data to deliver a coherent presentation and makes it even harder for the audience to understand what is being presented. Think about how hard it would be to follow a presentation about library services that started with juvenile circulation figures, moved to general budget numbers, took a side trip to present data about attendance at the summer reading program, then talked about adult circulation, and finally ended with information about the cost of new electronic resources.

Historical Order

When you use the historical order organizational model, you present information about trends in the areas being considered. These trends provide a context in which to consider data about current services or programs. This is a particularly useful model when you are presenting information about programs or services that are experiencing significant changes. If adult nonfiction circulation has dropped 20 percent in the past five years, that is important information to have when you are considering your materials budget. If media circulation has increased by 15 percent during the same period, that is also important to know. Of course, you can't use historical order if you don't have historical data, which is often the case when you are presenting data about new services or programs.

Priority Order

When you use priority order as the organizational model, you present the most important data first and then provide less important supporting data. It is a useful model if you are presenting a number of different data elements to support a specific proposal. Let's say you are reporting on the use of the library's electronic resources during the eighteen months since you began to allow users to dial in from off-site to use the library's databases and connect to the Internet. The most important data element would be the number of log-ons from off-site, and you would start your report with that. You might then choose to include data on the number of searches and the number of items retrieved to give the audience an idea of how the off-site access is actually being used.

Narrative Logic

When you use narrative logic as the organizational model, you arrange the data to tell a story. This model can be very effective when trying to sell a new idea or program. It allows you to create a script that moves the audience from one step to the next until they finally reach the conclusion you want them to reach. Often the story starts with information that the audience already knows (once upon a time . . .). Confirming prior knowledge builds credibility into the sales process. Then you select and present the data that best supports each of the key points in your story.

Designing the Document

The final thing to consider when presenting data is the layout and design of the data. In some ways, this is the most important part of the process. After all, if no one looks at the data you have selected and organized, all of your efforts will have been wasted. The first step in the design process is to create a document that is attractive and visually appealing. The document will have to look inviting enough to encourage busy people to take time to pick it up and start reading it. Next you want to be sure that the information in the document is clear and easy to read. Most of the people in your audience are too busy to spend a lot of time trying to decipher a jumble of confusing words and charts.

Graphic design is managing visual information through layout, typography, and illustration to lead the reader's eye through the page. The layout of the document is the first thing readers will see. They will observe the balance of white space and text and the proportion of text and graphics. A page that has little or no white space is not user-friendly; neither is a page filled with a jumble of graphics. You are looking for a balance between text and graphics surrounded by enough white space to provide an effective frame.

Create a basic layout and style sheet and use it consistently throughout the document. Select a single, readable font to use for text and graphics. Match your text and your graphics and try to keep the size of the visuals proportionate. A number of excellent books on graphic design are available that will provide additional suggestions and illustrations to help you create an effective document. Remember, in graphic design, as in so much else, simple is always better. You want the audience to focus on the content, not on the graphics.

Evaluating Methods of Presenting Data

Most library managers present data in three main ways: narrative descriptions, tables, and graphs and charts. Each can be used effectively in certain circumstances. You can also use two or all three of the methods together to improve the chances that your audience will receive and understand the information you are presenting. To help you select the best method or combination of methods for your purpose, think about the following:

> How long will it take to develop the presentation, and what level of skill will be required?
>
> How important is it that the information be presented in a visually attractive and interesting way?
>
> How easy will it be to read and understand the final product?
>
> Will the audience be expected to understand the relationships among various data elements?

These questions are addressed in more detail in the following sections.

Time and Skill

The first issue to consider when selecting a method of presentation is the time and skill required to develop the presentation. It can take considerable time and technical skill to create high-quality charts and graphs. Narrative descriptions and tables are normally much easier and quicker to develop. Consider the following questions when deciding how much time and energy to invest in developing a presentation:

> Is the target audience internal or external? Normally, library managers are willing to invest more time in presentations for external audiences.
>
> Is the data being presented for informational purposes, or do you want it to result in a decision? It makes sense to spend more time on presentations that are intended to help people reach a decision.
>
> How frequently will the final product be used? Some presentations will be used a number of times, while others will be used just once. It is worth investing the time and energy needed to ensure that the template for your monthly report to the city manager is a high-quality product because you will be using it repeatedly.
>
> What is the easiest and simplest method that can be used to achieve what needs to be accomplished?

Visual Appeal

The second issue to consider when selecting a method of presentation is the need to present the information in a visually attractive manner. It is always important that information be readable, but if you are presenting information to staff, you may be less concerned about making it attractive and interesting than you would be if you were presenting the same information to the members of the chamber of commerce. Most library managers routinely "clean things up" for external use. Visual presentations tend to be more appealing and interesting than text presentations. They also usually take considerably longer to develop.

Simplicity and Clarity

The third issue to consider when selecting a method of presentation is the ease with which the data can be read and understood. Some kinds of data are easier to understand than others. A single data point can be presented very nicely using a narrative description. On the other hand, as you will see in figure 52, it is difficult to use narrative description to present complex historical data about several different categories of information.

Depiction of Relationships

The last question to consider when selecting a method of presentation is whether there are relationships among the data elements that you want to highlight. Most people find it easier to see such relationships when they are presented in graphs and charts rather than in narrative form. The old saying "A picture is worth a thousand words" is as true about data as it is about describing a sunset.

FIGURE 52
Narrative Description

CIRCULATION BY TYPE OF MATERIAL

The circulation patterns in the library have changed over the past five years. The most significant change has been in the circulation of nonfiction materials. In 2004, 28 percent of the total circulation in the library came from adult nonfiction items and approximately 12 percent came from children's nonfiction; the combined circulation of children's and adult nonfiction items represented almost 40 percent of the total circulation. In 2008, the circulation of adult nonfiction materials was 19 percent of the total circulation and an additional 9 percent came from children's nonfiction. The combined circulation of children's and adult nonfiction materials was only 28 percent of the total circulation. That represents a 12 percent decrease over a five-year period.

On the other hand, the circulation of nonprint materials increased from 13 percent to almost 20 percent of total circulation between 2004 and 2008. The change in the percentage circulation of fiction materials has been more moderate. In 2004, 25 percent of the total circulation came from adult fiction materials and 22 percent of circulation came from children's fiction; total fiction circulation was 47 percent of the overall circulation. In 2008, 27 percent of the circulation came from adult fiction materials and 25 percent came from children's fiction; total fiction circulation was 52 percent, a 5 percent increase.

Methods for Presenting Data

Narrative Descriptions

Time and skills:
Low
Visual appeal:
Low
Simplicity and clarity:
Low to moderate
Depiction of relationships:
Moderate

Narrative descriptions use text to present quantitative and qualitative data and to describe the relationships, if any, among data elements. Before library managers had easy access to personal computers and spreadsheet programs, they presented a great deal of library information using narrative descriptions. Even now, some managers rely heavily on narrative descriptions because they are quick and easy to prepare and do not require any special computer skills.

At times narrative descriptions can be effective (especially for qualitative data that is itself narrative in form), but they have some serious drawbacks when used as your primary presentation method. The most obvious problem is that blocks of text aren't very attractive or interesting. It can also be confusing to read about a variety of data elements with no easy way to keep track of them. Although you can use narrative descriptions to describe the relationship among several data elements, the relationship would probably be clearer if you included a table or graph.

Figures 53 through 56 present the same data in a variety of ways. Read the description in figure 52, and then look at the table in figure 53 and the graphs and charts in figures 54 through 56. Which of the options do you think presents the information most effectively? Why?

When to Use

Narrative description can be an effective way to present information gathered through focus groups or other qualitative data-collection processes because qualitative data is often narrative rather than numeric. Narrative descriptions can also be used effectively to present a few simple statistics and to discuss the relationships among them. You might

---

FIGURE 53
Sample Table

CIRCULATION BY TYPE OF MATERIAL

	2004	2005	2006	2007	2008
Media (DVDs, CDs, etc.)	38,900	46,650	60,877	63,450	65,980
Adult fiction	78,090	79,950	82,074	85,375	87,430
Adult nonfiction	88,098	84,650	76,220	70,580	63,250
Children's fiction	67,991	71,600	76,909	81,649	83,230
Children's nonfiction	36,500	36,480	34,815	32,112	30,980
Total	**309,579**	**319,330**	**330,895**	**333,166**	**330,870**

FIGURE 54
Sample Bar Graphs

A. Bar Graph—Poor Example

CIRCULATION BY TYPE OF MATERIAL 2004–2008

B. Bar Graph—Better Example

CIRCULATION OF MEDIA 2004–2008

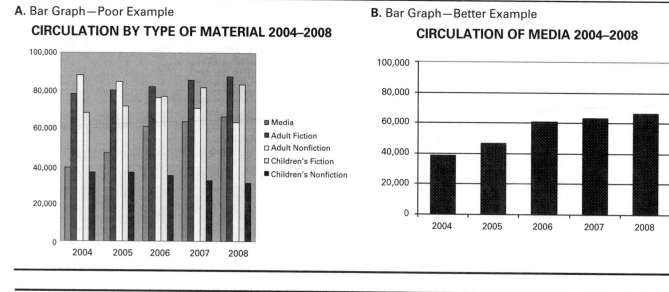

FIGURE 55
Sample Line Graph

CIRCULATION BY TYPE OF MATERIAL 2004–2008

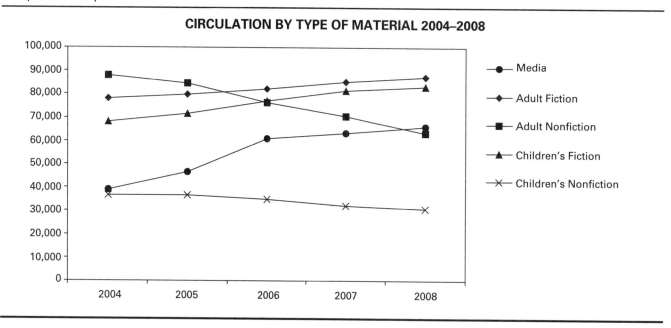

also find narrative descriptions helpful when you are presenting information that is new or unfamiliar to your audience. The narrative process makes it easy to include background and introductory information.

Whenever you use narrative description to present data, read the final product carefully to see if your points would be clearer if you included one or more tables or charts. In general, narrative descriptions work best when used in conjunction with one of the other methods of presenting data.

FIGURE 56
Sample Pie Charts

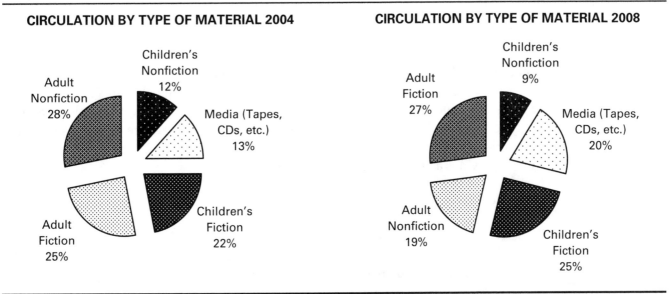

CIRCULATION BY TYPE OF MATERIAL 2004

CIRCULATION BY TYPE OF MATERIAL 2008

What to Do

1. Treat the narrative description as you would any other written presentation. Include an introduction, a body, and a conclusion. If the description is longer than a page, consider using heads and subheads to break up the text.
2. If it takes more than one short paragraph to describe the actual data, consider including a table or graph.
3. Keep it simple. Use short words and sentences.
4. Be very aware of layout and page design. Large blocks of text are boring and can be intimidating.
5. Include the date when the narrative description was written.

Tables

Time and skill:

Low

Visual appeal:

Moderate

Simplicity and clarity:

Moderate

Depiction of relationships:

Low

Tables present information in a grid format (see figure 53) and provide a relatively easy way to display a considerable amount of information. Library managers often use tables to present data because tables don't require sophisticated computer skills to prepare and can be put together fairly quickly.

Tables are more visually interesting than text, but they can be harder to read and understand than charts or graphs. It is often difficult to identify trends and relationships among the data presented in a table, particularly if the table includes a lot of data. State libraries publish public library statistical reports annually. These reports present data about public library services and resources in tabular form. The tables typically have five or more columns, and they can have hundreds of rows—one for each public library in the state. These endless rows of numbers are very difficult to read, and it is virtually impossible to use them to identify trends or relationships. Most state libraries are now making this statistical data available electronically, which allows the user to manipulate the data to create more focused tables and to develop charts that illustrate trends or relationships.

When to Use

You can use tables to present a variety of information, both numeric and textual. Tables work best when you are dealing with a limited number of data elements and a small set of data. The table in figure 51 is effective because it presents relatively simple data in an easily read and understood format. If the same information were presented in a narrative description, it would have taken more space and been more difficult to understand. Figure 51 also provides a visual break in a full page of text.

What to Do

1. Select a brief title that clearly identifies the focus of the table.
2. Put borders around tables to make them easier to see and read.
3. Number tables if you are using more than one.
4. Label each row and column clearly using simple words or short phrases.
5. Use different kinds of lines to separate labels from data when possible.
6. Identify the source of data for each table.
7. Round off numbers to the nearest whole number.
8. Use bold or italic type to indicate totals and subtotals.
9. Include the date when the table was prepared.

Graphs and Charts

Time and skills:
   High

Visual appeal:
   Moderate to high

Simplicity and clarity:
   Moderate to high

Depiction of relationships:
   High

Graphs and charts are visual depictions of numeric data. If you can't count it, you can't graph or chart it. Every graphic item in a chart represents two pieces of information:

1. The name of a measurable item (called a category), which is identified on the chart by a label
2. The quantity associated with the item (called a data point), which is plotted on the chart as a value[1]

Today, almost all charts and graphs are created using computer software programs, which provide templates for dozens of different types of charts and graphs. Microsoft Word includes fourteen standard chart styles and an additional twenty custom chart styles. Specialized chart and graph software packages provide even more options. Because all of these software programs take time to learn and use, graphs and charts are the most labor- and skill-intensive of the three presentation methods. However, if the message is important and the data is complex, the investment in time required to create graphs and charts is worthwhile.

The three main types of charts and graphs that most libraries use are bar graphs, line graphs, and pie charts. These three styles are illustrated in figures 54–56. In general, bar graphs are used to rank the relative size or importance of something over a period of time. Line graphs illustrate trends in several data elements over a period of time. Pie charts show the relationships of parts to the whole; pie charts always present 100 percent of a single category of data.

When to Use

Use graphs and charts when it is important that the audience understand the relationships among various types of information. The most effective graphs and charts focus on a single theme or message and contain only the data needed to deliver the message. Be sure to select the right type of graph or chart to present your data. Use graphs to show the relationship between two or more variables. Charts are used to represent data with a single variable.

Bar graphs work best when you want to present data about two variables, normally the changes in a single data element over a period of time. Look at the two graphs in figure 54. Bar graph A is difficult to read and confusing because it tries to present data about multiple data elements over a five-year period. Bar graph B, which presents data on one data element over the same five-year period, is much clearer and easier to understand.

Line graphs work well to illustrate the trends in multiple data elements over a period of time. Figure 55 presents exactly the same data as figure 54A. However, most people would agree that figure 55 is easier to read and understand than figure 54A. The horizontal lines make it easy to follow the trend in each category of circulation during the five-year period under consideration.

Pie charts are used to present data with a single variable. As noted previously, all pie charts reflect 100 percent of the data in the variable under consideration. Figures 56A and B illustrate the circulation of materials (the variable) in 2004 and again in 2008. To present the circulation data for 2005, 2006, and 2007, you would need to create three more pie charts. Pie charts are not normally the best format to present multiyear data. However, they are an effective way to illustrate the proportions of the pieces of any given data element.

What to Do

1. Select the right type of graph or chart for the data you are presenting.
2. Keep each graph or chart focused on a single message or theme.
3. Select a brief title that clearly identifies the focus of the graph or chart.
4. Put borders around graphs or charts to make them easier to see and read.
5. Number graphs or charts if you are using more than one.
6. Identify the source of data for each graph or chart.
7. Keep the background clear, and select simple contrasting patterns to fill bars or slices of a pie chart.
8. Round off numbers to the nearest whole number.
9. The x axis (bottom) and y axis (left) should meet at 0 for bar and line graphs.
10. Include the date when the graph or chart was prepared.

Note

1. Michael Talman, "Charts and Graphs: Visualizing Data," chap. 10 in *Understanding Presentation Graphics* (San Francisco: Sybex, 1992), http://www.talmanassociates.com/upg/ch10/ch10.html.

Part Four

Workforms

Instructions

Use this workform to develop a plan to communicate before, during, and after each task.

1. Complete a copy of this workform for each of the ten tasks in the planning process.

2. See Step 1.4 for more information on completing the workform.

Task ____: _____

A. Start Date: _____

B. End Date: _____

	C. Why do they need to know about this task?	D. What do they know now?	E. What will they need to know?	F. When do they need to know it?	G. How will they be informed?	H. Who will be responsible for informing them?
1. Board/ Governing Authority						
2. Library Managers						
3. Library Staff						
4. Planning Committee Members						
5. Other						

Notes:

Completed by _____ Date completed _____

Source of data _____ Library _____

Instructions

1. **Columns A and B.** You can either indicate the "Organization/Group/Skill" that you think should be represented on the committee in column A *or* you can suggest the names of specific people who should be considered for inclusion on the committee in column B *or* you can complete both columns A and B, listing a group or skill in column A and a person who represents that group or has that skill in column B.

2. **Column C.** Indicate the reasons for your recommendations in this column.

3. Factors to consider:

   - It is important to involve *stakeholders* in the process. Stakeholders can be defined as people or groups who can affect or will be affected by an action. There are two kinds of stakeholders for you to consider:

     Library stakeholders: The committee will include one library staff member and one library board member.

Community stakeholders: Start by identifying community decision makers. Who in your community can influence elected officials? Who are the leaders of the various groups and organizations that combine to make up the fabric of your community?

- You may also want to identify people with *special skills*. The skills that you want to have available on your committee will vary depending on local circumstances.

- The third thing to remember is that you want the committee to look like your community. Therefore, you are looking for representatives of the various demographic and socioeconomic groups in your community. You will also want people who live in all parts of your service area represented.

A. Organization/Group/Skill	B. Name(s) to Consider	C. Reason for Selection

Completed by _____ Date completed _____

Source of data _____ Library _____

Instructions

Picture your community ten years from now. Imagine that your community and its people have been successful beyond belief. Your community is a place everyone is proud to call home. Now describe what makes it so wonderful. What benefits do people receive because they live in your community? Why do people value those benefits? Think about children, teens, adults, and seniors. Consider educational level, income, race and ethnicity, religious groups, longtime residents, newcomers, jobs or professions, etc. List the target audiences, benefits, and results in the table below. Note that a sample has been provided.

Column A. Identify a target audience

Column B. Describe a benefit that the members of the target audience would receive in an ideal community and the result for the members of the audience if they received that benefit.

A. Who Will Benefit	B. Benefit and Result
Children	will receive the education they need to secure employment that provides a living wage

Completed by _____   Date completed _____

Source of data _____   Library _____

Instructions

Use this form to record the strengths, weaknesses, opportunities, and threats that will affect the community's ability to achieve the vision statements you have identified.

A1. Record the current conditions in the community that support achieving the vision statements.

A2. Record the conditions outside of the community that currently support achieving the vision statements or that might support them in the future.

B1. Record the current conditions in the community that will make it difficult to achieve the vision statements.

B2. Record the conditions outside of the community that currently or potentially will make it difficult to achieve the vision statements.

A. Support Achieving the Vision	B. Obstruct Achieving the Vision
A1. Community Strengths	**B1.** Community Weaknesses
A2. External Opportunities	**B2.** External Threats

Completed by _____ Date completed _____

Source of data _____ Library _____

Instructions

Use a copy of this form to record the strengths, weaknesses, opportunities, and threats that will affect the library's ability to achieve one of the preliminary service responses. Use a separate form for each preliminary service response.

A. List the title of the preliminary service response under review.

B1. Record the strengths that the library has in the area selected as a service response.

B2. Record the external conditions that will support the delivery of the service response.

C1. Record the weaknesses that the library has that will make it difficult to implement the service response.

C2. Record the external conditions that currently or potentially will make it difficult to implement the service response.

A. Library Service Response: _____

_____

B. **For Selecting the Service Response**	**C.** **Against Selecting the Service Response**
B1. Library Strengths	**C1.** Library Weaknesses
B2. External Opportunities	**C2.** External Threats

Completed by _____ Date completed _____

Source of data _____ Library _____

Instructions

Use this workform to analyze the information you gathered about the change environment in your library.

Column A. List the factors that you think will make it easier to implement the changes that will result from your planning process.

Column B. Use a scale of one to three to indicate how critical this factor is to creating an environment that will support change (1 = minimal, 2 = moderate, 3 = significant).

Column C. List the factors that you think will make it difficult to implement the changes that will result from your planning process.

Column D. Use a scale of one to three to indicate how critical this factor is to impeding an environment that will support change (1 = minimal, 2 = moderate, 3 = significant).

A. Factors That Create an Environment That Supports the Change(s) ——————————▶	B. Wt.	Change(s) under Consideration	C. Factors That Create an Environment That Impedes the Change(s) ◀——————————	D. Wt.

Completed by _____   Date completed _____

Source of data _____   Library _____

Instructions

Use this workform to develop one goal that supports one of your service responses. Each goal will target a separate audience, and you may have several goals for a single service response. Use as many copies of the workform as you need to develop goals for all of the service responses that have been selected

A. Write the service response on this line.

B. Copy the one-line description of the service response from "Service Responses" (part 2 of this book).

C. Write the audience that will be targeted in this goal. The target audience may be defined by demographics (age, etc.) or by condition (parents, business owners, immigrants, etc.).

D. Copy any vision statements that may apply to this service response. If there are no such vision statements, leave this section blank.

E. Write the benefit the members of the target audience will receive because the library offers the service described in the service response. The wording in sections C and D provides a starting point.

F. Complete the goal template.

1. Write the target audience from section C.

2. Write the benefit from section E.

G. Record the final goal, which is simply the combination of F1 and F2 in the goal template. You will probably have to add verbs and you may have to make other minor changes to make the goal read smoothly, but you should not have to make significant changes.

A. Service Response: _____

_____

B. Service Response Description: _____

_____

_____

C. Target Audience: _____

_____

D. Vision Statement(s), If Any: _____

_____

_____

_____

E. Benefit: _____

_____

_____

F. Goal Template

1. Audience	2. Benefit

G. Final Goal: _____

_____

_____

Completed by _____ Date completed _____

Source of data _____ Library _____

Instructions

Use this workform to develop the objectives for one of your goals. Complete a separate copy of the workform for each of the goals in your plan. There is space on this workform to create four objectives for a goal. If you want to develop more than four objectives for a single goal, use a second copy of the worksheet.

A. Write the service response on this line.

B. Write the goal on this line.

C. Copy the "Possible Measures" from the complete description of the service response that this goal supports here. The descriptions can be found in part 2 of this book.

D–G 1. Write the measure you will use to track your progress toward reaching the goal. You may use one

of the measures in the "Possible Measures" section or you may use a measure that is unique to your library.

D–G 2. Write the target you intend to reach.

D–G 3. Write the date by which you intend to reach the target (for example, 2XXX or annually)

D–G 4. Complete the objective template.

    a. Copy the time frame from D–G 3 here.

    b. Copy the target from D–G 2 here.

    c. Copy the measure from D–G 1 here.

D–G 5. Put the time frame, the target, and the measure into a sentence that reads smoothly and write it on this line. This is your objective.

A. Service Response: _____

B. Goal: _____

C. Possible Measures from Service Response Description: _____

_____

_____

_____

_____

_____

D. Objective 1

  1. Selected Measure: _____

  2. Target: _____

  3. Time Frame: _____

  4. Objective Template

a. Time Frame	b. Target	c. Measure

  5. Objective 1: _____

_____

_____

(cont.)

E. Objective 2

   1. Selected Measure: _____

   2. Target: _____

   3. Time Frame: _____

   4. Objective Template

a. Time Frame	**b.** Target	**c.** Measure

   5. Objective 2: _____

_____

_____

F. Objective 3

   1. Selected Measure: _____

   2. Target: _____

   3. Time Frame: _____

   4. Objective Template

a. Time Frame	**b.** Target	**c.** Measure

   5. Objective 3: _____

_____

_____

G. Objective 4

   1. Selected Measure: _____

   2. Target: _____

   3. Time Frame: _____

   4. Objective Template

a. Time Frame	**b.** Target	**c.** Measure

   5. Objective 4:

_____

_____

_____

Completed by _____   Date completed _____

Source of data _____   Library _____

Instructions

Use this workform to record the recommendations made during the branch staff meeting about the priority of the system goals for the branch.

PART I

A. Write the name of the branch library here.

B 1–10. List the goals in priority order as they were approved in concept by the library board. Add additional lines if needed. This column may be completed before the workform is sent to the branches.

C 1–10. Enter a number indicating the priority of each goal in *your branch* here. The goal with highest priority

for the branch will be number 1, the goal with the second-highest priority for the branch will be number 2, etc.

D 1–10. Write the rationale for each of your recommendations here. If the goal is a priority for your library, explain why it is a priority and why it ranks where you placed it in your list of priority goals. If the goal is a low priority in your branch, explain why.

PART II

The branch manager will sign here and submit to the appropriate administrators for approval.

A. Branch Name: _____

PART I: Branch Priority of Library Goals

B. Goal	C. Branch Priority	D. Rationale
1.		
2.		
3.		
4.		
5.		
6.		
7.		
8.		
9.		
10.		

PART II: Review and Approval

Reviewed and Approved by:

Branch Librarian _____   Date completed _____

Administrator _____   Date completed_____

Instructions

Use this workform to record the branch targets for the system objectives for one of the system goals. You will complete a copy of this workform for each of the system goals.

PART I

A. Write the name of the branch here

B. Write the system goal on this line.

C. Indicate the priority of the goal in your branch.

D 1–6. Write the objectives for the system goal on these lines.

E 1–6. Indicate the branch targets for each of the objectives on these lines.

- If the target for the system is expressed as a percentage increase, the target that is selected for the branch must be at least as large as the system target for that objective.
- If the target for the system is expressed as a number, the target for the branch will be a portion of that number.

F 1–6. Explain why you selected the target in E 1–10.

PART II

The branch manager will sign here and submit to the appropriate administrators for approval.

A. Branch Name: _____

PART I: Branch Targets for System Objectives

B. System Goal 1: _____

C. Branch Priority: _____

D. System Objectives	E. Branch Target	F. Rationale
1.		
2.		
3.		
4.		
5.		
6.		

PART II: Review and Approval

Branch Librarian _____ Date completed _____

Administrator _____ Date completed _____

WORKFORM K Organizational Competency Issues

Instructions

Use this workform to record information about the current conditions in your library in order to help you identify the areas in which the library should develop organizational competencies.

A–J 1 and 2. Read the questions in the table and place an X in the "1. Yes" or "2. No" box, based on conditions in your library.

A–J 3. List any other issues that relate to the topic that need to be addressed in your library.

A. External Partnerships. This includes formal and informal relationships with other governmental units, nonprofit agencies and organizations, and businesses.

1. Yes	2. No	
		Does the library maintain a comprehensive and accurate list of all organizations and agencies with which it has formal and informal partnerships?
		Is there a clear process that is observed when determining whether or not to partner with an organization or agency?
		Are all staff aware of the process to be followed when they wish to initiate a partnership agreement or respond to a request to establish a partnership?
		Have criteria been established that will be used when assessing existing or potential partnerships?
3. Other:		

B. Finance. This includes both operational and capital funding and addresses the allocation, expenditure, tracking, and reporting of those funds.

1. Yes	2. No	
		Are library funds allocated in accordance with the priorities in the strategic plan?
		Is the library's financial reporting system understood by staff and board members who have fiduciary responsibility?
		Are board members and library management aware of their legal responsibility vis-à-vis public and donated funds?
		Are accurate, timely, and easy-to-understand reports about library finances distributed to and discussed with library board members and the library management team on a regular basis?
3. Other:		

C. Fund-raising. This includes all gift and donation programs supported by the library, the Friends of the Library, or the library foundation.

1. Yes	2. No	
		Does the library have a fund-raising plan?
		Are the fund-raising responsibilities of the library foundation, Library Friends, library management, and library staff clearly understood, respected, and observed by all parties?
		Have the individuals with fund-raising responsibilities received the appropriate training to enable them to perform their assigned duties?
		Do members of the foundation, Friends, and staff have access to attractive and up-to-date fund-raising materials?
		Are all fund-raising efforts directed toward priorities in the strategic plan?
		Are donors promptly and appropriately acknowledged and recognized?
3. Other:		

(cont.)

D. Governance. This includes issues that arise in libraries that have policy or advisory boards or libraries that are a city or county department.

1. Yes	2. No	
		Are the library board's bylaws up-to-date? Do they reflect current practice?
		Is the committee structure of the board in accordance with the board's authority and does it reflect the board's responsibility in the accomplishment of the new plan?
		Are the board's actions transparent to the public? Are announcements of meetings posted on the library website and in other appropriate places?
		Are board agendas, minutes, and related documents available to the public and staff in a timely, convenient manner?
		If your library serves multiple jurisdictions, are the authority and responsibility of each jurisdiction clear? Is it clear to whom the director reports?
		If your library is a city or county library, is it clear to whom the director reports?
3. Other:		

E. Marketing and Public Relations. This includes all of the work the library does to promote the use of library services and programs in all media: print, video, audio, and online.

1. Yes	2. No	
		Does the library effectively use the print media, its website, and other electronic media to communicate with the public?
		Does the library produce information about its services and policies in languages spoken by community residents?
		Does the library have a recognizable logo, tagline, and/or image that is used consistently in promotional materials?
		Does the library have criteria that are used to evaluate the effectiveness of marketing or public relations activities?
3. Other:		

F. Measurement and Evaluation. This includes all of the data that staff collect for any reason. Data collection can be manual or electronic.

1. Yes	2. No	
		Does the library have a comprehensive list of the data elements that are collected by staff and how those data elements are used?
		Has the library provided staff with a definition of each data element and instructions on how and when to gather that data so that comparisons between units and over time are valid?
		Is the library currently collecting all of the data that will be needed to report progress on the objectives identified in the strategic plan?
		Is there a method in place to regularly report progress on library objectives to the board, the staff, and the community?
		Does the library respond accurately and on time, to the state library's request for information?
		Does the library participate in the Public Library Data Service sponsored by the Public Library Association?
3. Other:		

(cont.)

G. Operational Efficiencies. This includes issues related to current procedures that could be modified or eliminated to make the organization more efficient.

1. Yes	2. No	
		Are circulation procedures as efficient as they could be?
		Are technical services as efficient as they could be?
		Are reference procedures as efficient as they could be?
		Are procedures in all other units as efficient as possible?
3. Other:		

H. Organizational Structure. This includes all aspects of the library's organizational structure, including reporting relationships and primary areas of responsibility.

1. Yes	2. No	
		Does the organizational structure support the delivery of services envisioned by new goals and objectives?
		Do the library's job descriptions reflect the activities that will need to be performed to accomplish the new goals and objectives?
		Does the organizational structure and the team/committee structure support the accomplishment of the new goals and objectives?
		Does the organizational structure support effective communication between and within units?
3. Other:		

I. Policies. This includes all of the library's policies, regulations, procedures, and guidelines.

1. Yes	2. No	
		Do all of the library's policies support the new goals and objectives?
		Can staff and the public locate a specific policy when they wish to do so?
		Are policies being uniformly observed in all units or by all staff?
		Does the library board regularly review all policies and revise them as necessary? Are all policies in compliance with local, state, and federal laws and regulations?
3. Other:		

J. Training and Staff Development. This includes internal and external training programs for staff in all classifications.

1. Yes	2. No	
		Does the library have a new employee orientation that includes information about the service priorities and the library's strategic plan?
		Will staff need training to accomplish the activities that will be an integral part of the new plan? Is there a plan in place to provide that training?
		Does the library encourage staff to participate in continuing education and professional activities at the state and national levels? Is funding provided to support these activities?
		Does the library have a comprehensive continuing education plan that addresses the needs of all staff in all classifications?
3. Other:		

K. Other. Are there other areas in which the library needs to create or enhance organizational competency? If so list them here.

Competency: _____

1. Yes	2. No	

Completed by _____   Date completed _____

Source of data _____   Library _____

Instructions

A. List the target audience.

B. Indicate the priority of the audience (see Step 10.2).

C. Briefly describe the intent of the message that will be sent to the audience. You can only list one intent per line. You will create a separate message for each intended outcome.

D. Indicate who will be responsible for writing the message.

E. Indicate the date by which the message should be sent.

A. Target Audience	B. Priority	C. Intent of Message	D. Person Responsible	E. Date Due

Completed by _____ Date completed _____

Source of data _____ Library _____

Instructions

A. Write the target audience for the message.

B. Write exactly what you expect the target audience to do as a result of the message. Use a separate copy of this workform for each intended outcome.

C 1–4. List the facts that members of the target audience will have to know in order to do what you want them to do.

D 1–4. List the feelings/emotions/beliefs that will make the members of the target audience want to do what you want them to do.

E 1–4. List the medium or media you will use to send the message you develop. Be specific. Don't just list "print." Describe the print medium you will use (brochures, newspaper articles, bookmarks, etc.).

F 1. Write the measure you will use to determine if your message was effective.

F 2. Write the target you expect to reach if the measure is effective.

G. Attach copies of the final message(s) you create to this workform. If you create audio or visual media, indicate where those electronic files are stored.

A. Target audience: _____

B. What we want them to do: _____
_____
_____

C. What they need to know in order to do what we want them to do:

   1. _____
   2. _____
   3. _____
   4. _____

D. What they need to feel or believe in order to do what we want them to do:

   1. _____
   2. _____
   3. _____
   4. _____

E. Media to be used to deliver the message:

   1. _____
   2. _____
   3. _____
   4. _____

F. Evaluation measure and target

   1. Measure: _____
   _____
   2. Target: _____
   _____

G. Attach copies of the final message(s) to this form.

Completed by _____ Date completed _____

Source of data _____ Library _____

Instructions

Assign a number to each of the items you are prioritizing. This worksheet will help you evaluate up to 15 items against every other item on list, each time determining which of your choices is the more important. Begin in Column A below. Compare the first and second items and circle the number of the one you think is more important (1 or 2). Continuing in Column A, compare the first item and the third item, again circling the service response you think is more important (1 or 3). Continue through all of the columns.

```
A
1   2      B
1   3    2   3      C
1   4    2   4    3   4      D
1   5    2   5    3   5    4   5      E
1   6    2   6    3   6    4   6    5   6      F
1   7    2   7    3   7    4   7    5   7    6   7      G
1   8    2   8    3   8    4   8    5   8    6   8    7   8      H
1   9    2   9    3   9    4   9    5   9    6   9    7   9    8   9      I
1  10    2  10    3  10    4  10    5  10    6  10    7  10    8  10    9  10      J
1  11    2  11    3  11    4  11    5  11    6  11    7  11    8  11    9  11   10  11      K
1  12    2  12    3  12    4  12    5  12    6  12    7  12    8  12    9  12   10  12   11  12      L
1  13    2  13    3  13    4  13    5  13    6  13    7  13    8  13    9  13   10  13   11  13   12  13      M
1  14    2  14    3  14    4  14    5  14    6  14    7  14    8  14    9  14   10  14   11  14   12  14   13  14      N
1  15    2  15    3  15    4  15    5  15    6  15    7  15    8  15    9  15   10  15   11  15   12  15   13  15   14  15
```

To score your ratings, add the number of times you circled each number and place the total by the appropriate line below. Note that you must add vertically and horizontally to be sure that you include all circled choices. The service response with the highest number is the one you think is most important.

1 _____   4. _____   7. _____   10. _____   13. _____

2. _____   5. _____   8. _____   11. _____   14. _____

3. _____   6. _____   9. _____   12. _____   15. _____

Completed by _____   Date completed _____

Source of data _____   Library _____

Index

Note: The letter *f* following a page number denotes a figure.

Sandra Nelson is a consultant, speaker, trainer, and writer specializing in public library planning and management issues. She has worked in both small and large public libraries and in two state library agencies. She has presented hundreds of training programs and facilitated strategic planning processes in dozens of libraries during the past thirty years. She was named Librarian of the Year by the Arizona State Library Association in 1987, received the ASCLA Professional Achievement Award in 1996, and received the Outstanding Alumni Award from the University of North Texas School of Information Science in 1999. She chaired the committee that developed the original *Planning for Results: A Public Library Transformation Process* (1997). She is the author of *Planning for Results: A Streamlined Approach* (2001) and is coauthor of *Wired for the Future: Developing Your Library Technology Plan* (1999), *Managing for Results: Effective Resource Allocation for Public Libraries* (2000), and *Creating Policies for Results: From Chaos to Clarity* (2003), all published by the ALA. She is the Senior Editor of the PLA Results series.